BEYOND THE ROARING FORTIES

Beyond the Roaring Forties

NEW ZEALAND'S SUBANTARCTIC ISLANDS

Conon Fraser

GOVERNMENT PRINTING OFFICE PUBLISHING

WELLINGTON, NEW ZEALAND — 1986

Black-browed mollymawk chick at
Bull Rock colony, Campbell Island.

Front cover photograph: Snares crested
penguins in a clearing in the *Olearia*
forest on the Snares.

Title page:
The south-west coast of Campbell
Island has been heavily eroded by
the sea, leaving numerous islets and
rock stacks. One of the most striking
is La Botte — The Boot — near the
entrance to Monument Harbour.

ISBN 0 477 01362 7

Typeset by Wordset Enterprises Ltd, Wellington and
printed by Woolmore Printing Ltd, Auckland.

Unless otherwise stated, the photographs in this book
are by Conon Fraser.

Foreword

BY SIR PETER SCOTT

I have always been interested in the more remote corners of the earth, and especially the unique birds found in isolated places. New Zealand's subantarctic islands certainly qualify as remote, and some of them have even been left alone by man to "evolve undisturbed since their creation" as Conon Fraser puts it. This makes them enormously valuable to all of us, not only to naturalists. We need to know that there are some completely unmodified parts of the world, even if we are never able to visit them.

I have had the good fortune to visit some of these islands twice, first in 1971 and again in 1979 when travelling as a lecturer on board the *Lindblad Explorer*. The first time we were on our way to Antarctica, and my wife and eighteen-year-old daughter were with me. Our first stop was at Enderby Island, which is off Port Ross on Auckland where my father (Captain Scott) landed in 1904. I wrote in my diary:

> Alas a morning of low cloud and drizzle which persisted for the first 2 hours of our visit to stupendous Enderby Island. Two qualities made it as good as any wildlife island we have seen since the Galapagos. The first was its rich diversity of bird species and the second the extreme tameness of almost all of them. The skuas were absurdly tame, the penguins agreeably tamer than the Yellow-eyed are supposed to be . . . the Red-crowned parakeets were also very tame. . . . the New Zealand pipit was the tamest of all. . . . For the last hour the rain had held off and we went up onto the closely rabbit-cropped turf with Hooker's sea lions all around. . . . Dafila looked inside the tiny hut near the landing and found it full of baby sea lions sleeping in rows.

Eight years later we were coming back from another expedition to Antarctica, and stopped again at Campbell, Auckland, and Enderby Islands. On Campbell Island I recorded in my diary that we found

> a fairly large concentration of Royal Albatross nests. In one area there were some 15–20 nests, and later we climbed a ridge and found several more. The immense poise and dignity of these birds was deeply impressive – their huge size, their peaceful acceptance of the people around them, their astonishing elegance as they sat on their raised nests.

Beyond the Roaring Forties contains an absolute wealth of fascinating detail about the birds and other wildlife of the subantarctic islands. It also provides a lively picture of the history of man's involvement with the islands. Some of the history was shameful, such as the ruthless exploitation of the seals, and some of it much nobler, such as the "Cape Expedition" during the Second World War. Groups of men were stationed on Auckland and Campbell Islands to watch for enemy shipping. They hardly saw any ships, but many of them carried out immensely valuable scientific work when they were off-duty.

These islands are now being managed with a high standard of care and expertise by the New Zealand authorities. However, even in these remote waters new threats to the islands and their wildlife constantly emerge, such as the rapid expansion of the squid fishery around the Auckland Islands which is now threatening the endangered Hooker's sea lion. A considerable number of the sea lions become entangled in the trawlers' nets and drown, and new management methods will have to be worked out to prevent this.

The whole of the Southern Ocean, and especially the areas around the subantarctic islands, is undergoing a rapid build-up of massive over-fishing. This is potentially as serious a threat to the sea birds and the marine mammals as it is to the stocks of fish, squid and krill. Everyone who cares about the world's wild places must keep a constant watch on all the developments which threaten them, and be prepared to speak out in their defence. Conon Fraser's book provides excellent support for this task.

Peter Scott.

Sir Peter Scott
Slimbridge, July 1986

Preface

I became deeply interested in New Zealand's subantarctic islands while researching and then directing the filming of the documentary *Beyond the Roaring Forties* for the National Film Unit. Gradually, the idea grew of bringing together all the varied resources I had used, with my own experience of the islands, and of writing an account of their fascinating ecological and social history.

Filming was demanding, the logistics exacting, and still photography for this book, particularly during the first summer with the *Acheron* in 1983–84, had to be snatched, sometimes with only seconds to spare. There were inevitably opportunities we caught on film, which I missed for the book; one such lost chance I regret was the take-off of thousands of sooty shearwaters at dawn, on the Snares.

On that first round to the Snares, Aucklands, and Campbell Island, we experienced the sort of weather that had fooled some of the early Antarctic explorers into thinking the Aucklands an idyllic paradise, although the untypically good weather meant that we filmed for long hours with few breaks for forty-eight incredibly full days. Landing on sheltered eastern shores, we would immediately be surrounded by bellbirds, which would stay for several minutes, filling the air with "the most melodious music. . .almost imitating small bells but with the most tunable silver sound imaginable," as Joseph Banks described it, when he first landed on the New Zealand mainland with Captain Cook. We knew what he felt like; for although we were filming, there was a certain sense of going back in time, and of being removed in more than just distance from our familiar populated world.

The HMNZS *Monowai* expedition in early 1985 was very different: no intimate atmosphere of shared experiences, but five weeks within a highly organised unit of civilisation, from which we made our daily sorties to the islands by helicopter, boats, or inflatable dinghies. Because of the planning I was involved in, there was again little time for taking any but the most hurried notes. But these, my photographs, and the film log were vivid reminders of the time, for example, when a rather aggressive adolescent male Hooker's sea lion, after a threatening advance, flopped under the camera tripod, sprawled there motionless for a few seconds and then, as if feeling accepted, got up and ambled off without a backward look. The cameraman, with his eye to the viewfinder, had never even noticed!

Salvin's mollymawk in flight, Bounty Islands.

Although a remote part of the world, New Zealand's subantarctic has an unexpectedly rich past, and I have quoted quite often from the early explorers, seamen, adventurers, and scientists, because the observations they made at the time seem so particularly relevant and vivid.

I am extremely grateful to the many people who have helped me with innumerable aspects of the further and much deeper research needed in writing this book. The Acknowledgements which follow give some idea of the extent of that help. Their advice was always readily given, and I could not have written about the subantarctic islands in any depth at all without such generous encouragement and support.

Conon Fraser
Wellington, New Zealand
1986

Acknowledgements

Firstly, I am greatly indebted to Rowley Taylor of the Ecology Division, DSIR, and Paul Dingwall, of Head Office, Lands & Survey, for reading through the entire manuscript, and to Rowley Taylor for the generous loan of much of his own personal research on the history of New Zealand's subantarctic. The following people were kind enough to read through one or more specific chapters: Dr Chris Adams, Dr Ron Balham, Martin Cawthorn, Sir Charles Fleming, Dr Cameron Hay, Peter Johns, Ron Keen, Dr Colin Meurk, Chris Robertson, Dr John Warham, and Dr John Yaldwyn. I owe much to them, and must stress that any errors that are left are mine. Others, too, were generous with their advice, experience, and time: Sandy Bartle, Brian Bell, John Campbell, Martin Foggo, Dr Eric Godley, Dr Murray Gregory, Mike Hurst, Norm Judd, John Kendrick, Laurie Pollock, Dr Mike Rudge, Ramari Stewart, Chris Thomas, Graham Turbott, Dr Kim Westerskov, Dr Murray Williams, and Dr Peter Wilson. My thanks also to Alex and Colleen Black of RV *Acheron*, and their crew, for their skill and good company; to Mark Crompton, Grant Harper, and others on Campbell Island; to Hugh Best and Ron Nilssen; to Cdr Willie Jacques; to Cdr Ken Robertson, Lt Cdr Owen Hanley, and Lt Cdr Dave Washer, pilot of HMNZS *Monowai*'s helicopter; to my National Film Unit colleagues Lynton Diggle, Bayly Watson, John Cooper, and Steve Upston for shared experiences — and to the management of the National Film Unit, who encouraged this project and granted me leave to complete it.

I am grateful to Dave McKerchar and Wayne Devine of the Department of Lands & Survey for their help and interest; to Dr David Waite for permission to quote from William Mackworth's unpublished diaries, in the possession of Mr Des Downes of Auckland; to the British Admiralty Hydrographical Office; and to Russell Beck of the Southland Museum for the loan of a *General Grant* "messenger". My thanks for the use of photographs to Alexander Turnbull Library (12 photos), T. E. Atkinson, Alex Black, Canterbury Museum, Martin Cawthorn, Fisheries Research Division of the Department of Agriculture and Fisheries, *The Illustrated London News*, Norm Judd Collection (2), I.S. Kerr Collection, Department of Lands & Survey, Simon Mitchell (3), Monash University, Australia, National Library of Australia,

National Museum, Wellington, New Zealand National Film Unit, Laurie Pollock, Ramari Stewart (8), Graham Taylor, Chris Thomas, Bayly Watson, Wellington *Evening Post*, Kim Westerskov (7), and New Zealand Wildlife Service (2). My thanks also to Tim Galloway for his careful preparation of the maps and diagrams.

Finally, my special thanks to Tom Ballard, formerly Director of Publications at the Government Printing Office, for responding to my enthusiasm for this project from its very early stages; to Chris Lipscombe and Lynne Ciochetto for their patience over the illustrations; to Paula Wagemaker for her skilful editing; and to my wife Jackie for her support and advice, from start to finish.

C.F.

The author being investigated by a Hooker's sea lion while photographing a southern skua at Northwest Bay, Campbell Island.
Photo: Bayly Watson.

Key to Maps and Diagrams

New Zealand fur seal at the Bounty
Islands.

Contents

PART ONE

Homes in a Wild Ocean

Rugged southern coast of Adams
Island, near entrance to Victoria
Passage, looking east.

1
The Elemental Islands

Scientists used to assignments in the remote Antarctic and the Arctic have called New Zealand's subantarctic islands the most inaccessible in the world. The British explorer Sir James Clark Ross referred to the stormy ocean between the southern end of the world's continents and Antarctica, with its constant heavy swell, as far more hazardous than the Arctic. Thomas Musgrave, shipwrecked on the Auckland Islands in 1865, wrote of the "incessant gales, constant hail, snow and pelting rain. . . . I have been round Cape Horn and the Cape of Good Hope and crossed the Western Ocean many times, but never have I experienced . . . anything in the shape of storms to equal those of this place."[1]

The ocean dominates the islands scattered upon its wild unbroken reaches. Even on the largest of New Zealand's subantarctic islands, the main Auckland Island and Campbell Island, one is never far from its overwhelming influence — whether of rapid fronts and squalls sweeping in from the sea, the unleashed wind on the barren high country, or the permanent lanes which gales have carved in the close canopy of stunted scrub and forests. The mammals and birds are those of the ocean.

Nowhere else on earth could one find islands more totally influenced by the surrounding sea than the Bounty Islands: a stark, desolate group so exposed that the storms of centuries have kept the guano of millions of sea birds from building up, by constantly washing it to the sea, leaving only a treacherous enamelled surface on the harsh granite rock. There is not a trace of vegetation, apart from the occasional green tinge of algae, on these barren, worn outcrops in the ocean, no colours other than the grey of rock and sea and sky, the grey and white of circling and nesting mollymawks, the slaty blue-grey of fulmar prions, the black and white of crested penguins, and the dark brown of fur seals. Pungent smells of guano and sea and a cacophony of sound assault the senses: the plaintive staccato chorus of mollymawks, the abrupt screeching of penguins, and the incessant cooing and bickering of prions mingle with the rumbling and crash of the surf.

The Antipodes, to the south, are only slightly less inhospitable. The main island has dark volcanic cliffs rising to an open, exposed plateau of tussock and fern, dotted with the isolated nests of wandering albatrosses. The second-largest island, Bollons, and adjacent Archway Island, make up two

Salvin's mollymawks and
erect-crested penguins massed on
Depot Island at the Bounty Islands.
The absence of soil and vegetation
emphasise the birds' dependence on
the surrounding ocean for food.

thirds of the rim of a once perfect volcano, now partially destroyed by the sea. The Windward Islands have their bases pierced by high, narrow caves, so that they seem rooted to the sea floor by powerful splayed fingers of rock. Night falls, with the lonely cry of the sooty albatross and the mocking laughter of parakeets giving way to the moaning, mewing, and crooning of vast numbers of petrels and prions returning to their burrows from the ocean.

Closest to New Zealand are the Snares, covered with heavy tussock grass and a twisted, leaning forest which gives them a very different character. They are protected from people not so much by distance as by their rocky, exposed shores and hazardous seas.

There are an estimated six million sooty shearwaters on North East Island. This island, the largest of the Snares, is just over three and a half kilometres long.[2] The sooty shearwaters have relatively few taking-off places where the ground is open and facing the sea, and one of my first and most memorable experiences of the subantarctic islands was filming a mass departure of these birds at dawn on the first day of 1984.

After seeing the New Year in at the scientific station, we woke up well before dawn and blundered our way with torches through the *Olearia* forest with its low snagging branches and the burrows of the sooty shearwaters honeycombing the soft ground among the network of tree roots. At Punui Bay, on the north-east coast, an amphitheatre of rough tussock grass sweeps down towards a sheer drop to the sea. There is a small cliff at the back, under which we huddled because, with millions in mind, we had been warned in all apparent seriousness that we might be knocked down and bowled into the sea by a wall of birds!

Erect-crested penguins at Anchorage Bay on the main Antipodes Island.

As dawn began to break, hundreds of sooty shearwaters began to emerge from the *Olearia* forest, and soon there was a great row of them behind us and above our heads, fluttering their wings and getting ready to take off. They floundered onto our heads and shoulders, and crawled through the clumps of tussock and up onto our legs, sometimes taking off from our knees. One could stroke them; they were very soft and smoky brown, and totally unafraid of us. As the light grew, they continued to pour from the island, and we got up because there was no sudden wall of birds at all, and filmed them leaving and sweeping out over the sea.

Campbell Island, with its weather station, is New Zealand's only inhabited subantarctic island. It is an island of pale, tussock-covered hills and craggy, rounded mountains; of often inaccessible penguin colonies at the base of steep volcanic cliffs; and of harbours and bays where huge elephant seals lie dozing in foul mud wallows in the tussock. Rare right whales gather in winter to mate in Northwest Bay, and Campbell is the world's major breeding ground of the majestic southern royal albatross. Like the wandering albatross, the royal nests in solitary state, and from a distance the white mushrooms of individual birds thinly dot the wide, rolling landscape. The huge size and unruffled dignity of a sitting albatross induce an instinctive awe and respect in anyone approaching. One feels a mere visitor, here for a few hours or days, in the presence of a bird which spends most of its life in effortless flight over the vast reaches of the subantarctic seas.

The Auckland Islands, between Campbell Island and the Snares, are large enough to have elements of most of New Zealand's other subantarctic islands, and a wider range of native flora and fauna than anywhere else in the subantarctic. The exposed western coasts have stark, rugged cliffs which face

Sooty shearwaters, which gather from late afternoon until they reach their greatest numbers at nightfall, fill the sky over North East Island at the Snares, before returning to their burrows in the *Olearia* forest.

the prevailing south-westerly winds and gales that come spinning and circling off the Antarctic Continent — gales so strong that waterfalls are frequently blown back by the force of the wind as they leave the cliffs, and sent whirling across the land like jets of steam.

The eastern side of the group is relatively sheltered, with numerous inlets and two large and indented harbours. Each bay has its guardian sea lion or two, and the broad sweep of Sandy Bay on Enderby Island (the Riviera of the subantarctic) is crowded in the summer breeding season with hundreds of Hooker's sea lions — massive bulls, sleek, blonde females, and pups in closely crowded nurseries.

The prostrate trunks of the stunted rata forest show that westerly storms still reach this side. The soil scientist B. C. Aston, in his report to the Secretary of Agriculture in 1907, wrote with feeling of conditions in the scrub and open country above the sheltering rata:

> As we proceeded up the hill the weather rapidly became worse. Torrents of rain soon drenched us to the skin. . . . With frozen fingers Mr Field endeavoured to photograph a solitary albatross on the nest while I dug down into the soil for samples. . . . Severe hail showers compelled us to take shelter behind rocks . . . the wind was bitterly cold. . . . We were . . . about half a mile above the camp and commenced to descend through the scrub breast high which concealed all traces of gullies, logs and pitfalls of various kinds. In the next few hours by dint of brute force we managed to scramble, push, crawl under or roll over the intervening half mile. Owing to the steepness of the declivity and the fact that gravity was on our side we, though greatly impeded by specimens, finally reached the bottom . . . and made our way back to the camp about dark.[3]

The most striking feature of the Auckland Islands is the massive rampart of their southern and western cliffs, which contrast with the varied conditions

Between fifty and one hundred young Hooker's sea lion bulls haul ashore at the Snares each year. Sea lions swallow pebbles while foraging for food, and the mystery of small pieces of basalt occurring on the granitic Snares is explained by the fact they were regurgitated by animals which had travelled here from the Auckland Islands.

Left: The north-west coast of Campbell Island, looking towards the Courrejolles Peninsula. The French, who were here in 1874 to observe the Transit of Venus, named many of the island's geographical features.

9

A vast colony of tens of thousands of shy, or white-capped, mollymawks on the eastern slopes of Disappointment Island, the Auckland Islands.

of the east. Where the *General Grant*, or possibly the *Anjou*, was wrecked, these cliffs rise absolutely sheer for 460 metres, or 1500 feet, with not a blade of grass or ledge for a sea bird to cling to. Along this awesome coast the sea pounds into deep caves at the base of the cliffs, exploding like gunfire into hurtling spray and forever undercutting them. Henry Armstrong, on the *Amherst*, wrote of the main Auckland Island: ". . . I have seen nothing to surpass, or even equal, the grandeur, the savage majesty of its grim storm-beaten sea walls; standing up bold and defiant, sullenly challenging old Ocean to a trial of strength."[4]

The conflict has been going on for millions of years, and is illustrative of the forces which have shaped not only New Zealand's islands but other lonely groups of islands round the subantarctic — elemental islands, surrounded by the overwhelming presence of the climate and the sea.

Young adult Hooker's sea lion bull at
Northwest Bay, Campbell Island.

2
Specks in the Ocean

To the south of Africa, Australia, New Zealand, and South America, beyond the South Atlantic Ocean, the Indian Ocean, and the South Pacific, lies the stormy, open expanse of the Southern Ocean, encircling the Antarctic Continent.

Cape Horn, some 900 kilometres distant from it in a direct line, is the tip of the land mass nearest Antarctica, but between this bleak extremity of South America and the Antarctic Peninsula, a looping chain of widely scattered and small island groups, in comparatively shallow seas, indicates that long ages ago these two great continents may have been linked. The biggest concentration and best known of the Antarctic and subantarctic islands are here.

The islands which cluster against the Antarctic Peninsula are so close to it that they can be regarded as part of it. The South Shetland Islands, dotted off the tip of the Peninsula, were originally claimed in part by Argentina, Chile, and Great Britain, while Russia and Poland have bases on them, although they never claimed land in the competitive years of exploration and whaling. The South Sandwich Islands and South Georgia, in the South Atlantic, are now Dependencies of the Falkland Islands, and any conflicting claims to land south of 60° south are now frozen under the Antarctic Treaty. The South Orkneys and South Shetland Islands lie within the Antarctic Circle.

Moving clockwise round Antarctica, Britain's Gough Island lies some 2500 kilometres north-east of South Georgia, while due east of South Georgia lies Norway's small, barren Bouvetøya Island. Another 3000 kilometres or so east, south of South Africa and south of the Indian Ocean, are South Africa's bleak Marion and Prince Edward Islands. Continuing clockwise, France's Îles Crozet lie another 1000 kilometres east, and 1500 kilometres east again are France's Îles Kerguelen. All of these islands, including Amsterdam Island and St Paul Island to the north-east, are volcanic, with the Îles Kerguelen being the largest and most important group in the Indian Ocean. The main island here has mountains rising to 1800 metres, with permanent snowfields and glaciers. Yet because of deep sounds and fiords, no part of the island is more than twenty kilometres from the sea, even though it is up to 120 kilometres across.[1]

Australia's Heard Island and McDonald Island group are only 500 kilometres south-east of the Îles Kerguelen, but then there is a stupendous

The bleak and barren Bounty Islands, partially obscured by a rain squall, were named by Captain William Bligh in 1788, on the voyage which culminated with the mutiny on the *Bounty*.

The Subantarctic and Antarctica

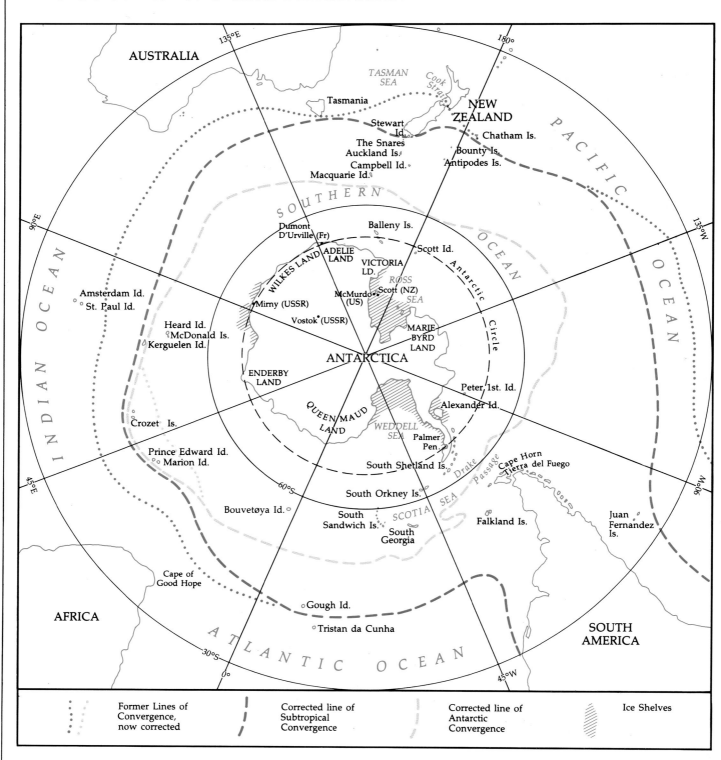

The Subantarctic Region, lying
between the Antarctic and the
Subtropical Convergences.

Sooty shearwaters "rafting" at the Western Chain islets of the Snares, before dispersing to range over wide expanses of the sea in search of food.

distance of some 6000 kilometres to Macquarie Island, slightly nearer to New Zealand than to Tasmania, and roughly the same distance from the Antarctic Continent. Although Macquarie belongs to Australia it has strong links with New Zealand, its weather station having been serviced on several occasions by the Royal New Zealand Navy, its resources exploited in the past by New Zealanders, and its ecology studied by New Zealand scientists. Its plants and wildlife have more in common with the New Zealand region than Australia, and in many ways it can also be considered geophysically part of New Zealand's subantarctic region, for just to the north-east of it lie New Zealand's subantarctic islands — the Snares, Auckland, Campbell, Antipodes, and Bounty Islands.

South of New Zealand's subantarctic islands, off North Victoria Land and the Ross Sea, and within the Antarctic Circle, lie the Balleny and Scott Islands, part of New Zealand's Ross Dependency. From these Antarctic outposts it is yet another vast distance of 4000 kilometres clockwise and eastwards again to Peter Island, the first land ever sighted within the Antarctic Circle, by Bellingshausen of Russia; while the distance from the Bounty Islands, the most easterly of New Zealand's subantarctic islands, round the Southern Ocean to the South Shetlands where this circuit began, is 8000 kilometres.

New Zealand's special place, in having five out of the twenty-four islands or island groups in this great ocean — Tristan da Cunha belonging more truly to the South Atlantic — is discussed in Chapter 4.

A comparison between similar latitudes in the Southern Hemisphere, where sea predominates, and the Northern Hemisphere, where land predominates, is particularly striking. For example, in the Northern Hemisphere, the British Isles, Germany, Poland, a swathe through the middle of Russia, and the southern half of Canada all lie between latitudes 50° and 60°. The ratio of land to sea is approximately 1.3 to 1. Within the same latitudes in the Southern Hemisphere, the only land is Punta Arenas and Tierra del Fuego in the south of South America. The rest is ocean. The ratio of sea to land is approximately 53 to 1. The islands, mere specks of land separated by enormous distances, seem infinitely remote outposts, dominated by unrestrained winds and the surrounding sea.

This is the realm of vast numbers of sea birds, which spend the greatest part of their lives at sea, riding the winds and stormy reaches of the Southern

Ocean. Among them are the legendary giant albatrosses and smaller molly-mawks, which soar in superb dynamic flight or skim the turbulent waves on a wingtip; shearwaters which make transequatorial migrations in their millions each year up into the cool offshore waters of the North Atlantic and North Pacific Oceans; prions which flutter like pale grey flakes above the sea; and small diving petrels which will frequently pass through waves rather than over them. Even the shags, with their shorter flying range, battling along with rapid wingbeats, and the many penguins, awkward in their movements on land, are birds of the sea, using the land and islands only for intensive periods of activity during which they breed and raise their young. But for this need of land for nesting, we would know very little about the birds of the subantarctic, just as we know little about the huge oceanic wilderness where they live and feed.

For the people who venture onto it, the Southern Ocean is a stormy and dangerous environment. It is vast enough to be full of mystery and change-able moods; sometimes wild, sometimes calm, with its skies fitfully lit by the glow and strange power of the aurora, often almost magical, as Edward Wilson, on Sir Robert Scott's first National Antarctic Expedition, discovered three days south of the Auckland Islands:

> Sat 12 March 1904. . . . Towards evening we got some very heavy black squalls blowing force 9 to 10, with enormous hail stones, which averaged 16–13 milli-metres, all having the same shape. This was the most weird and brilliant night I have ever seen at sea. The water was ablaze with phosphorescence. Acres of bril-liant light flashed by and the seas that broke over our deck were all ablaze. Ahead and astern were large luminous balls in the water, like gas lamps as far as one could see in every direction. Overhead was pitchy black, with aurora towards the horizon and occasional flashes of sheet lightning. And to crown all, St Elmo's fire settled every now and then on every masthead and on the two ends of all the upper yard arms, just one bright clear star on every point. It was a very beautiful sight in the pitchy black above, to see these crosses sweeping backwards and forwards as the ship rolled to and fro. The lights were as big and bright as the Gemini. One is lucky to see this electric phenomenon, for many men have spent their lives on the sea without ever coming across it.[2]

More typically, these latitudes are dominated by grey skies, stormy seas, frequent squalls, and a heavy subantarctic swell. Larson, the old Norwegian builder of the *Ranui*, had assured the coastwatchers who went south on his ship to the Auckland and Campbell Islands during the Second World War, " 'She'll never drown you', which was true enough provided that you were lucky enough to stay on her deck, but she might, and did on one occasion toss a passenger out of his bunk and knock him senseless against the mast."[3]

Mr F. Bates, chief mate of the barque *Compadre*, which went aground on the Auckland Islands in 1891, caught the weather-beaten bleakness of the sub-antarctic when he declared, "The Auckland Islands in the winter are as drear and desolate a place as one can imagine. They are swept by furious tempests and almost incessant rain. They are the homes of such seabirds as love the storm."[4]

The sea birds

Albatrosses, petrels, shearwaters, prions, and fulmars are all tube-nosed sea birds which belong to the order *Procellariiformes*. Adapted to an oceanic environment, all have grooved bills with protruding tubular nostrils, which give them a keen sense of smell and allow for the excretion of excess salt from their food, through the nasal glands, then along the grooves and off the heavily curved downward hook at the end of the bill.

Of the eighteen varieties of albatross which breed in the Southern Hemi-sphere, New Zealand has thirteen. These consist of races of the royal, wan-dering, and light-mantled sooty albatrosses, and eight of the smaller molly-

mawks. Campbell Island, with five breeding varieties, is outstanding among the world's albatross islands.[5]

The wandering and royal albatrosses, *Diomedea exulans* and *Diomedea epomophora*, have by far the longest wings of any flying birds, with spans of up to eleven feet, or 3.3 metres. A wandering albatross banded in Western Australia in 1957 had a reputed wingspan of 3.6 metres.[6] The only other comparable span is that of the Andean condor which, like several other birds, can weigh more than the albatrosses, but has a lesser wingspan of three metres.

The wandering albatross, *Diomedea exulans*, is more widespread than the royal, and breeds throughout the subantarctic. On New Zealand's islands it nests in large numbers on the Antipodes (2500 pairs), and on the Auckland Islands, where there are between 7000 and 7500 pairs, almost all of them nesting on the high southern half of Adams Island, the world's largest breeding ground for this species.[7] Wandering albatrosses also nest in small numbers on Campbell and Macquarie Islands.

The royal albatross, *Diomedea epomophora*, is restricted to four breeding places in the world. The slightly smaller northern species nests in very limited numbers at Taiaroa Head on the Otago Peninsula, near Dunedin, and in larger numbers (some 7700 pairs) on the Chatham Islands. The larger southern royal albatross of the subantarctic nests only at Campbell Island (with some 7500 pairs) and on Enderby Island in the north of the Auckland group (with less than sixty pairs), although numbers there appear to have

A wandering albatross sheltering its chick in gale conditions on Campbell Island. The dark crown and delicate patterning of the neck differentiate it from the royal albatross, which has a pure white head and body. *Photo: Ramari Stewart.*

been increasing since their protection from the predations of the sealers, castaways, and collectors of last century.

The great albatrosses have an unusually long breeding season, averaging eleven months for royals and a year for wanderers. The eggs of the royal albatross take some eighty days to hatch, and it is another 250 days before the chick flies. If successful, pairs breed every second year, and these birds can live for at least fifty years.[8] Once the young have fledged, they circle the Southern Ocean with the prevailing westerly winds, spending their lives at sea, and do not return home until they are four to six years old. Another three or four years pass before they start breeding, and during this time they form sociable groups for the highly stylised ritual of "gamming". In this ceremony, groups of adolescents and adults alternately bow, extend their huge wings, clapper their bills, and point their heads skywards, to the accompaniment of liquid rattlings, ecstatic shrieks, and melodious wheezings. As the birds mature, they form pair bonds at the nest site, by continuing a lesser form of their elaborate gam displays interspersed with rest periods.

The light-mantled sooty albatross, *Phoebetria palpebrata*, is considerably smaller, similar to the mollymawks in size. Like the larger royals and wanderers, it is generally a solitary breeder, choosing not open spaces but narrow

An aerial view of the vast numbers of mollymawks and penguins massed on the barren granite rocks of the Bounty Islands during the breeding season. The fractured structure of the rock can be clearly seen. Although a few seals are present, the large concentrations are closer to the sea.

A light-mantled sooty albatross near its nest on the slopes of Moubray Hill, Perseverance Harbour, Campbell Island. Generally, solitary nest sites are more commonly found on rocky and inaccessible ledges.

cliff ledges or craggy inland peaks. While other albatrosses are predominantly white and black, "sooties" are dark brown and grey, with a striking half circle of white behind the eye. They are beautiful birds, which frequently fly in pairs with perfect co-ordination against the sheer misty ramparts of the islands. Their haunting antiphonal call penetrates the sound of wind and waves, and is one of the loneliest sounds of the subantarctic. The sooty albatross breeds on many subantarctic islands, including Campbell, the Aucklands, and the Antipodes, and ranges the Southern Ocean as far as the Antarctic pack ice.

Mollymawks are the most numerous and gregarious of the albatrosses. Because the period from mating to the fledging of their young is eight to nine months, the birds nest every year, with the exception of the grey-headed mollymawk which breeds every two years. Mollymawks congregate in large colonies on steep, open slopes by the sea, although Buller's mollymawks on the Snares also nest within the *Olearia* forest up to a kilometre from the coast. With their white bodies and dark wings and backs, mollymawks resemble the larger albatrosses, but differ in the fierce and proud stare which the dark eyebrow or line from beak to eye gives them. It is the heads and bills which distinguish the different species and subspecies — ranging from the pale horn-coloured bill and pale grey head of the Salvin's mollymawk to the striking black and chrome-yellow bill of the Buller's and grey-headed mollymawks, and the white head and paler pink-tipped yellow bill of the black-browed.

The shy mollymawk, *Diomedea cauta*, so called because it seldom follows ships — is the largest of the mollymawks, and has three subspecies. The New Zealand subantarctic has two of these: the white-capped, *D. c. steadi*, which breeds on the grassier slopes of the western cliffs of the main Auckland Island and on Disappointment Island; and Salvin's, *D. c. salvini*, which has chosen barren islands without vegetation in the Bounty group and the stark Western Chain of the Snares. The Chatham Island subspecies, *D. c. eremita*, is outside the region.

On the lower slopes of Disappointment Island, shy mollymawks nest among tussock grasses and the huge "megaherbs" of ragged-leafed *Anisotome latifolia* and the broad, rib-leafed daisy *Pleurophyllum speciosum*.

Black-browed mollymawks and chicks at North Cape, Campbell Island. Years of occupation have denuded the site. The cylindrical nests, of mud and vegetation, grow taller each succeeding year.

The New Zealand black-browed mollymawk, *Diomedea melanophrys*, is the most numerous species, with an estimated population of 75 000 at the northern end of Campbell Island. Grey-headed mollymawks, *Diomedea chrysostoma*, nest in smaller numbers alongside the black-broweds on Campbell Island and several other subantarctic islands such as Macquarie and South Georgia.

The beautifully shaded Buller's mollymawk, *Diomedea bulleri*, has a northern subspecies at the Chatham and Three Kings Islands. Smaller estimated populations of the southern subspecies (approximately 5000 pairs) plus an unknown number of non-breeders are found on the Snares, and 2000 pairs exist on Solander Island off Fiordland. Buller's mollymawk is endemic to New Zealand, as are the three subspecies of the shy mollymawk mentioned above, and the New Zealand black-browed mollymawk.

An interesting feature of birds such as mollymawks which look very similar is that, regardless of latitude, they vary considerably in the time of year at which they court, lay eggs, and raise their young. The timing of the mollymawks' breeding is thought to depend on their differing sources of food and its seasonal availability, factors which have evolved them into different species and subspecies. Many Buller's mollymawks on the Snares are thus still courting in January when shy mollymawks on Disappointment

Left: On the Bounty Islands, the fulmar prion nests in crevices under the granite boulders. It also breeds at the barren Western Chain of the Snares, at the Auckland and Chatham Islands, and on Australia's Heard Island. It is the rarest of the three prions found in the New Zealand region.

Below: A southern giant petrel, or "Stinker", with its chick, in December snow on Campbell Island. The bird's heavy bill and single nasal tube are prominent distinguishing features. *Photo: Ramari Stewart.*

Island, further south and colder, are sitting on eggs. At the same time, New Zealand black-browed mollymawks, on Campbell Island to the south, and Salvin's mollymawks, on the Bounty Islands to the north, will have large down-covered chicks. The young of the different species fly as early as April and as late as August and September.

The many petrels, fulmars, prions, and shearwaters range from the southern giant petrel, *Macronectes giganteus*, sometimes called the "Stinker" or "Nelly" and nearly as large as a mollymawk, to the tiny fluttering prions and diminutive storm petrels. The giant petrel, even more than the skua on land, is the vulture and scavenger of the subantarctic. Its awkwardness on land and heavily tubed nose and beak make for an unattractive bird, but like the albatross it is a superb flier over the wild ocean.

The smaller cape pigeon, *Daption capense*, with its distinctive black and white flecked, barred, and patterned upper surface, is an instantly recognisable member of the petrel family, and is often seen following ships with larger giant petrels and albatrosses. Cape pigeons breed on many subantarctic islands and the Antarctic Continent, and range from the Antarctic to Cook Strait and occasionally further north. The Snares variety, *D. c. australe*, is endemic to New Zealand.

The little blue-grey fulmar prion, *Pachyptila crassirostris*, is possibly the rarest of the three prions in the New Zealand region. It breeds at the Chatham Islands, on rocky islets off the Auckland Islands, and at the

Western Chain of the Snares and the Bounty Islands. Among the jumbled rocks of the Bounties it presses flat against the granite, gripping tight even when no gale is blowing, or hides in dark fissures, from which sounds of crooning or chuckling, quarrelling, screeching, and bickering issue forth to add to the general pandemonium.

By contrast, the sooty shearwater, *Puffinus griseus*, is one of the most numerous of this large group of *Procellariiformes*, and it nests in underground burrows on many of New Zealand's offshore and subantarctic islands where there are no predators such as cats or rats. It is absent from the Bounties because there is no soil, but is found on several islands round the Southern Ocean and on Cape Horn and the coast of Chile. It is well known as the commercially exploited muttonbird of the islands around Stewart Island where, in April and May, the plump chicks, which, shortly before they leave their burrows weigh more than the adult birds, are caught, salted, and preserved for food.

A world authority, Dr John Warham of Canterbury University, tells how petrel oil has been used medicinally and as a lubricant and illuminant in other parts of the world:

> The northern fulmar was a mainstay of the St Kildan's economy, supplying "oil for their lamps, down for their beds, a delicacy for their table, a balm for their wounds, and a medicine for their distempers." . . . In some years the St Kildans exported part of their oil harvest, as the Australian mutton-birders still do with oil from the chicks of [*Puffinus*] *tenuirostris*. This has been used as a basis for sun-tan lotions, but most nowadays is used as a food stock supplement: a small quantity is said to impart a shiny coat to horses. Some 2797 gallons (12 711 litres) were sold after the 1976 season as a by product of the harvesting of 549,352 squabs [or chicks]. . . .[9]

Salvin's mollymawks ride the turbulent upcurrents at the Bounty Islands. To the right is a small fulmar prion. Moulting erect-crested penguins stand on the bare rocks below.

22

The Bounty Island shag is endemic to the group, and one of the world's rare birds, with fewer than 600 counted in 1978.

On the Chatham Islands, it is recorded that the Moriorors would hold young petrels over their mouths and allow the oil to drain straight into them![10]

New Zealand's muttonbird industry is reckoned to have no significant effect on the bird's population, but on the Snares, where the muttonbird is protected and conditions are ideal, the population is astounding, as are the results of Dr Warham's detailed and painstaking research:

> some 3,287,000 burrows were calculated for Main Island, the highest densities being 1.9 per square metre in *Poa* [tussock] meadows, with 1.2 [burrows per square metres] under the trees of the Olearia forest. . . . Assuming a 75% occupancy rate, we get a total population of about 2,750,000 burrow-holding pairs on the 328 hectares of the two largest islands . . . together with an unknown number of burrowless non-breeders . . . while, in addition to the shearwaters, some hundreds of thousands of other petrels and of penguins also breed there. Indeed, this small area supports a bird population similar in size to that of the whole of the seabird population of Britain and Ireland — some 3 million pairs — and although the shearwaters can travel far for food, the surrounding sea must be highly productive to support such a biomass . . . With populations of such magnitude it is not surprising that the southern shearwaters *P. gravis, tenuirostris* and *griseus* can come to dominate the northern waters into which they migrate during the southern winter. For example, [it has been] calculated that the Sooty Shearwater [population migrating north from Cape Horn] is the major seabird consumer during its fall passage off the Oregon coast, taking some 24,000 metric tons of anchovies during its 2 months' stay.[11]

A pair of Auckland Island shags, with two small chicks, at their nest on the northern coast of Enderby Island.

Shags, with their long necks and natural curiosity for people, on islands where people are seldom seen, are birds of the rocky coast, never far from the sea or turbulent surf. They usually breed in noisy, crowded colonies on untidy nests of dried seaweed, and observe stylised rituals of arrival, greeting, and departure. Their backs are dark with a metallic sheen and their chests and stomachs white. They stand on large webbed feet, balanced by a stubby tail. Their faces in breeding condition have striking colours, and it is these reds, mauves, greens, and purples which distinguish the different species. The New Zealand subantarctic has three species endemic to their own particular islands: The Bounty Island shag, *Leucocarbo ranfurlyi*, with

While moulting, penguins cannot go to sea for food, and are frequently lethargic and easily approached, as with this erect-crested penguin at Anchorage Bay on the Antipodes.

fewer than 600 birds, is one of the world's rarest;[12] the Auckland Island shag, *Leucocarbo colensoi*, which breeds at the north and south ends of the Auckland Islands, numbers about 5000; and the Campbell Island shag, *Leucocarbo campbelli*, has a population of under 10 000.[13]

The southern great skua, *Stercorarius skua lonnbergi*, is an aggressive and powerful bird, with an overall dark brown colouring, and white wing flashes. It is found widely round the subantarctic, and like the giant petrel is a scavenger, eating anything dead — the afterbirths, faeces, and regurgitations of sea lions, and the eggs and chicks of petrels and penguins — whenever it gets the opportunity. It is quite fearless, only hopping away with reluctance when approached, and is sometimes discovered hanging low above one's head on the wind. If threatened, it attacks with swift aerial passes which justify its alternative name of sea hawk.

Southern black-backed or Dominican gulls, *Larus dominicanus*, the little red-billed gull, *Larus novaehollandiae scopulinus*, and antarctic terns, *Sterna vittata bethunei*, with their scarlet bills, forked tails, and sharp, graceful wings, also breed on many of New Zealand's subantarctic islands.

Penguins are truly birds of the subantarctic and the colder regions of the Southern Hemisphere, although they also live in temperate seas and may well have evolved from warmer climates. As Sir Robert Falla put it, they are "characteristically Antarctic birds" and "swimming, floating, and diving are so much their normal form of activity that if it were not for the necessity of moulting and nesting like other birds they would have no more need than a porpoise to leave the water."[14]

The penguin's forelimbs have overlapping rows of stiff, almost scale-like feathers, which make these limbs marine flippers rather than aerial wings. When swimming and diving deep for food, the penguin becomes a superbly streamlined creature, in its true element. Being unable to fly, penguins leap ashore on the incoming swell, which can have as much as a nine to twelve metre rise and fall at the Bounty Islands. They generally concentrate in large colonies where there are suitable landing places and the coast is not too steep.

The New Zealand region has five of the six basic groups or genera of the world's penguins. While Australia's Macquarie Island, west of Campbell Island, is one of the world's great penguin strongholds, with king, royal, rockhopper, and gentoo penguins breeding there in numerous rookeries, which sometimes contain hundreds of thousands of birds, the New Zealand subantarctic can claim the greatest diversity of species.

The rockhopper, *Eudyptes chrysocome*, is the smallest but most common of the crested penguins. With untidy yellow head tassels, for which it was once slaughtered, it congregates in noisy colonies regulated by a highly ordered social system. It breeds on Campbell Island — where the population has declined drastically in recent years to some 5000 breeding pairs[15] — and on the Antipodes and Auckland Islands. Its distribution is widespread round the subantarctic.

The Bounty Islands are the stronghold of the endemic erect-crested penguin, *Eudyptes sclateri*, which breeds among the mollymawks. Erect-crested penguins also predominate over rockhoppers on the Antipodes, and can be distinguished by their tidier crests and deep braying voices, which contrast with the screams and yells of the rockhoppers. Erect-crested penguins breed in much smaller numbers on Campbell Island and the Auckland Islands.

The Snares crested penguin, *Eudyptes robustus*, is slightly stouter, and unique to the Snares. It nests in moderate-sized colonies of up to 300 birds, in muddy clearings in the *Olearia* forest, often long distances from the sea, which it reaches by well-trodden pathways leading from the coast. To see these penguins solemnly and silently filing through the bush is one of the most unlikely sights of New Zealand's subantarctic.

The yellow-eyed penguin, *Megadyptes antipodes*, is New Zealand's most distinctive and unusual penguin, and probably the world's rarest. It has pale eyes and a pale, gold- and black-striped head, and is noticeably anti-social. Whereas most penguins number into the tens of thousands or millions, the total population of yellow-eyeds is estimated at between 2400 and 3600.[16] It breeds on the Campbell and Auckland Islands, as well as on Stewart Island, the Otago Peninsula near Dunedin, and Banks Peninsula. It is an extremely nervous bird, both of human beings, of which other species take little notice, and of Hooker's sea lions, with better reason. On one part of Enderby Island yellow-eyed penguins have to run the gauntlet of Sandy Bay to get from the sea to their solitary nests in the scrub and rata, and occasionally sea lions will kill them on the beach, and have in fact been seen to skin one with a single shake of the head.

Sometimes stray king, royal, gentoo, and chinstrap penguins arrive as stragglers or to moult on New Zealand's subantarctic islands, but do not breed on them. On the New Zealand mainland are the shy Fiordland crested penguin, *Eudyptes pachyrhynchus*, and the little blue penguin, *Eudyptula minor*, which, with its various subspecies, is the smallest of all penguins, and well known for its catlike mewings, growling, screaming, and trumpeting under seaside baches at night! Both these species visit the Snares.

The Southern Ocean is so vast, and breeding places so few, that concentrations of birds and marine mammals are both enormous and astounding. The naturalist Andreas Reischek was ashore on the Bounty Islands at the height of the breeding season: "The stench from the guano was dreadful, and the noise deafening. There was no space, even of a few feet, free from birds, and I have never before seen such a sight."[17]

The Bounties are approached for such an assemblage of life only by the Snares. All the other island groups have their free, open spaces, with the colonies of birds and marine mammals crowded at strategic places: penguins and seals on the coasts, mollymawks and shags on the cliffs and ledges, petrels and prions honeycombing the soil, and albatrosses dotting the tussock plateaus. Their impact affects the very nature of the land.

Two Snares crested penguins strive to out-shriek each other. Such displays will frequently subside into long periods of silence, or end with one bird establishing its dominance.

3
Creatures of the Sea

New Zealand's subantarctic islands have no land animals, other than those introduced as food for sealers and castaways, or for past farming ventures. Sheep, cattle, pigs, goats, rabbits, cats, and dogs all arrived on ships, and only the dogs failed to survive. Fortunately, these animals are confined to certain islands, and there are still a significant number of islands without any of them. Less fortunately, rats and mice also got ashore with stores and food, although so far rats have only reached Campbell Island, and mice have only slightly affected the Antipodes, the main Auckland Island, and Enderby Island.

The first impact of people on the subantarctic was one of exploitation, particularly of the marine mammals — the whales, fur seals, elephant seals, and sea lions, although at Macquarie Island penguins were also slaughtered in large numbers for their feathers and oil. The pigs put ashore and the cats left behind created havoc with the vegetation and ground-nesting birds of the main Auckland Island, and rats similarly wiped out most of the ground-burrowing sea birds on Campbell Island.

The full story of these often disastrous changes, and of why farming was attempted on what are now protected islands, is told in later chapters, but essentially these changes came about because of practices which were not tempered by the realisation that there is a price to pay for exploitation, that environments can have intrinsic value far beyond commercial gain, and that these islands possess a flora and fauna unique in the world. Certainly, this realisation is widespread today, although not yet universal.

Land was still being farmed on Campbell Island and the main Auckland Island when Adams Island was made the first flora and fauna reserve in the New Zealand subantarctic in 1910. Gradually, other islands followed, with an increasing awareness of the need for their protection. It took a long time, but by 1961 all five of New Zealand's subantarctic groups were flora and fauna reserves. In 1978 they were gazetted as Nature Reserves, and by 1986 were National Reserves, giving their total environment the fullest internationally recognised degree of protection.

New Zealand fur seals with young, at the Bounty Islands. Virtually wiped out by 1810 due to the sealing trade, there were still only fifty animals at the Bounties in 1926, over a century later. There are now more than 16 000.

This complete change in policy, from plunder to preservation, has had a particularly marked effect on the marine mammals of the subantarctic which depend on these small outposts in the ocean as vital breeding grounds. Whales, elephant seals, sea lions, and fur seals converge on the sheltered bays and coasts of the islands every year to mate and give birth to their young.

The Marine Mammals

The rare right whale, *Eubalaena australis*, is a slow swimmer with a preference for the inshore waters of shallow, protected bays in which to give birth, and these characteristics made it especially vulnerable during the years of intensive international whaling last century when the species was almost exterminated. It was considered the "right" whale to hunt, not only for its oil but also for the length and quality of its baleen, the three-metre long curtain of flexible bone plates between its jaws — once used for umbrella ribs, corset stays, and riding crops — through which baleen whales sieve their food. Even the pelagic, or ocean-going, whaling ships found it profitable to anchor close inshore during the winter calving season. Once seldom seen, right whales are making a comeback at the Auckland Islands. Few people visit the Aucklands in winter, but large groups of up to seventy animals have been seen by Martin Cawthorn of the Fisheries Research Division,[1] and by regular fisheries patrolling flights of the RNZAF.

More than sixty right whales were killed by shore-based whalers on Campbell Island between 1909 and 1916, and soon became scarce.[2] But observations during the Second World War and by meteorological staff on the island since then indicate that numbers are also increasing there. The right whale is now totally protected by international law, and seems to be gradually regaining its former widespread distribution.[3]

The sperm whale, *Physeter catodon*, is the largest and best known of the toothed whales and reaches up to twenty metres in length. These whales have been seen in North East Harbour and Perseverance Harbour on Campbell Island.[4] Humpback whales, *Megaptera novaeangliae*, have been sighted in Perseverance Harbour and at Port Ross in the Aucklands.[5] J. H.

Pilot whales, sometimes incorrectly known as blackfish, accompany HMNZS *Monowai* near the Bounty Islands. The species feeds mainly on squid and often swims in large groups. Thirty-one mass strandings, involving more than 2000 animals, have been recorded on the coasts of mainland New Zealand. *Photo: Kim Westerskov.*

Right whales mating at Northwest Bay, Campbell Island. The wart-like callouses on their heads, the largest of which is called the "bonnet", can be clearly seen on the nearest animal. These excrescences help researchers to identify different animals. *Photo: Ramari Stewart, Fisheries Research Division.*

Sorensen, who was at Campbell Island during the Second World War, records that sperm whales, blue whales, and dolphins were sometimes sighted at sea. On one occasion he approached to within four metres of a right whale in Perseverance Harbour, noting that "the noise of the 'blow' at this distance was rather awe inspiring"![6] Both still photographs and film taken at the time proved useless because of a camera defect or, more likely, the excitement of the moment.

Whales are air-breathing, warm-blooded animals, with a blood temperature much the same as humans. They usually live in the colder oceans where the huge concentrations of shrimp-like krill, or fish and squid on which the different species feed, occur in the greatest quantities. Some 300 mm or so of insulating fat, or blubber, serves as a food reserve and protects them against heat loss. The blue whale, *Balaenoptera musculus*, is the largest creature that has ever lived on earth, growing up to thirty metres, or a hundred feet in length, and weighing 130 tonnes, the equivalent of thirty elephants or 1600 people. The right whale, growing up to eighteen metres in length, was hunted for the longest and most valuable baleen, and Campbell Island is one of the best places in the world to study this rare and usually solitary mammal, for it congregates in shallow waters there during the breeding season.

Pinnipeds, the group of flippered marine mammals which includes seals, elephant seals, sea lions and the northern walrus, differ from whales, or cetaceans, in that most species come ashore to give birth, suckle their young, and mate for the following season. This made them particularly vulnerable to hunters in search of their insulating fur and blubber. Years later these animals are only just beginning to breed again in certain places, and to approach their former numbers on once prolific grounds.

Elephant seals, *Mirounga leonina*, are the largest of the pinnipeds, weighing up to almost four tonnes. Unlike fur seals and sea lions they cannot walk on their flippers, but like gargantuan slugs move on shore with a rippling, undulating motion, dragging their rear flippers behind them. The southern elephant seal occurs throughout the subantarctic, and is particularly numerous on South Georgia, with 300 000 animals, Kerguelen and Heard Islands, with about 200 000, and Macquarie Island, with 100 000 animals.[7] The Campbell Island population of less than 500 animals is small by these standards, and breeding numbers are even smaller at the Antipodes.

Elephant seal bulls come ashore to moult in February, at the end of the breeding season. The swollen trunk-like snouts from which they get their name are at their largest during the mating period. Mature animals like these can weigh almost four tonnes.

Elephant seals visit the Auckland Islands and the Snares, and are occasionally seen on the New Zealand mainland as far north as the Bay of Islands. The northern elephant seal is found in smaller numbers and is distributed from Mexico to Alaska.

Elephant bulls are often heavily scarred from territorial battles, and can be up to six metres in length. They come ashore about the middle of August, some two weeks before the cows, to establish their territories. The largest males may have harems of up to twenty cows, which are about half their size, and mating begins as soon as the pups have been weaned, three weeks after birth. The pups, which will have gained weight at about five kilogrammes a day, leave for the sea to fend for themselves after only two months. The harems break up and are gone by the end of November.

Elephant seals also come ashore to moult; the younger ones in November, while breeding is still going on, followed by the breeding cows in January and the bulls in February. During this period, which can last from thirty to forty days, they laze on open beaches, such as Northwest Bay on Campbell Island, or lie in deep and foul-smelling mud wallows in the peat and tussock, behind Northwest Bay or at Tucker Cove at the head of Perseverance Harbour. If disturbed, they rear up, flecks of white spume flying from their nostrils on a breath fetid with stale fish, their pink balloon-like tongues rising and falling in their gorges with each sickening rattle of protest. However, if approached or passed quietly, they take very little notice of people.

The leopard seal, *Hydrurga leptonyx*, is the only other true or earless seal found round New Zealand's subantarctic islands. Their hearing is keen, but they have no external ear. Not only are they very much rarer than elephant

New Zealand fur seals were widely hunted in the early nineteenth century for their inner pelt of soft, reddish-brown fur. They were exterminated on Macquarie Island and the Antipodes, and reduced to very low numbers on the Auckland and Bounty Islands.

seals, they are very different in appearance. They have sleek, large, serpentine heads with sharp multi-pointed teeth, and streamlined bodies with mottled markings. Females are larger than males, which is unusual. Like elephant seals they swim with fishlike lateral undulations of the body and rear flippers. Leopard seals mate at sea and do not form colonies ashore. Little, therefore, is known about them. The solitary animals which occasionally visit the subantarctic islands are generally vagrants from the Antarctic Continent.

The New Zealand fur seal, *Arctocephalus forsteri*, is by far the most numerous of the eared seals in this region. They have small external ears, and differ from the "true" seals in that they are able to bring their hind flippers up beneath their bodies and walk rather than haul themselves along. Attractive to hunters for their inner pelt of soft, reddish-brown fur, they were the main seal hunted, and were exterminated on Macquarie Island and the Antipodes, and reduced to very small numbers indeed on the Auckland and Bounty Islands. On the Bounties only five were seen in 1831 at the height of the breeding season,[8] and recovery was extremely slow, because fur seals return to the same place to breed each year, and do not normally seek out new territories. Only one fur seal was seen on Enderby Island in the Aucklands in March 1954 and a few in November of that year, although it is thought there were probably small colonies along the inaccessible western coast.

On the Bounty Islands, where the seals have been protected since 1894, numbers had risen to only fifty by 1926. But this was a nucleus. By 1950 there were between 5000 and 6000, and by 1982, 16 000, with an estimated rate of increase of about five percent each year. On the Antipodes, it took until 1985 for the first indications that fur seals were beginning to breed there once again. On Campbell Island, there were about 800 fur seals in 1958, and 2000 in 1969.[9] On the Snares, there are some 1200 animals on the main islands and the outlying Western Chain. There are also breeding colonies and rocky hauling-out grounds round the New Zealand mainland, and the total population is thought to be about 40 000, including 2000 in South and Western Australia.

Fur seals feed largely on squid and octopus, and are able to stay under water for up to ten minutes, with a mean dive time of about two minutes,

Sandy Bay on Enderby Island, looking east. Each of the two large beachmaster bulls presides over a harem of smaller, fawn-coloured females, some of them with pups.

during which their circulation is greatly limited to save oxygen, and their heart beat slows from eighty to twenty beats per minute. Males and females are much closer in size, and it is often hard to distinguish between females and young males. Harems, of up to ten cows, are smaller than those of elephant seals or sea lions, and in further contrast to the elephant seal, fur seals suckle their pups for 300 days and are found ashore for most of the year.

Hooker's sea lion, *Phocarctos hookeri*, is the least known and one of the rarest of the world's five species of sea lion. There are, for example, well over 100 000 Californian sea lions (*Zalophus californianus* — the species used as a performing animal) and over 240 000 Steller sea lions — *Eumetopias jubatus* — in the Northern Hemisphere, and more than 100 000 South American sea lions — *Otaria byronia*.[10] But there are only about 5000 Australian sea lions — *Neophoca cinerea* — and between 6500 and 7000 Hooker's sea lions.[11]

Hooker's sea lions are consistently larger than fur seals, and are strictly hair seals, in that they have no under-fur. The males are very much larger than the females — 400 kilogrammes and 160 kilogrammes respectively. The bulls are massive, dark brown animals with powerful shoulders, blunt, black faces, and heavy manes which protect them in their territorial fights. The females are lithe and graceful, and a pale greyish fawn, cream, or tawny gold in colour.

Most bays in the harbours of the Auckland Islands have their guardian sea lion or two, and these are invariably females or inquisitive young males.

Although the Hooker's sea lion is an eared seal, like the New Zealand fur seal, it is strictly a hair seal, with no soft under-fur. It has no fear of people, and clearly enjoys its greater manoeuvrability and speed in the sea. *Photo: Kim Westerskov.*

An eight-month-old Hooker's sea lion pup at Campbell Island. Note the clearly defined "fingers" of its flipper, and its small external ear. *Photo: Ramari Stewart.*

Edward Wilson of Scott's Antarctic Expedition wrote in his diary of a memorable encounter with sea lions at night:

> It was very dark indeed when we neared Erebus Cove and the phosphorescence in the water was beautiful. We then saw a sight which I shall not soon forget. There were from two to four or five Sea Lions following our boat in the water, rising with a snort to breathe every minute or two and then diving under the boat. There wasn't a scrap of light in the sky to spoil the effect and each beast was ablaze with phosphorescence, so that one could follow its every motion — every movement of the flippers, every curve in its flashing pathway.[12]

There is a feeling of empathy in this description which is very understandable, for sea lions are less wary than fur seals, and provided one moves quietly and avoids eye contact, especially with the bulls and "stroppier" males, they will soon ignore one and continue their normal activities.

After the sealing era, castaways on the Auckland Islands occasionally killed sea lions for food, but the species has been fully protected since 1881 and is the subject of a detailed on-going study.

The world population of Hooker's sea lion is centred on the Auckland Islands, with the main rookeries on Dundas Island, with 3550 sea lions, and Enderby Island, with 1200 animals at Port Ross and a small colony of 150 among the trees on Figure-of-Eight Island in Carnley Harbour.[13] There is a small colony at Northwest Bay on Campbell Island, where some fifty to a hundred pups are born annually. Between two and five pups are born each

Young elephant seals in a foul-smelling mud wallow at Windlass Cove, Northwest Bay, on Campbell Island. Like sea lions, elephant seals often show a preference for resting close to each other.

year at the Snares. The Snares are also visited by fifty to a hundred unsuccessful young bulls which migrate north from the Auckland Islands during the breeding season.

The breeding season begins in November with the arrival of the bulls and the fighting which settles their territories. Sandy Bay, on the sheltered side of Enderby Island, is the most accessible colony and is ideal for sea lions, which prefer beaches and bays to the rocky exposed coasts sought out by fur seals. As the females reach the colonies early in December they assemble into harems of up to twenty-five animals. The bulls guard their territories fiercely if challenged, and do not eat, drink, or leave them for two months.

Pupping starts after a few days and continues into January, with most pups being born in the second half of December. Seven or eight days after giving birth the females mate for the following year's cycle. At two weeks of age the pups gather into large, closely packed "pods", and as they become more adventurous begin to move onto the grass sward behind the beach or to play in streams and rock pools. In spite of this their mothers have to coax them into the sea for the first time and overcome their initial fear, much as fledgelings have to be taught to fly.

Outside the breeding season, sea lions are more widely dispersed and reach Macquarie Island, Stewart Island, and Foveaux Strait, with individual animals landing on the Otago coast and Banks Peninsula.

Whereas the tropics have a vast variety of species, each of which is not very numerous, both on land and in the sea, the subantarctic has a few species which occur in vast numbers. This is particularly true of the ocean, with its countless swarms of shrimp-like krill, squid, and zooplankton.

The main commercial fish of the Southern Ocean are orange roughy, squid, southern blue whiting, mackerel, warehou, barracouta, sharks, oreo dory, and blue cod. Inshore varieties are very limited and often low in numbers, as around Campbell Island. There are some five species of the Antarctic cod *Notothenia*, a blenny, a pipefish, a flatfish common to the seas round the New Zealand mainland, and an endemic sucker fish. There are also fresh water *Galaxias*, which tolerate saltwater and are interesting because, with land invertebrates, they support a long-standing argument for the former existence of land bridges — an argument which has been just as convincingly refuted, and which is discussed in Chapter 5.

The inshore fish of the subantarctic islands are almost without exception heavily infested with parasitic worms. This was noticed at the Auckland Islands by the Antarctic explorer Dumont D'Urville, in 1840.

> For the first few days that we were in harbour here, our sailors thought that these worms were merely veins and ate them freely, without ever suffering any ill-effects. But later on, when they saw that most of the officers turned with disgust from this infected fish, they too preferred to eat their ordinary rations of salted fish. . . . The most vigorous of [the fish], no less than the others, were riddled with huge worms of astonishing thickness and length.[14]

Sorensen also expressed horror at this discovery, and wrote that fish did not

Fish, Crabs, and Shellfish

An exquisite species of *Cyanea* jellyfish, which grows up to forty centimetres across, photographed in clear water at a depth of twenty-four metres, at Northwest Bay, Campbell Island. The small fish is of an unknown species. *Photo: Kim Westerskov.*

A well camouflaged southern spider crab stirs the marine silt for food, at Campbell Island. These crabs are also common in shallow waters at the Aucklands. The southern king crab inhabits deeper waters. *Photo: Kim Westerskov.*

figure prominently on wartime subantarctic menus, and that what fish they did have came from New Zealand in tins![15] An exception was flounder, which appeared to be free of parasites.

The most interesting of the crustacea, particularly numerous round the Auckland Islands, is the giant spider crab, *Jacquinotia edwardsii*, which can measure up to 200 mm across the shell, with a total span, including legs, of up to a metre. During the time they shed their shells they are preyed upon by sea lions, which then have a characteristically pink colour to their regurgitations. The prospect of fishing these crabs commercially has been considered, but is unlikely because of the difficulty of extracting their meat.

Shellfish are common, and most of the early explorers tried them. Large cockles of up to fifty millimetres in diameter were found at the head of Laurie Harbour. Edward Wilson considered them "like watery oysters, nothing like as good as Welsh cockles",[16] but thought the mussels at Port Ross excellent. The crew of the German merchant ship *Erlangen*, hiding in Carnley Harbour at the start of the Second World War, found "an enormous quantity of mussels"[17] at the first low tide. This was particularly welcome, as the crew's provisions were critically low. The shellfish helped them to extend their stay to gather the wood vital for fuel, and

> every day, at the ebb tide, the [Chinese] cook and his mate were busy gathering sackfuls of mussels. On good days we could haul 7 sacks on board. . . . [To preserve the shellfish] the flesh of the mussels was wound round cables and hung out on deck to dry.[18]

Limpets, which wander in search of food and return to the eroded ovals of their anchoring positions as the tide retreats, grow to a large size. There is also a small white-footed paua or abalone, *Haliotis virginea huttoni*, on Campbell Island and in the north of the Auckland Islands. The paua has been brought back from Enderby Island to cross with the larger black-footed paua, *Haliotis iris*, in the hope of producing a variety more acceptable to the Japanese market.

A lively scientific interest makes no direct impression on the coastal waters or shore life of the subantarctic islands, but the commercial exploitation of the southern king crab, *Lithodes murrayi*, found in deeper waters on the Campbell

Above: Mussels grow prolifically round the shallow shores of Carnley Harbour, in the south of the Auckland Islands, and were a welcome source of food for shipwrecked mariners, the crew of the German cargo steamer *Erlangen*, and World War II coastwatchers.

Left: Looking up at flora and fauna on the underside of rocks near the south head of Perseverance Harbour, at a depth of eleven metres. The numerous bottle-shaped animals with round siphons are sea squirts, some of a still unnamed species. The fish on the left is a thorn fish, *Bovichtus variegatus*, and the purple coralline patches are a marine alga. *Photo: Kim Westerskov*.

Plateau, is always a possibility. Crayfish — *Jasus edwardsii*, or rock lobsters — also occur in sparse numbers at the Auckland Islands, which is probably the southernmost limit of their range, as well as the limit of their commercial viability.

Our future influence on the animals of the subantarctic may not be direct, as in the past, but through line, pot, and trawl fishing could take the form of increased competition for the food on which they totally depend, in the ocean where they spend the greater part of their lives.

4
The Nature of the Subantarctic

The Southern Ocean, that grey region of storms and restless seas which surrounds Antarctica, can be loosely thought of as the subantarctic. Yet some of its islands, like South Georgia, with glaciers and permanent snow, or those within the Antarctic Circle, clearly belong to the Antarctic, while Gough Island, at 40° south in the South Atlantic, still remains a subantarctic island.

It is not temperature or latitude alone, but the character of the ocean — its currents, surface temperature, the life it spawns and supports, and its effect on the environment and ecology of the islands upon it — which defines the nature of the subantarctic.

At the northern boundary of the subantarctic region, the surface waters of the Southern Ocean, drifting in a slowly widening circumpolar flow under the influence of the prevailing westerly winds, meet the warmer subtropical waters of the Pacific, Indian, and South Atlantic Oceans. This meeting of cold and warm seas is known as the Subtropical Convergence (see map, page 14). The convergence is not always a clearly defined boundary, but sometimes a times a general region where waters mingle and mix. Just the same, surface temperatures differ from one side to the other by at least four degrees: from 8° to 12°C in winter and from 12° to 16°C in summer. At the convergence, the cold subantarctic waters sink and turn back south as the uppermost of several complex subsurface currents.

The southern boundary between the subantarctic and the Antarctic is better defined, although it can vary seasonally, and from year to year, by up to 160 kilometres in its position north or south. Across this Antarctic Convergence there is a temperature difference of about 2°C; a variation of 1° to 3°C in winter and of 4° to 6°C in summer. As they meet, the colder and denser Antarctic water sinks quite sharply beneath the subantarctic surface water.

Just as the Subtropical Convergence defines the limit of certain fish and marine organisms, and therefore seabirds, so the Antarctic Convergence limits the range of various plankton and fish. This then is the true boundary of the Antarctic: the Antarctic Circle is no more than a line on the map.

Detail of ground cover on Disappointment Island: a cushion of purple *Gentiana cerina*, the broad leaves of some small *Stilbocarpa polaris*, the long liliaceous leaves of *Bulbinella rossii*, and the prickly burs of biddy-bid — *Acaena minor antarctica*.

The large, sage-green, leathery leaves of *Olearia lyallii*, the giant tree daisy which, with *Hebe elliptica* (shown here), *Senecio stewartiae*, and tussock grasses, forms the prevailing cover on North East Island, the main island of the Snares.

In a lecture, Dr Dilwyn John, of the 1933 *Discovery II* Expedition, described the Antarctic Convergence in this way:

> The zoologist need know only the species of prawns of the genus *Euphausia* to which *Euphausia superba*, whale food, belongs. They are so numerous in the surface that his net will always catch some. If, in the neighbourhood of the convergence, he takes *Euphausia vallentini* or *Euphausia longirostris* he is in sub-Antarctic water. He will have crossed the convergence and be in the Antarctic when his net brings back *Euphausia frigida* and not *vallentini* nor *longirostris*. But we, whether sailors or scientists, know and will remember the convergence best in another way: as the line to the north of which we felt one day . . . after months in the Antarctic, genial air again and soft rain like English rain in the spring. . . . It was like passing at one step from winter into spring. In the southernmost lands in the sub-Antarctic, the islands about Cape Horn, the earth smells as earth should smell and as it never does in the Antarctic.[1]

The islands off Cape Horn, and the Falkland Islands to the east of the tip of South America, are indeed in subantarctic seas, for the cold Falkland Current diverts the Subtropical Convergence north of them until it meets the east coast of South America at latitude 30° south, as can be seen on page 14. On the other side of the continent the Humboldt Current takes subantarctic waters even further north, and influences its entire western coast. The Juan Fernandez Islands, between latitude 33° and 34° south, on which Alexander Selkirk was marooned, to become the inspiration for Daniel Defoe's *Robinson Crusoe*, are even further north than Gough Island in the Atlantic. However, like the Falklands, they are influenced by the nearby South American continent, and have a milder summer temperature than the subantarctic's true exposed oceanic islands.

Giant subantarctic herbs on Campbell Island — the daisy *Pleurophyllum speciosum*, the yellow heads of *Stibocarpa polaris*, and the carrot-like leaves of *Anisotome latifolia*. Beyond are the leaves of the lily *Bulbinella rossii*.

Rugged, volcanic Gough Island, 350 kilometres south-south-east of Tristan da Cunha, is also south of the Subtropical Convergence, and therefore subantarctic. It has vast numbers of penguins and seals, besides being a breeding island for wandering albatrosses and the most northerly limit of the giant petrel.

The list of subantarctic islands now becomes restricted in more ways than one. French surveys of the Southern Ocean in 1982 indicate that in the region of the Kerguelen and Crozet Islands, formerly regarded as subantarctic, the Antarctic and Subtropical Convergences actually merge into a single convergence zone, of about three degrees of latitude, "effectively eliminating the subantarctic region".[2]

Most of the islands scattered round the Southern Ocean, and mentioned in Chapter 2, belong to the Antarctic — islands such as South Georgia, Bouvetøya Island, Heard Island, and the Balleny Islands. Prince Edward Island lies

Southern rata in flower on Rose
Island, Port Ross.

just within the Antarctic Convergence. Others are borderline cases just
outside the Subtropical Convergence: Tristan da Cunha, which has subantarctic penguins and albatrosses, as well as subtropical noddies; and the
Chatham Islands, which have subantarctic prions, fulmars, albatrosses, and
a subtropical petrel, breeding on them.

The only remaining islands between the convergences are Australia's
Macquarie Island and New Zealand's Campbell Island, Bounty Islands, and
the Antipodes, Snares, and Auckland Islands. Gough Island in the South
Atlantic, Macquarie Island, and the five New Zealand groups are arguably
the world's only true subantarctic islands.

Although the subantarctic is essentially an oceanic region, ornithologists
associate it with the large number of sea birds which live within it and
nowhere else. Botanists, too, regard it as quite a special region for plants; but
while there is a distinct subantarctic flora, there are still scientists who find
certain aspects controversial. For example, some argue that a true subantarctic island cannot have trees, while others point out that stunted trees
are the last step before the timber line and the tundra or true Antarctic
beyond, and are thus less than antarctic — in other words subantarctic.[3]

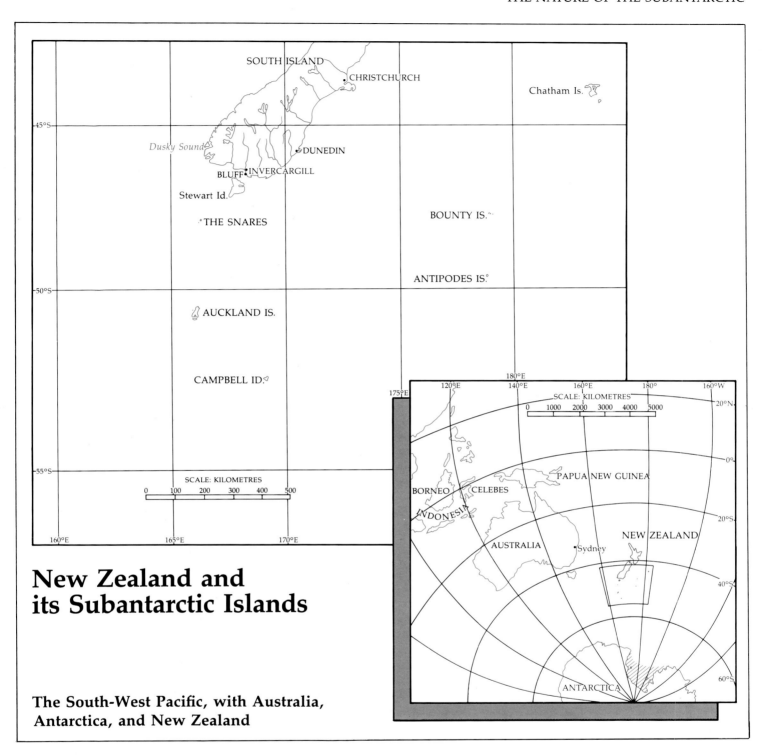

New Zealand and its Subantarctic Islands

The South-West Pacific, with Australia, Antarctica, and New Zealand

There is, for example, an introduced Sitka spruce, *Picea sitchensis*, in a reasonably sheltered spot at Camp Cove on Campbell Island, which has been growing there for between sixty and eighty years. Although it is green and healthy, it is stocky and about six metres high. In Northwest America it can grow, in about the same time, to a height of sixty metres, as one of the world's great trees.

The *Olearia* and rata forests on the Snares and Auckland Islands are severely affected by wind and temperature except in the most sheltered places, and their compressed, contorted forms resemble subalpine forests growing at high altitudes near the timberline in New Zealand. Sir Joseph

Interior of the *Olearia lyallii* forest, on the Snares. *Olearia* is a giant tree daisy, or leatherwood. The leaning trunks are due to the strong prevailing winds and soft ground. The rhubarb-like *Stilbocarpa robusta* grows in the lighter clearings.

Hooker, the botanist on Sir James Clark Ross's British Antarctic Expedition in 1840, described the Auckland rata as "a dense thicket of stagheaded trees . . . gnarled and stunted by the violence of the gales";[4] and Dr Leonard Cockayne wrote that "more than one half of their length lies prone upon the ground" and that "they would have little chance if they stood erect, as do ordinary forest trees".[5]

Although the subantarctic environment is generally inhospitable to temperate vegetables and cultivated plants, which seldom flourish, it is ideal for the native vegetation. This is well adapted to its acid peat soil, which has formed from the decaying vegetation over the centuries. Sometimes, in fact, in what Dr Cockayne called "an important and peculiar characteristic"[6] of their perpetually wet surroundings, plants such as the *Danthonia* and *Poa* tussock grasses build up thick trunks, "forming peat in their lower portions and growing above with vigour, the living part putting forth roots and subsisting on its own dead remains"[7] — thus avoiding the worst of the acidity and the waterlogged ground.

Far from simply representing a southern extension of New Zealand, many species of flowering plants are characteristic of the circumpolar subantarctic, having been distributed round it by sea birds and ocean currents. Sir Joseph Hooker found a seventh of the plants on the Auckland Islands common to other subantarctic regions, while on Campbell Island, further from the influence of mainland New Zealand, as much as a quarter of the plants were found to occur on other islands in the Southern Ocean, and a sixth discovered to be common to Tierra del Fuego, 16 000 kilometres away.[8]

The surrounding ocean is critical to the ecology of the subantarctic islands — to their plants, animals, and physical environment. Remote outposts such as Campbell Island and the Antipodes may seem bleak and barren, but sterile surfaces without any vegetation at all are virtually unknown in New Zealand's subantarctic, apart from the Bounty Islands, where wind, waves, and the incessant traffic of birds and seals on the bare granite rock prevent the growth of even the most primitive vegetation, except for a few algae and lichens in stagnant pools and on a few vertical rock surfaces.

On all other basalt islands, much of the rock is covered with encrusting lichens — some of which resemble grey, white, or black rock — or by plants, large and small, growing in peat from the sea to the summits.

The Plant Communities

Subantarctic plants, like all others, have four simple requirements: light, heat, water, and nutrients. Although most of the sunlight is rather weak and the skies predominantly overcast, light is seldom a limiting factor and summer days are extremely long. Because of the ocean, summer temperatures vary only by a few degrees, and while the wind chill may be very severe, the plants have special characteristics, or adaptations, which allow them to soak up all the available heat. The most striking are the giant herbaceous plants, or "megaherbs", which Dr Cockayne called "the special glory of these subantarctic islands",[9] and which prompted Sir Joseph Hooker to declare that here were "species more remarkable for their beauty and novelty than the flora of any other country can show".[10] These unexpectedly rich-looking plants, with their purple or yellow flowers, have leaves up to half a metre in diameter, which act as solar panels, soaking up the sun's radiation. Being close to the ground they avoid most of the wind chill, and leaf temperatures may be five to ten degrees warmer than the surrounding air. Similarly, moss cushions can feel quite warm to the touch.

The ocean also favourably reduces extremes of temperature. There is only five degrees average difference between the summer and winter months. Heavy frost is unheard of and snow infrequent. As botanist and plant ecologist Dr Colin Meurk explains, "There is thus a virtual year round growing season at sea level which even North Auckland cannot boast because of summer drought."[11] Moisture is certainly not short in the subantarctic, and although nutrients tend to be deficient in peaty, acid soils, the maritime influence again greatly enhances the natural fertility near the coast. A steady rain of dilute sea spray, as well as bird and seal excrement, makes parts of the islands extremely fertile, as Dr Meurk points out:

> Along the coasts where the giant tussock grasslands and herbfields grow, total above and below ground production may be an enormous five to seven kilogrammes of new dry matter growth in each square metre per year. This is comparable to New Zealand's top yielding sheep and dairy pastures. But as various failed farming ventures have shown, this subantarctic growth is too localised and cannot sustain trampling and grazing.[12]

A fell-field on the top of Adams Island, photographed while looking north towards Carnley Harbour and the main Auckland Island. Mosses and the shiny leaves of *Pleurophyllum hookeri* cover the stony, saturated ground.

Cold, wind, and excessive moisture are limiting factors to plant growth at high elevations. On exposed coasts, severe salt burning from storms may detract from the greater fertility which lesser amounts of salt induce. For these reasons the taller trees and dense scrub are found in the more sheltered harbours and valleys. Tussock grass and the lusher herbfields grow on the exposed coastal areas, where woody growth is discouraged. The more stunted herbfields, mosses, lichens, and bogs occur on the high country where the soil is thin and leached and the land frequently covered in low cloud.

Colin Meurk has described the subantarctic as "awful for people, wonderful for plants!"[13] High on the open fell-field, with its stony, boggy ground scarred by the force of the wind, one cannot help feeling unsure about the environment for plants as well. The *Pleurophyllum hookeri*, with its silvery green leaves pressed flat to the saturated, blackish soil, is hardly worth calling a "megaherb" at this altitude. But the highly diffused light is surprisingly bright, and even as squalls sweep across, there are sheltered places where delicate plants flower, and where gentians, in pockets of calm, bloom in clusters that range in colour from deep reddish purple to mauve and white.

Conditions in the subantarctic may be likened to sinking mainland New Zealand into the sea, so that the stunted trees normally found just below the

The predominant ground cover of the central plateau of the main Antipodes Island — pale *Poa litorosa* tussock grass, and deep-green *Polystichum vestitum* fern.

bushline occur at sea level, and the alpine herbfields at low elevations. This pattern of vegetation growth is particularly noticeable on Enderby and Rose Islands, which rise less than fifty metres above the sea. F. R. Chapman, on Rose Island in 1891, found gentians close to the shore and

> tiny creeping Coprosmas with bright berries, telling the visitor in the plainest terms that he was now entering a sub-antarctic region, and that the sea-level plants here were equivalent to mountain plants nearly 3,000 feet above the sea in New Zealand.[14]

In the centre of Enderby Island, between the open sward to the north and the scrub and rata forest to the south, is a low-lying moorland of *Cassinia* and *Oreobolus*, with bright green moss cushions and scattered plants of *Myrsine* scrub, stunted *Dracophyllum*, and dwarfed southern rata. Open and pleasant on a fine summer day, this tundra-like bog of the greater part of the year is the result of poor drainage, highly acid peats, and a low level of fertility.

Tussock grass is slowly returning on Rose Island, and would be widespread on the exposed northern side of Enderby Island but for the rabbits and cattle. On the undisturbed Antipodes, a clumpy *Poa litorosa* tussock meadow is the dominant cover of the islands, and appears as a strangely pallid green from a distance, with the darker, stronger green of *Polystichum vestitum* fern marking the gullies.

Where the high plateau of the main Antipodes island descends towards the coast and the salt spray, this *Poa* meadow is borne up to 1.5 metres above the ground on its own massive trunks of dead and rotting leaves. To try and push a way through, neck deep, is almost impossible, and the "fastest" way is to risk frequent falls by stepping from the wobbling top of one shock-headed mass to the next. This exhausting means of progress is humorously described by the naturalist H. Guthrie-Smith:

> Vainly attempting to keep his balance the walker might at one stride be sema-phoring high and tall, desperately gesticulating, the next his shoulders only might be visible above the treacherous mat of grass. Sometimes deeper still only a lonely head with ears like handles to lift the thing by might remain oscillating from side to side, spying out the best line for a new struggle![15]

Poa litorosa tussock is also the predominant cover of Disappointment Island, with two similar tussocks, *Poa foliosa* and *Chionochloa antarctica*, less

The lily *Bulbinella rossii*, unpalatable to grazing stock, occurs in large and spectacular splashes of colour on Campbell Island and Enderby Island in early summer. *Photo: T. E. Atkinson, Lands & Survey.*

common. On Campbell Island, *Chionochloa antarctica* was heavily reduced by burning and grazing, as was the maritime *Poa foliosa*, which is only slowly returning.

Below the tussock on Campbell Island the tall native *Dracophyllum* — or "Draco" as the meteorological station staff call it with perverse affection — is the main scrub, taking the place of rata on the Aucklands and *Olearia* on the Snares. *Dracophyllum* species may technically attain dwarf tree status, growing to about five metres in height in the more sheltered places and harbours. In New Zealand, another *Dracophyllum* species is known as the Inanga, or grass tree, and grows to twelve metres, with spearlike leaves.

Between the tussock and the rata forest on the Auckland Islands, the scrub is more complex, and almost impenetrable. It contains brittle, needle-like *Dracophyllum* and stunted rata, tough *Hebe* and *Coprosma*, and a rigid inter-laced shrub called *Myrsine divaricata*. At its worst it has caused scientists, battling through it, after a few frantic hours snatched as the chance of a lifetime, to abandon their priceless specimens in desperation. B. C. Aston described it in 1907 as

> one of the worst drawbacks we had to encounter; from four to six feet high it is quite impassable with reasonable exertion; walking on the top can be undertaken only by a very light man. Only with the severest exertion can it be pushed aside to enable a man to pass, crawling under it is quite out of the question.[16]

To R. McCormick, on Sir James Clark Ross's Antarctic Expedition in 1840, the scrub was

> as impervious as a thicket of thorns to get through, and so matted and interlaced at the top that I sometimes had to roll myself bodily over their flat summits. . . . [In places] The bottom was of so swampy a nature that I sometimes sank knee-deep in the morass, rendering all progression most laborious and toilsome. . . . Heavy rain . . . had been incessantly falling since I started, accompanied . . . by a cold, chilling state of the atmosphere, which all along had been overcast, thick and gloomy . . .[17]

However, he was finally rewarded by a large bed of the lily which Hooker was to name *Chrysobactron rossii*, and which is now known as *Bulbinella rossii*, in full bloom.

> The rich golden-yellow flower spikes contrasting with the deep leek-green of their long liliaceous leaves and the framework of ferns, grasses, and short thorny scrub in which they were set, combined to produce a charming effect, much heightened, too, by the vicinity of an umbelliferous plant having flowers of a purplish hue.[18]

The giant daisy, *Pleurophyllum speciosum*, a magnificent herbaceous plant with flower heads a metre above the ground, and corrugated leaves up to half a metre in diameter, growing amongst the tussock on Campbell Island. The foreground fern is *Polystichum vestitum*.

The flowers of the tall, herbaceous plant *Pleurophyllum criniferum* have no petals. The large leaves grow close to the ground to absorb the sun's warmth. The tussock grass is *Poa litorosa*.

Anisotome latifolia, a giant umbelliferous herb of the carrot family, which thrives in the cold but generally equable subantarctic climate.

At some cost, McCormick had stumbled upon "the special glory of these subantarctic islands";[19] for the mauve flowers, growing waist high, were *Anisotome latifolia*, a giant herb of the carrot family. The yellow *Bulbinella* flower was a close relative of the Maori onion, which gives a golden glow of colour in season to the high country of South Canterbury and Otago and other parts of New Zealand. It grows thickly over a wide area on Enderby Island, and on Campbell Island was noticed by Hooker as giving a yellow tinge to the landscape clearly visible two kilometres from shore.

Being unpalatable, *Bulbinella rossii* was not grazed by sheep on Campbell Island, whereas other herbaceous plants were trampled and eaten, and are only slowly returning. In the same way, the giant "megaherbs", several of them unique to New Zealand's subantarctic islands, are found on the Auckland Islands only on steep cliff ledges where introduced cattle or pigs cannot reach them. It is only on the Snares, Disappointment Island, the Antipodes, and Adams Island that they can be seen in their natural state and in the wonderful profusion with which they once covered Campbell Island and the main Auckland Island.

Perhaps the most magnificent of these megaherbs is the giant daisy, *Pleurophyllum speciosum*, which has flower heads standing about a metre above ground and rich, deeply corrugated leaves up to half a metre in diameter. Even taller is *Pleurophyllum criniferum*. It is a strange plant, as the flowers are dull, purplish-brown buttons or ray florets without petals, and is related to the smaller and similarly flowered *Pleurophyllum hookeri* of higher, more exposed places.

Sealers and castaways quickly recognised the palatability and nutritional value of the giant herbs, and found *Stilbocarpa polaris*, with its heavy, pale green flower heads, particularly useful on Macquarie and Disappointment Islands. The survivors of the *Dundonald* baked the roots and then peeled and

The rata forest, on Enderby Island, with its moss-covered floor, tends to be lower and less dense than on the main Auckland Island.

The long, cable-like strands of a forest of *Macrocystis pyrifera*, the largest of all seaweeds, photographed at thirteen metres at Northwest Bay, Campbell Island. This seaweed is the world's fastest growing plant — up to fifty centimetres a day.
Photo: Kim Westerskov.

ate them like potatoes. At other times they grated them. An allied plant, the ginseng, is still highly valued for its widespread and almost mystical medicinal properties in China. On the Snares, the similar, rare, and rhubarb-like *Stilbocarpa robusta* grows in the clearings and lighter parts of the *Olearia* forest, and is confined to this island group and some of the smaller islands off Stewart Island.

The *Olearia* forest of the Snares covers four-fifths of the main island and gives it a unique and unmistakable character. *Olearia lyallii* is one of the largest of several New Zealand species of the leatherwood, Tupare, a tree daisy which grows from two to ten metres tall, its gnarled trunks leaning with the wind, and its large, leathery leaves making a pale sage-green canopy, broken only by the occasional darker greens of *Senecio stewartiae* or *Hebe elliptica*. The bare peat of the forest floor, scattered with dead leaves and twigs, is a network of *Olearia* roots riddled with the burrows of sooty shearwaters.

Apart from the same prostrate trunks, "pressed down by the weight of the wind",[20] the rata forest on the Auckland Islands is very different. The canopy is thicker and astonishingly compact, with the result that the interior is even more protected and calm than the *Olearia* forest. Huge mounds of dead vegetation and accumulations of peat are covered in green mosses, liverworts, and ferns. There is no southern beech here, or anywhere else in the subantarctic, but there are occasional tree ferns, and *Dracophyllum*, *Coprosma*, and fuchsia.

This is the most sheltered part of New Zealand's subantarctic. The wooded shores of Carnley Harbour and Port Ross, in rare days of summer calm and bellbirds' song, fooled several of the early explorers into thinking they had finally found Utopia. Those who stayed long enough discovered that this paradise was an illusion.

These bays and inlets are one of the few parts of the subantarctic islands where sea and land do not wage constant war. But there are still powerful skirmishes. The *Grafton* was wrecked by a storm well into Carnley Harbour, and on Campbell Island furious williewaws, which whip the surface off the water, are common as the wind funnels down Perseverance Harbour.

Sea conditions are still not as violent as on the open coast, and in the harbours the long fronds of the largest of all seaweeds, the bladder kelp, *Macrocystis pyrifera*, lie golden-brown on the water's surface in shallow bays, necessitating a careful approach to land by inflatable dinghy. In deeper waters the kelp's long, cable-like stipes rise in branching forests from massive holdfasts which anchor it to the sea bed at depths of up to twenty metres. Each stem is held aloft by a pear-shaped bladder of air at the base of its long, lanceolate "leaf".

Macrocystis is less common on the outer coasts, but Hooker, who considered it a "botanical phenomenon", found both this bladder kelp and the bull kelp *Durvillaea antarctica* as detached plants far out on the ocean "in large vegetating floating patches, nearly as far south as any open water remaining free of bergs, in lat. 61°S".[21]

Durvillaea antarctica is the massive, leathery kelp of the exposed ocean coasts. It grows in a broad band in the lower intertidal zone round all the subantarctic islands and extends well into the harbours. It is only dwarfed or absent on the sheerest cliff faces where the waves are particularly powerful. Elsewhere, its huge, dark, writhing straps, honeycombed inside their tough covering with air-filled tissue for buoyancy, divide into long, whiplike thongs which surge and undulate with the rise and fall of the sea and cushion the ocean's impact on the shore. This aptly named bull kelp is anchored to the rock by a strong, dome-shaped holdfast and a stout, flexible stem. Charles Enderby noticed that the Maori on the Auckland Islands in 1850 partly split open its thongs to make "a bag, which is capable of holding from seven to ten gallons of water, in which are put a large number of mutton birds that float in their own oil and which keep for a long time thus prepared".[22] The mutton-

birders of Stewart Island used it for the same purpose until comparatively recent times, when kerosene tins took its place.

Another large kelp, *Lessonia flavicans*, forms submarine forests at the Auckland Islands from the low water mark to a depth of ten metres. On the Snares a newly discovered species of *Lessonia* forms extensive forests from three to twenty metres in depth, while at the Aucklands, at the entrance to Carnley Harbour, there are thick submarine forests of *Marginariella*, found only in the New Zealand region.

These seaweeds, and the many smaller varieties, are as vital to animal life in the sea as plants are to life on land, and being dependent on sunlight grow in depths of less than sixty metres. They are at their most prolific in shallow waters close to the shore.

The New Zealand subantarctic has, at present, 212 known species of seaweed. The range of the submarine flora of the Snares, Antipodes, and Aucklands is quite extensive, the groups having 114, 116, and 112 species respectively, with the Snares having the largest number of seaweeds common to the New Zealand mainland. By contrast, the Bounty Islands, with their small area and uniformly exposed coastlines, have only thirty-three recorded species, although this tally may be partly due to the danger and difficulty of diving there.[23] Few of these species are unique to the New Zealand region, notable exceptions being the *Lessonia* of the Snares, the *Marginariella* of the Aucklands, and a *Durvillaea* kelp, which so far has been found only on the east coast of the Antipodes.

Plants and a considerable depth of peat cover most islands, while the marine flora gives way at the high tide mark to bare rock or cliffs. It is on these exposed and weathered shores and coasts that most of the clues are found as to the origins of these remote islands in the ocean.

The writhing thongs of the massive kelp *Durvillaea antarctica*, at the Bounty Islands. The brighter golden-yellow of this generally brown seaweed is due to the elevation of the kelp band by the particularly vigorous wave action at these islands.

5
Origins

The Earth is constantly changing. New Zealand did not exist in its present form until about 135 million years ago, when it was much closer to Antarctica and Australia, and the Tasman Sea separating it from Australia was much narrower, if indeed it existed at all. Australia was also joined to Antarctica as part of the ancient super-continent of Gondwanaland, and at this time, the newly created land mass of New Zealand extended south to include the Campbell Plateau and the area now occupied by its subantarctic islands.

During a major mountain building period, many of New Zealand's ancient and unique animals and plants, such as the tuatara, the kiwi, and numerous ferns, migrated by various means across relatively narrow sea gaps to the new land, although distances were too great for snakes to arrive from Asia, or marsupials from Australia.

As the Tasman Sea widened, New Zealand moved further away from Australia and Antarctica, which were still joined together, and became increasingly isolated. By about sixty-five million years ago, mountains of this early New Zealand land mass had been eroded away close to sea level and were sinking. By thirty million years ago less than a third of present day New Zealand remained above the sea, and the sea had flooded the Campbell Plateau to the south of Stewart Island and the Snares.

Australia started to move away from Antarctica later than did New Zealand. It did so about fifty million years ago, as the huge and ancient southern super-continent of Gondwanaland began to break up into its separate land masses. A well defined submarine mountain ridge, at least two thousand metres high and part of an almost continuous rift round Antarctica, marks the upwelling of volcanic magma and point of outward spreading of the sea floor between Australia and Antarctica. The division began on this ridge, and a gap widened until a circumpolar current was able to flow in the Southern Ocean.

The Earth's crust is made up of several plates which move constantly in many directions, floating on the molten magma beneath. At some plate boundaries, magma is injected from below, pushing the plates apart and cooling to add to them as it does so. Where plates collide, mountains such as the Southern Alps or the Himalayas are formed by upward buckling. The movement of one plate sliding beneath the other and down into the earth's mantle causes ocean deeps, zones of earthquakes, and island-arc volcanoes, such as in the "Ring of Fire" round the Pacific, which includes the volcanoes of White Island, the central North Island, and Taranaki. The present stage of mountain building, which is lifting the Southern Alps and the main ranges of both the North and South Islands, began twelve to fifteen million years ago.

Erect-crested penguins at Anchorage Bay on the main Antipodes Island. Having recently come ashore, the birds' crests are still flat against their heads. In the background is Bollons Island.

Volcanic activity has ceased on the subantarctic islands, but the earthquakes associated with the north-west movement of the submarine plateau they stand on continue, and have produced numerous violent shocks in the past. R. E. Malone, at Port Ross on 22 July 1852, wrote that

> at about a quarter to nine A.M., we felt the shock of an earthquake; it lasted about three-quarters of a minute. The ship trembled like a steamer getting up her steam, and there was a noise like the rolling of casks on the deck. It was felt by nearly every one ashore; some describing it as lasting ten, and others half a minute. The day after we exercised firing: at the first shot millions of a very small fish rose instantly to the top of the water (some jumping clear out of it), and appeared greatly frightened. We had fired often before, and this had never happened: could the earthquake have had anything to do with it?[1]

The survivors of the *Grafton*, at Carnley Harbour on 1 June 1864

> were aroused from our sleep by a shock of earthquake. The movement went in the direction of N.N.E. to S.S.W. It was accompanied by a singular noise, like the rattling of a thousand chariots down a rocky declivity. The vibration lasted for ten or fifteen seconds: our beds, our table, the very house, shook heavily. We were frozen with terror.[2]

But perhaps the most protracted series of shocks was reported by a Mr Thomson, in charge of a sealing and oiling gang on Macquarie Island, in 1815: "The first which took place on the 31st of October, 1815, at one in the afternoon, overthrew rocks, and gave to the ground the motion of a wave for several seconds. Several men were thrown off their legs, and one was considerably hurt by his fall . . ." Three more quakes followed that day "all accompanied with a noise in the earth like that of distant thunder . . ." In all, there were at least fifteen quakes between October and April, but the first was the most severe. "The people were much alarmed and expected nothing short of the island's total disappearance, or being engulphed [sic] within its bowels."[3]

The subantarctic islands rise above the surface of the Southern Ocean in the shallow seas of the Campbell Plateau and Bounty Platform, which stand on the extensive southern part of New Zealand's continental crust. The Snares and Bounty Islands are composed of the oldest rocks — 105–120 million years and 170–190 million years respectively.[4] They are the weathered remnants of once much larger land masses, and were formed beneath the sea floor, to be later uplifted and attacked by the weather and the ocean.

The Auckland, Campbell, and Antipodes Islands are not only very much younger, but volcanic. In recent years, it became apparent that the Antipodes were particularly new because they had geologically fragile minor craters and features which had not yet been eroded away as they must have been on the older Campbell and Auckland Islands. This disparity in ages gave rise to a fascinating theory, confirmed by careful analysis in the field. Dr C. J. Adams, writing in the scientific journal *Nature*,[5] suggests that these volcanic islands were formed as the Pacific tectonic plate of old granitic and sedimentary rocks passed over a linear hot zone in the Earth's mantle. The hot zone can be envisaged as a belt of some hundred kilometres in width, which twenty million years ago extended for 1000 to 1500 kilometres, from southern New Zealand to the south edge of the Campbell Plateau. The Auckland Islands were formed at this time, but have now moved a thousand kilometres to the north-west. Ten million years ago, Banks Peninsula came into being as it passed over the zone; between five and ten million years ago, Campbell Island was directly over it; and less than two million years ago the Antipodes erupted from the sea.

At the present time the zone should lie close to several submarine features, which are possibly volcanic and which rise from 5000 metres to less than 3000 metres beneath the surface. However, this is still deeper than the Campbell Plateau, and it is unlikely that further subantarctic islands will be created in

Volcanic Origins

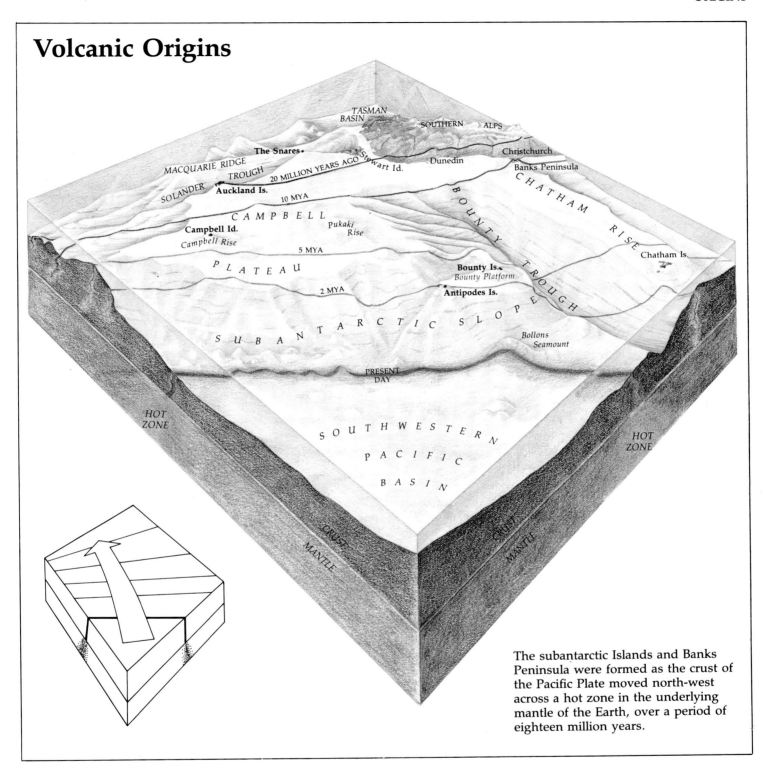

The subantarctic Islands and Banks Peninsula were formed as the crust of the Pacific Plate moved north-west across a hot zone in the underlying mantle of the Earth, over a period of eighteen million years.

the future, as the hot zone now lies to the south-east of the Plateau, down the Subantarctic Slope and beneath the deeper waters of the South West Pacific Basin.

Working on an expected age differentiation of between five and ten million years, Chris Adams has accurately determined the ages of rock samples from these islands by potassium-argon dating, a method broadly similar to the more familiar radio-carbon dating used for younger materials. Volcanic rock contains a radioactive potassium gsotope, ^{40}K, the age of which is clocked at zero at the moment the rock cools and solidifies from the heat of the eruption.

Volcanic dykes of intruded igneous rock form natural jetties at Tucker Cove on Campbell Island. On the background hill is the first fenceline, built in 1970 to keep sheep to one half of the island.

As this potassium undergoes radioactive decay at a known rate, it produces a gas, argon −40 — and from the ratio of potassium to argon the age of the rock can be determined.

At the Department of Scientific and Industrial Research's Institute of Nuclear Sciences, the rock samples were crushed and then melted, at a heat of 1800°C, to expel the minute trace of the argon gas contained. This was then collected, purified, and measured in a mass-spectrometer. A computer — which controls the measuring of the argon isotopes — finally produced a readout giving the age of the sample in millions of years. The result quite surprisingly extended the volcanic period expected from a much younger age of 1.5 million years for the Antipodes, to a more advanced age of twenty million years for the Auckland Islands. The Pacific plate, bearing the Campbell Plateau and the subantarctic islands upon it, moves north-west at just under six centimetres a year, which equates with the eighteen million years in time between the formation of the Antipodes and Auckland Islands, and the actual sea distance between them, of approximately one thousand kilometres.

These volcanic groups are far too young to support the old argument of land bridges being necessary for the common distribution of so many plants, flightless insects, and freshwater fish round the scattered islands of the subantarctic. The existence of land where there is now sea, and vice versa, has of course long been obvious from marine fossils occurring in sedimentary rocks thousands of feet above sea level, and from coal seams beneath the sea.

The outstanding systematic botanist T. F. Cheeseman, writing in 1909,[6] found the problem of the distribution of flora and fauna as vexing as Hooker and Darwin had done before him. It was still six years before the publication of Alfred Wegener's theory,[7] widely ridiculed at first, on the origin of continents and oceans and the concept of continental drift, which was to prove the basis for modern plate tectonics. At the time, former land bridges seemed the only answer.

Cheeseman, probably quite rightly, and after corresponding with Hooker, assumed that Antarctica and South America were once linked by the stretched loop of islands following the line of an ancient land bridge, but he also suggested that Antarctica and New Zealand's subantarctic islands may once have been very much closer, if not actually joined, when Antarctica reached further north and the long shallow extension of New Zealand to the south was above the sea. Thus, Cheeseman argued that South America and New Zealand with its subantarctic islands would have been linked through an Antarctic Continent warmer than it is now. Cheeseman acknowledged the distribution of seeds and some insects by wind, ocean currents, and birds, and noted the fact that the flora and fauna of islands such as the Azores, the Galapagos, and Hawaii must have somehow reached them over vast ocean distances.

Nowadays, in spite of the extraordinary discoveries of plate tectonics, many mysteries remain, especially when land masses and islands such as Hawaii are too young for differences in land or sea level, or plate tectonics, to have affected them. Just how some terrestrial animals have managed to cross oceans is one of the outstanding problems of biogeography. The fact is, they have done so. An old map of 1816, incorporating Cook's voyages, has a mark in the middle of the Pacific, with the words "19th of July. Piece of wood seen" — a strangely impermanent thing to find on a map, but significant. Such driftwood could have had life on it. Skinks and geckos are thought to have reached New Zealand on driftwood from the islands towards Southeast Asia, while several years ago a log of Tasmanian beech was found in southern Chile. Sizeable pieces of pumice from a submarine volcano near Chile have reached Campbell Island, the Aucklands, and southern New Zealand after travelling three-quarters of the way round the subantarctic ocean. But floating debris is not always needed to transport life, for recently a live flight-

Penguin Slope, on the north-east corner of North East Island, main island of the Snares, clearly shows the granite rock of which the group is made. The coarse, granular structure gives a foothold on what would otherwise be an impossibly steep surface.

less beetle, common to the Antipodes, Auckland Islands, and South America was picked up in a Neuston net tow to the east of the Antipodes.[8]

Professor Philip Darlington, in his *Biogeography of the Southern End of the World*, was certain that "all the plants and animals that have reached New Zealand have done so across water . . . just as, somehow, they have reached every other remote island in every ocean."[9] The absence of native land mammals on remote islands is further evidence against former land bridges, and Professor Darlington concluded that no land connections are needed anywhere across the southern end of the world to explain the distribution of animal or plant life in the Southern Ocean.

Speculation must remain as to how some of the life on New Zealand's subantarctic islands first reached them. How, for example, did the Bounty Islands get their endemic weta? Wingless flies and beetles offer tantalising

The Bounty Islands are of basement granite. The large, angular blocks are the result of fracturing, due to the release of enormous pressures with the buckling of the rock and uplifting of the islands.

clues, which are looked at in Chapter 6, and while the broad origins of the islands themselves may be known, many details are still puzzling, or surprising.

The Snares, the subantarctic group closest to New Zealand, have rocks very similar to those of the southern part of Stewart Island; they are probably eroded remnants of the same single batholith of granite, formed some 120 million years ago by the slow cooling of magma below the Earth's surface. This gradual cooling has allowed quartz, feldspar, and other minerals to crystallise, giving the Snares' granite rock its characteristic coarse granular structure.

The Bounty Islands are the other granitic group, a cluster of some twenty small islands and rocks, rounded by severe weathering and battering from the sea, and no more than fifty to seventy-five metres above sea level. Their pale grey basement granite, into which later granite dikes have intruded, provides a rare sample of the rock which lies beneath the submerged continental crust of the Campbell Plateau. Formed deep under the sea floor, the granite has fractured with the release of enormous pressures into huge angular blocks which are locked into the eroded topography of the island or lie jumbled upon its surface.

The Auckland Islands, the largest group, were formed by the two adjacent Ross and Carnley volcanoes breaking through submarine basalt domes. These volcanoes were of the Hawaiian type, erupting as a succession of lava flows separated by layers of ash and scoria. Examples of these stratified layers can be clearly seen on the slopes of Adams Island and on the hills round Carnley Harbour. Some of the Ross lava flows are up to thirty metres thick and are best seen in the northern cliffs, with their volcanic colourings, soon after leaving Port Ross. These cliffs have superb examples of horizontal strata overlaid by vertical columnar structures.

A radial pattern of valleys and ridges indicates that the Ross volcano had its centre near Disappointment Island, which may be a hard, resistant core, or volcanic plug. Erosion by the sea along the west coast of the main Auckland

Stratified rocks, which have collapsed to form a deep cave, overlaid with columnar basalt, in the large bay between North Point and North East Harbour, at the north of Auckland Island.

The rampart of the western cliffs of the main Auckland Island, rising sheer by almost 600 metres, contrasts with the gentler slopes and glimpses of Carnley Harbour to the east.

Island has been extremely severe and is the cause of its steep cliffs, which form an almost continuous wall for more than thirty-two kilometres.

In places, these western cliffs have two "stories" or distinct stages in their development, which is rare in the New Zealand region. The upper, sloping part was cut back during the last period of high sea levels between the ice ages, and then more gently eroded by streams until, although steep, they became largely covered in tussock grass and vegetation. The lower, stark, and almost perpendicular cliffs are still being actively formed by the sea, and vary in height from 120 metres to almost 600 metres. Sir Charles Fleming, who first described these cliffs, has estimated that the sea has eroded away as much as fifteen kilometres from the western side of the Auckland Islands.[10]

To the north-east, the regular pattern of the two overlapping volcanoes is broken by the low-lying rocks and reefs of Rose, Enderby, Ocean, Ewing, and other islands, which were probably produced by later lava flows from the

Erosion of the Ross and Carnley Volcanoes at the Auckland Islands

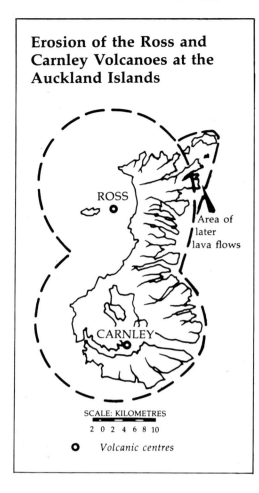

ROSS

Area of later lava flows

CARNLEY

SCALE: KILOMETRES
2 0 2 4 6 8 10

O *Volcanic centres*

secondary vents of Shoe Island and Dea's Head, at Port Ross. These features, with their columnar basalt rock, are the hard plugs of dikes which have forced their way up through fractures in the volcano. The conspicuous angular knob on the top of Mt Eden is a similar plug core.

The Carnley volcano overlaps with the Ross volcano at Tandy Inlet, half way up the east coast. Carnley Harbour is its caldera, or collapsed and eroded crater, and Musgrave Peninsula its core. Granite rock on the peninsula is part of the much older basement rock through which the volcano erupted. A small area of sandstone on the east coast of Musgrave Peninsula is also interesting because it contains sea shells about fifteen million years old of a sort which indicate that the sea was much warmer at that time.[11]

Ice ages have also left their mark, and the valleys of the east coast and some of those draining into Carnley Harbour show clear signs of glaciation, with typically U-shaped profiles. Lakes Hinemoa, Tutanekai, and Speight on the main Auckland Island are dammed behind old glacial moraines.

Layers of glacial silt are exposed in small cliffs close to the main sea cliffs on the northern shore of Enderby Island, and these gently deposited sediments contain vertical "carrots" of rough rock fragments, which were almost certainly released from above, with the melting of seasonal ice floes on the surface of a land-locked lake.[12] This phenomenon is a further indication of erosion, and proof that Enderby Island once covered a considerably greater area than it does now.

Campbell Island, like the Aucklands, has been heavily eroded along its western flanks, and its original circular form is almost unrecognisable. But rocks in North East Harbour, Perseverance Harbour, and South East Harbour have a radial pattern with a likely centre of the eruption at Northwest Bay, on the opposite coast. Here, there are small outcrops of basement schist and quartz veins dating from 640 million years ago, which could have been uplifted prior to the eruption of the volcano. Dent Island, lying offshore, is of massive intrusive columnar rock and, like Disappointment Island, is probably the hard core of a dike which has resisted the sea, while the land which once surrounded it has been worn away. Beeman Hill, immediately behind the meteorological station, is the core of another and later eruptive cone.[13]

Carnley Harbour from Adams Island, photographed while looking north up the main Auckland Island. The distant headland seen projecting from the right is Musgrave Peninsula, the old core of the severely eroded Carnley volcano.

Above: Lake Turbott, gouged out by a small cirque glacier and dammed behind a rock threshold, is on the south coast of Adams Island. Its steep sides clearly show the successive strata of lava flows of the Carnley volcano. *Photo: New Zealand Wildlife Service.*

Left: The effect of glacial action can be seen at the head of many of the fiord-like inlets and valleys on the east coast of Auckland Island. *Photo: Department of Lands & Survey.*

Left: A male Hooker's sea lion emerges from the sea like a leviathan, at Northwest Bay on Campbell Island. Beyond are limestone cliffs from the sea floor, lifted before the main volcanic eruption, and veined with lines of later-intruding volcanic lava.

Below: Dea's Head, at Port Ross, is the eroded core of a secondary lava flow on the flanks of the older Ross volcano, at the Auckland Islands.

Campbell Island has sedimentary rocks of sandstone, conglomerate, and mudstone which have been pushed above sea level, and there are striking limestone cliffs at Northwest Bay above the schist basement, which were heaved out by the sea by enormous forces before the volcanic eruption. Because of these marine formations, Campbell Island has many fossils, which are rare on the Auckland Islands. Almost half the island is covered by the Shoal Point Formation, a marine deposit of eroded volcanic sediment which includes fossils, and this in turn is covered by further lava flows. North East Harbour, Perseverance Harbour, and South East Harbour all show signs of glaciation, and inland valleys have tell-tale glacial profiles, although glacial moraines and sediments are small and infrequent.

The main Antipodes island, rising from the south-east edge of the Bollons Platform, is predominantly an extinct ash volcano formed by huge fire fountains rather than lava flows. Its collapsed central vent is thought to lie under the peat and tussock between Mt Galloway and Mt Waterhouse on the gently sloping central plateau.[14] Steep cliffs, rising to 300 metres, surround most of the island. There are several subsidiary cones, particularly on the eastern side, with spattered viscous material and black clinker-like scoria. The most striking of them is a large, steep-sided crater of 150 metres in diameter, on the slopes above Crater Bay. Deep reddish ash and scoria can be clearly seen here, as well as in the coastal cliffs and on the vertical sides of nearby Leeward Island. This unscalable erosion remnant is eighty metres high, and its top dips inwards from the rim like a shallow saucer.

Of the few lava flows, one of the clearest is a long tongue of ropy texture which descends to sea level at South Bay on the south-west coast. There are also dramatic columnar basalt cliffs at Anchorage Bay.

Two kilometres to the north, the broken rims of Bollons Island and adjoining Archway Island, the remnants of a crater invaded by the sea, unmistakably show the volcanic nature of the group, and illustrate in a most dramatic way the creation of land from beneath the sea.

Above: Bollons Island and Archway Island, in the foreground, are the remnants of a rapidly eroding volcanic crater at the Antipodes. Leeward Island and the main Antipodes Island lie beyond.

Left: Subsidiary cones and craters, of which this is one of the best examples, are a feature of the plateau bordering the east coast of Antipodes Island, between Stella Bay and Crater Bay.

6
Islands of Contrasts

The south end of Anchorage Bay, on the comparatively sheltered north-east coast of the main island, is one of the few safe places to land on the Antipodes (map, p. 74).

The group lies at 49°41' south and 178°45' east, and is dominated by its largest island, which is roughly oval and seven kilometres long by four to five kilometres wide. It covers 2100 hectares and is the most remote of the sub-antarctic islands, being 872 kilometres south-east of Bluff. Yet because it is almost exactly opposite latitude 0° at Greenwich, in England, it is probably the only group whose name is even vaguely familiar beyond New Zealand.

When the sea is calm enough, a landing can be made on the flat coastal shelves, where the black kelp surges, at the foot of a steep rocky beach backed by spectacular columnar basalt cliffs. There is a large colony of erect-crested penguins here, through which one has to pass to climb a steep pitch to waist-high tussock and a first sight of the island's huts. The pale brown Antipodes pipit, with dull yellow striped markings, of a subspecies endemic to the island, picks insects, flies, and grubs from among the penguin excreta and crevices in the rocks. Andreas Reischek, referring to the pipit as a ground lark, "named it *Anthus [novaeseelandiae] steindachneri*, after Dr Franz von Steindachner, Privy Counsellor, and Director of the Imperial Museum at Vienna, in recognition of his kindness to me".[1]

There are two huts. The old castaway hut was built in 1886, and the Department of Lands and Survey's one in 1978, for use by scientists and visiting expeditions. The huts stand on one of the few level areas near sea level on the island. Mice, the only surviving animal accidentally introduced by humans to colonise the island successfully, are abundant, but appear to have had little impact on the environment.

Towards Reef Point the tussock grasses are thick and almost head high, while inland a broad, shallow valley climbs with an increasing gradient towards the Central Plateau. Here, too, the vegetation of long-leaved tussock and sedge, fern, and Coprosma scrub can be waist or head high, making progress difficult. An endemic subspecies of snipe, *Coenocorypha aucklandica meinertzhagenae*, lives on the Antipodes, but is rarely seen. It is fast flying but prefers swift, evasive action along the ground.

The view from half way up Col Ridge towards the entrance to Perseverance Harbour, on Campbell Island. The meteorological station is on the promontory at the foot of Beeman Hill.

The high, rolling, central plateau of Antipodes Island has an unmistakable character, with its vegetation of pale tussock and dark fern emphasising the wetter ground, and the occasional wandering albatross appearing as a mere white dot.

The old wartime coastwatchers' camp at Tagua Bay in Carnley Harbour, well concealed from the sea by the rata forest. The permanent lines of wind-sheer caused by frequent gales can be clearly seen in the forest canopy.

There are also numerous parakeets, living in burrows in the peat or tussock and feeding on grasses, seeds, flowers, and berries. The Antipodes has its own distinct species, the Antipodes Island parakeet, *Cyanoramphus unicolor*, which is entirely green, and the Antipodes red-crowned parakeet, *Cyanoramphus novaezelandiae hochstetteri*, a subspecies which closely resembles those found in New Zealand. They are the result of two separate invasions, each evolving into a distinct species and sub-species respectively, and although they frequently occur together they do not normally interbreed on the island.[2] The green parakeet prefers tall tussock, which also forms the greater part of its diet, while the red-crowned lives on the more open parts of the island, and eats seeds, flowers, berries, and insects.

On the plateau the vegetation is shorter and the going easier. The short, deep green fern is interspersed with mosses and lichens, and the tussock clumps are only knee high and no longer a barrier. Wandering albatrosses sit silently on their widely scattered nests. Streams are few, and water sinks quickly into the peaty ground. The wet places are lush with the huge leaves and stems of *Stilbocarpa* and of *Pleurophyllum*. The mist can roll in swiftly, blotting out the unfamiliar landscape.

Easy access to the coast is limited to Anchorage Bay, Reef Point, Stella Bay, Alert Bay, Ringdove Bay, South Bay and a few other parts of the south coast, for the volcanic cliffs of the Antipodes are in sharp contrast to its interior. The cliffs contain numerous caves. A gigantic one at Cave Point, to the west, was named "Remarkable Cave" by Captain Fairchild and arches to ninety metres above sea level. Another, almost as vast, is one of several eating into the outer south-east coast of Bollons Island, while a huge surging cavern has hollowed out the island's inner volcanic rim where it adjoins Archway Island. The overall impression of the Antipodes is that of a curiously undulating, pale green interior and a harsh black volcanic coast under determined attack from the sea.

Campbell Island (map, p. 70), the most southerly of the subantarctic islands, is 52°53' south and longitude 169°10' east. It has an area of 11 331 hectares and is seventeen kilometres from east to west and fifteen and a half from north to south. Perseverance Harbour, at least a kilometre wide, runs inland for eight kilometres between steep hills and the high ridges of Mt Lyall and Mt Honey. The meteorological station and jetty do not come into view for several kilometres, but the harbour entrance is visible by climbing up the slopes of Beeman Hill, immediately behind the buildings.

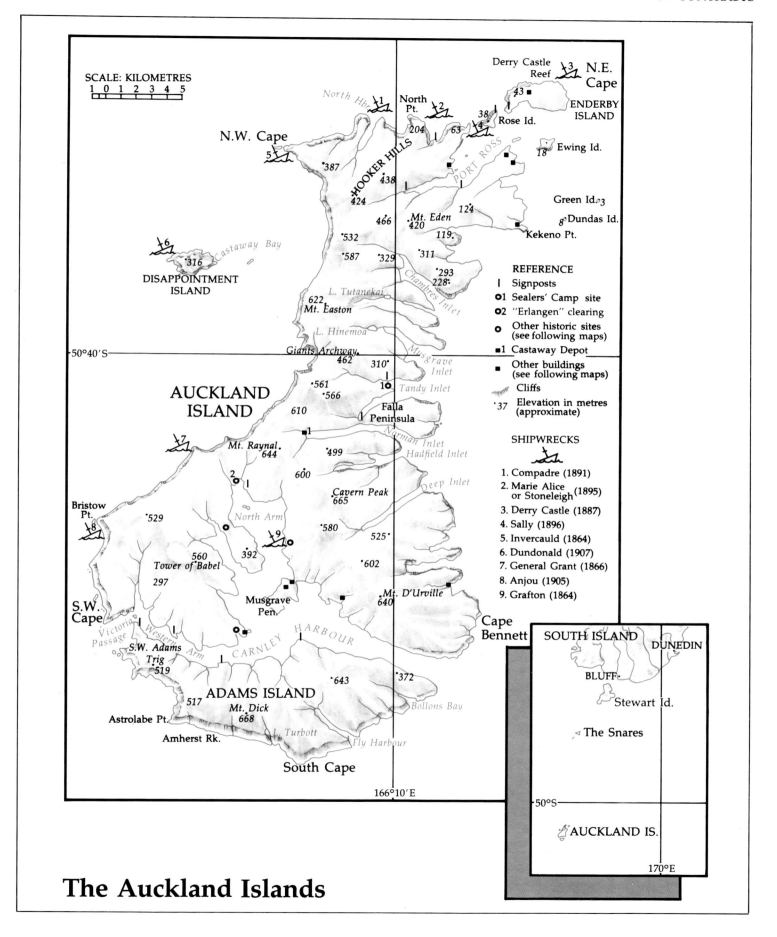

SCALE: KILOMETRES
1 0 1 2 3 4 5

Derry Castle Reef
N.E. Cape
3
43
ENDERBY ISLAND
North Hbr
1
North Pt.
2
204
63
38
14
Rose Id.
N.W. Cape
5
18
Ewing Id.
387
HOOKER HILLS
438
424
Green Id. 3
466
Mt. Eden
420
124
8 Dundas Id.
532
119
Kekeno Pt.
587
329
311
293
228

REFERENCE
| Signposts
o1 Sealers' Camp site
o2 "Erlangen" clearing
o Other historic sites (see following maps)
■1 Castaway Depot
■ Other buildings (see following maps)
Cliffs
·37 Elevation in metres (approximate)

DISAPPOINTMENT ISLAND
6
316
Castaway Bay

L. Tutanekai
622
Mt. Easton
L. Hinemoa

Chambres Inlet

Musgrave Inlet

50°40'S
Giants Archway
462
310
561
1
Tandy Inlet
566
AUCKLAND ISLAND
610
Falla Peninsula
Norman Inlet
Hadfield Inlet

7
Mt. Raynal
644
499
600
Cavern Peak
665
Deep Inlet

SHIPWRECKS

1. Compadre (1891)
2. Marie Alice or Stoneleigh (1895)
3. Derry Castle (1887)
4. Sally (1896)
5. Invercauld (1864)
6. Dundonald (1907)
7. General Grant (1866)
8. Anjou (1905)
9. Grafton (1864)

Bristow Pt.
8
529
North Arm
2
9
580
525
560
Tower of Babel
392
602
297
Musgrave Pen.
Mt. D'Urville
640
S.W. Cape
Victoria Passage
Western Arm
CARNLEY HARBOUR
Cape Bennett
S.W. Adams Trig
519
643
372
ADAMS ISLAND
517
Mt. Dick
668
Astrolabe Pt.
L. Turbott
Amherst Rk.
Fly Harbour
Bollons Bay
South Cape

166°10'E

SOUTH ISLAND
DUNEDIN
BLUFF
Stewart Id.
The Snares

50°S

AUCKLAND IS.

170°E

The Auckland Islands

Campbell Island, bleak, open, and windswept, has a wild beauty. This photograph was taken while looking south, towards the inner reaches of Perseverance Harbour, with the erosion-scarred slopes of Mount Honey to the left.

A clearing in the *Olearia* forest on the Snares, formerly occupied by a colony of Snares crested penguins. As former colonies are abandoned in favour of new sites, *Hebe elliptica*, chickweed, grasses, and *Olearia* seedlings cover the old site. Most will be crowded out as the forest canopy becomes re-established.

The head of the harbour divides into several shallow bays — Tucker Cove, where the early farming venture was based, Camp Cove, Garden Cove, and Venus Bay. Low tide at each of these bays exposes their mudflats. A fence-line, built in 1970 to confine the feral sheep to the southern half of the island, runs up a steep incline from Tucker Cove to Col Ridge and the cliffs of the western coast. From here one can look south to sheltered Northwest Bay (presumably named because it faces north) or north along the steep coast to the rugged Courrejolles Peninsula. Poled walking tracks lead to small huts at Northwest Bay and North Cape.

The track to Sorensen Hut, or Bull Rock Hut, near North Cape, starts on a boardwalk round the flank of Beeman Hill, and passes St Col Peak, climbing close to the coast on the way to Mt Azimuth, and giving a high view down a broad valley towards North East Harbour, long and narrow like Perseverance Harbour, and the site of a former whaling station.

Faye Ridge, north of Mt Azimuth, is high, open country, with misty views towards the Courrejolles Peninsula, thinly dotted with royal albatrosses nesting or in small groups. The vegetation is sparse tussock and stunted herbfield, with moss, lichens, and rocks. Large areas of bare peat have been scoured out by the wind after grazing by sheep.

From the Sorensen Hut near North Cape, open scrubland slopes towards the coast and a large colony of New Zealand black-browed mollymawks, which breed only at the northern end of this island. Other huts on Moubray Hill, at South East Harbour, Penguin Bay, and at Northwest Bay are used by scientists on field survey or by meteorological station staff taking a break from the routine of the base. Away from tracks, walking can be exhausting across the deceptively gentle-rolling tussockland.

The lower scrub is home to white-eyes, starlings, hedge sparrows, chaffinches, and redpolls. Welcome swallows and pukeko have also been seen. Thrushes and blackbirds are rare, and rats appear to have wiped out Campbell Island's pipits and rare flightless duck, which are now found only on outlying islets.

Like the Antipodes, there is a sharp contrast between the interior of Campbell Island and its coast. Not all of the island's coastline is sheer, for the land frequently slopes to bays and harbours, but the western side is stark, with precipitous cliffs where peaks like Mt Paris have been shorn in half and rise straight from the coast. Jacquemart Island and Dent Island are the largest of several craggy offshore islets and rocks, reminding one again of the harshness of the land and the power of the sea.

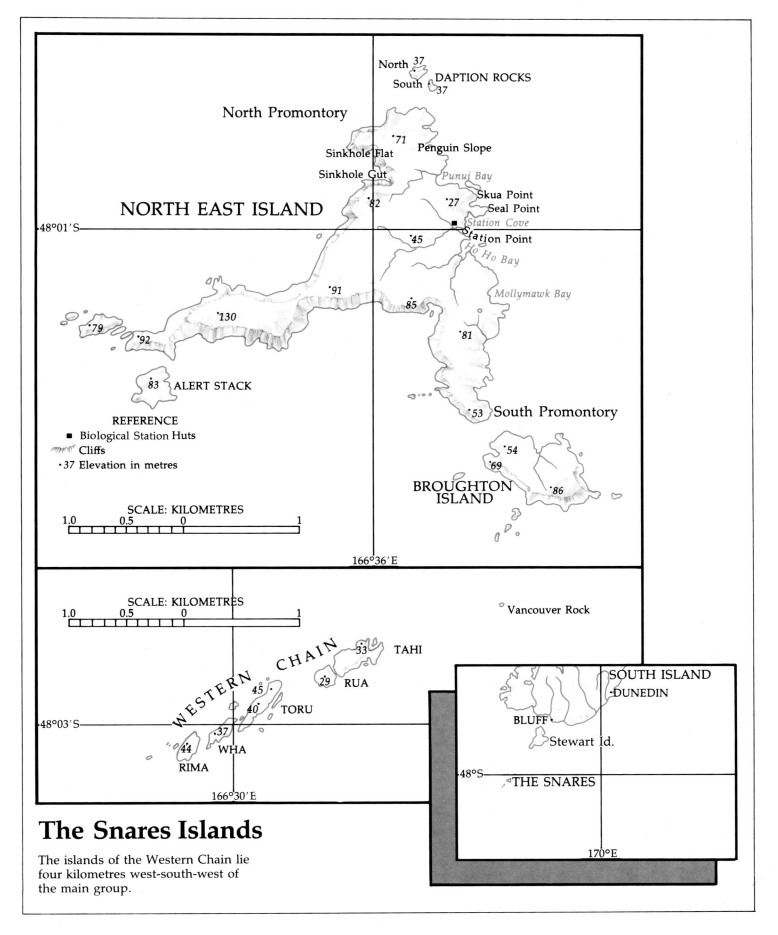

North 37
South DAPTION ROCKS
37

North Promontory

·71 Penguin Slope

Sinkhole Flat

Sinkhole Gut *Punui Bay*

NORTH EAST ISLAND

·82 ·27 Skua Point
Seal Point

·48°01′S *Station Cove*

·45 Station Point

Ho Ho Bay

·91 *Mollymawk Bay*

·85

·79 ·130 ·81

·92

·83 ALERT STACK ·53 South Promontory

REFERENCE

■ Biological Station Huts
Cliffs
·37 Elevation in metres

·54
·69
·86

BROUGHTON
ISLAND

SCALE: KILOMETRES

1.0   0.5   0   1

166°36′E

SCALE: KILOMETRES

1.0   0.5   0   1

° Vancouver Rock

·33 TAHI
W E S T E R N   C H A I N

SOUTH ISLAND
·DUNEDIN

2·9 RUA

45·
BLUFF·
40· TORU

·48°03′S
·Stewart Id.

·37
44 WHA

RIMA 48°S THE SNARES

166°30′E

170°E

The Snares Islands

The islands of the Western Chain lie
four kilometres west-south-west of
the main group.

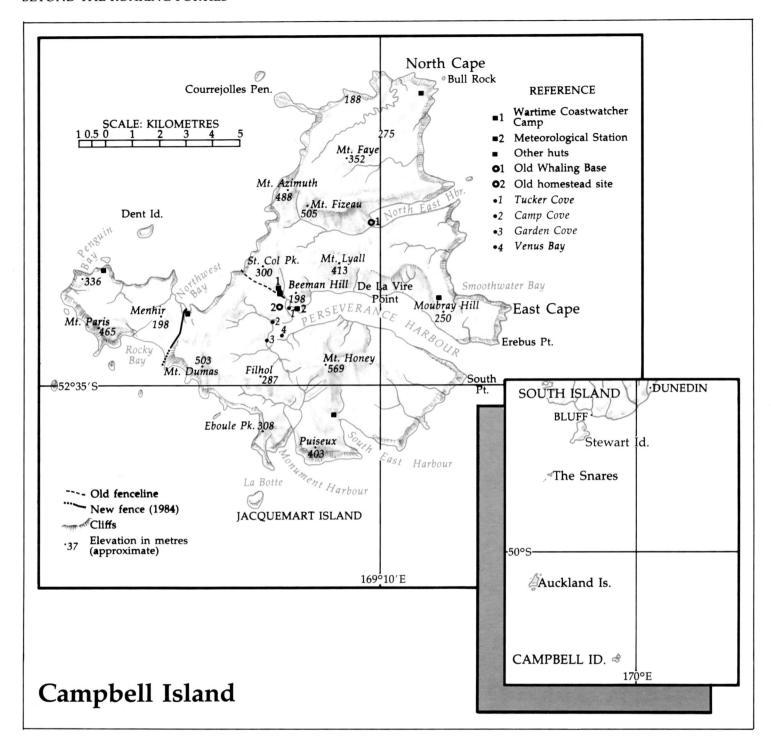

SCALE: KILOMETRES
1 0.5 0   1   2   3   4   5

REFERENCE

■1 Wartime Coastwatcher Camp
■2 Meteorological Station
■   Other huts
◎1 Old Whaling Base
◎2 Old homestead site
•1 *Tucker Cove*
•2 *Camp Cove*
•3 *Garden Cove*
•4 *Venus Bay*

North Cape
Bull Rock
Courrejolles Pen.
188
275
Mt. Faye
·352
Mt. Azimuth
488
·Mt. Fizeau
505
Dent Id.
North East Hbr.
Penguin Bay
·336
St. Col Pk.
300
Mt. Lyall
413
Beeman Hill
De La Vire Point
Smoothwater Bay
Northwest Bay
198
2◎ •1 ■2
1
Menhir
198
Moubray Hill
250
East Cape
Mt. Paris
465
•2
4
PERSEVERANCE HARBOUR
Rocky Bay
•3
Erebus Pt.
503
Mt. Dumas
Filhol
·287
Mt. Honey
·569
South Pt.
52°35′S
Eboule Pk. 308
Puiseux
403
South East Harbour
La Botte
Monument Harbour
JACQUEMART ISLAND
169°10′E

- - - Old fenceline
···· New fence (1984)
〜 Cliffs
·37 Elevation in metres (approximate)

SOUTH ISLAND ·DUNEDIN
BLUFF·
·Stewart Id.
·The Snares
50°S
Auckland Is.
CAMPBELL ID.
170°E

Campbell Island

The Auckland Islands (map, p. 67), 465 kilometres from Bluff, are by far the largest group, and lie between latitudes 50°30′ and 50°60′ south and longitudes 165°50′ and 166°20′ east. The distance from South Cape on Adams Island to North East Cape on Enderby Island is all but fifty kilometres, and it is twenty-six kilometres from Bristow Point on the west coast to Cape Bennett on the east. Adams Island (slightly smaller than Campbell Island) is 10 117 hectares, and the main island 51 000 hectares.

Besides a large number of long, fiord-like, sheltered inlets on the east coast, there are two excellent harbours. The largest is Carnley Harbour in the south, which separates Adams Island from the main island. Victoria Passage

The Main Group of the Bounty Islands. Numerous seals can be seen on the nearer rocks, while thousands of birds pepper the higher slopes of Depot Island beyond.

on the west is narrow, with treacherous currents, and the main approach is from the east. Rata forest and dense scrub clothe the slopes of promontories and bays, but the high ground and inward facing slopes of Adams Island, with their pale grass and layered outcrops of volcanic rock stepping up the misty hills, remind one of the Highlands of Scotland and particularly the Isle of Skye.

It is only three kilometres, but a considerable climb, from the innermost North Arm of Carnley Harbour to the tremendous contrast of the western cliffs. B. C. Aston, a soil scientist, made the crossing in November 1907.

> The day was now clear and fine and the awful nature of the coast could well be seen. Cliffs about 1500 ft rose sheer out of the water. One could look over and see the waves beating at the foot, leaving no foothold on which the unfortunate castaway could land. A few fur seals were observed lying on the ledges at the foot of the cliffs. Here was the scene of much slaughter of seals in bygone days when the sealers were let down by ropes over the perpendicular rocks to the ledges on which the animals rested. The seals were then butchered, their skins hoisted to the top and borne across four or five miles of country on men's shoulders to the N. Arm. The Maoris [on the boat] say that there are only two places where one may land on this coast, and it is easy to believe them.[3]

This iron-bound coast, the scene of at least four known shipwrecks, begins on the south-west of Adams Island and runs as a great wall of rock to the north. For most of the time the cliffs rise into cloud, discouraging travel on the high country which, in spite of the saturated peat bogs and rocky ground, offers reasonably good going.

Port Ross is the smaller harbour to the north. Here, the climate is slightly better. In fact, Enderby Island, which is open and low-lying and covers 688 hectares, gets considerably more sunshine than the hills round the harbour on the main island. Ewing Island is small and densely wooded and has the best surviving population of the rare Auckland Island flightless duck; Dundas Island is open and scrub covered, with a large colony of Hooker's sea lions; and Rose Island is particularly attractive, even though modified by introduced animals, with its wild sea cliffs, sheltered shores, and open sward.

The Aucklands have the most varied bird and insect life of all the groups. Almost fifty species of birds are thought to breed on them, including, among the land birds, endemic subspecies of pipit, tomtit, snipe, and the rare, coastal-dwelling banded dotterel. There are also red-crowned and yellow-crowned parakeets, skylarks, blackbirds, silvereyes, and tuis, as well as

The sheer western cliffs of the Auckland Islands were dreaded by mariners, using the Trade Winds of the Roaring Forties in the days of sail, en route from Australia to Cape Horn.

The Antipodes Island parakeet is the largest of the New Zealand species, and endemic to the group. It nests in burrows which are often more than a metre deep.

An endemic Auckland Island tit, on Rose Island.

The Snares Island tit is endemic to the main group.

chaffinches, hedge sparrows, goldfinches, redpolls, and starlings. House sparrows, liberated in New Zealand by Acclimatisation Societies, are occasionally seen. The first welcome swallow recorded in the New Zealand region was caught by a cat at Ranui Cove on the main island in 1943.[4] The second sighting was at Ahipara in Northland. Since then, the species has become widespread throughout New Zealand.

By far the most numerous bird of the rata forest is the bellbird, *Anthornis melanura*. Its song varies quite distinctly from Port Ross to Carnley Harbour. Bellbirds almost invariably appear as soon as one lands ashore and will come to within a metre or two, staying for several minutes and singing with a fluent mixture of strangulated jarring sounds and purest melody.

The simplicity or limited range of insect fauna is typical of the subantarctic, but still numbers several hundred species. Sixty percent of the beetles and weevils and twenty-one percent of the moths are endemic, and most are smaller than their counterparts on mainland New Zealand.[5]

A high proportion of the subantarctic's insects is flightless. Insects tend to adapt and change much faster than plants, and the evolution of flightless forms, including kelp flies, which have only stunted, rudimentary wings, may be due not so much to long isolation as to intense natural selection in the high winds and cold environment of the subantarctic, and to the last period of glaciation.

These flightless insects are almost certainly derived from ancestors which flew, and which could have been carried great distances on the strong winds circling the Southern Ocean. Philip Darlington points out that certain flight-less *Migadopine carabid* beetles found on subantarctic moorlands occur in only three general regions of the world, separated by vast ocean barriers. These are South America and the Falkland Islands; Tasmania and South East Australia; and New Zealand and the Auckland Islands.[6] This distribution of the beetle was at first thought to support the theory of former land bridges and the break-up of Gondwanaland, but a study of winged species of the same family now suggests that all of this particular group of beetles was once capable of flight and could therefore have been dispersed by the wind.

Few visitors to the subantarctic have shared Antarctic explorer Edward Wilson's delight at "the novelty of some blue-bottle flies that found their way on board and were soon buzzing round the ward-room".[7] Thomas Musgrave, marooned by shipwreck at Carnley Harbour in 1865,

> suffered torment from the sandflies. Their virulence surpasses my powers of description. . . . Unless the wind were blowing a whole gale they were flying about in myriads from daylight to dark, alighting upon us in clouds, literally covering every part of our skin that happened to be exposed; and not only that, but they got inside our clothes and bit there.[8]

Graham Turbott, who spent a year of the Second World War on the Aucklands, recalls that

> The first thing I remember noticing in the hut when we went in was a notice saying: "Auckland Island Calendar. Every day is Fly-day." [This was one of Sir Robert Falla's irrepressible puns, for which he was to become renowned.] There's no doubt that one of the problems of living in the Auckland Islands for any length of time is the blow flies. All of us learnt very quickly to take extreme precautions when we left the tent during field trips. We had to wrap everything up extremely carefully and make sure that we didn't come back to an unlivable tent.[9]

Allan Eden, another Cape Expeditioner, found the sandflies terrible and the blowflies

> Disgusting. . . . Leave a blanket or a pair of socks in an accessible place and you will return to find a crust of eggs an inch or more deep, with blowflies completely embedded in the mess. It is fiendishly difficult to get the eggs out of the woollen articles.[10]

Such experiences represent the flies of the subantarctic at their worst, and are one of the drawbacks of field camps. For much of the time, when passing

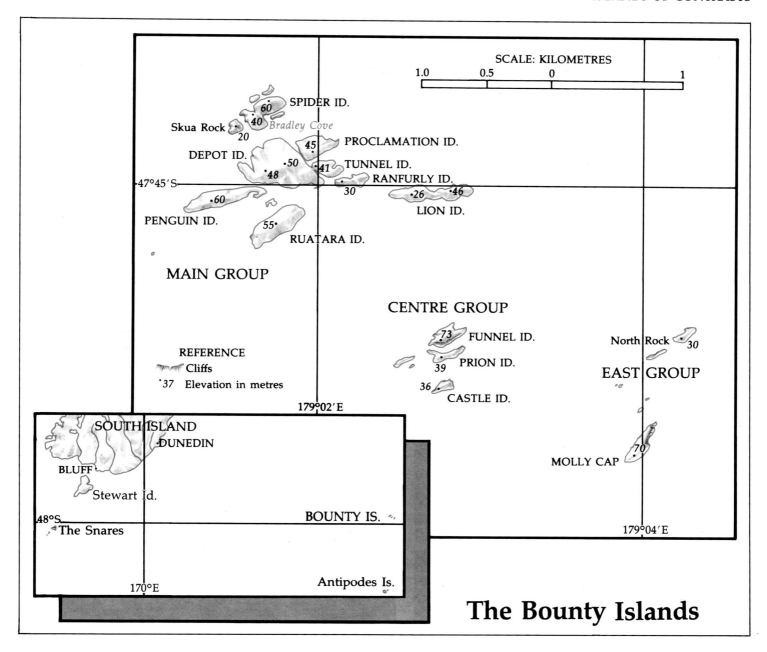

The Bounty Islands

through the bush, or on beaches where sea-wrack and kelp provide rich breeding grounds for insects, and even in sea lion and birds colonies, flies and other insects are very little problem.

The fourth island of the Auckland group, Disappointment Island, covers 392 hectares and stands apart from the others to the west. It is a lonely oceanic island with only one safe bay in which to land, and has steep, tussock-covered slopes dotted with innumerable nesting white-capped mollymawks.

The Snares Islands (map, p. 69) are the closest to New Zealand, being approximately a hundred kilometres from Stewart Island, 209 kilometres south-west of Bluff, and situated at 48°01' south and 166°36' east. The main island covers 280 hectares and Broughton Island forty-eight hectares. The main island is roughly triangular, and just over three and a half kilometres from east to west and three kilometres from north to south. The Western Chain, named after the Maori numerals for one to five as they extend westward, lies some four and a half kilometres to the south-west.

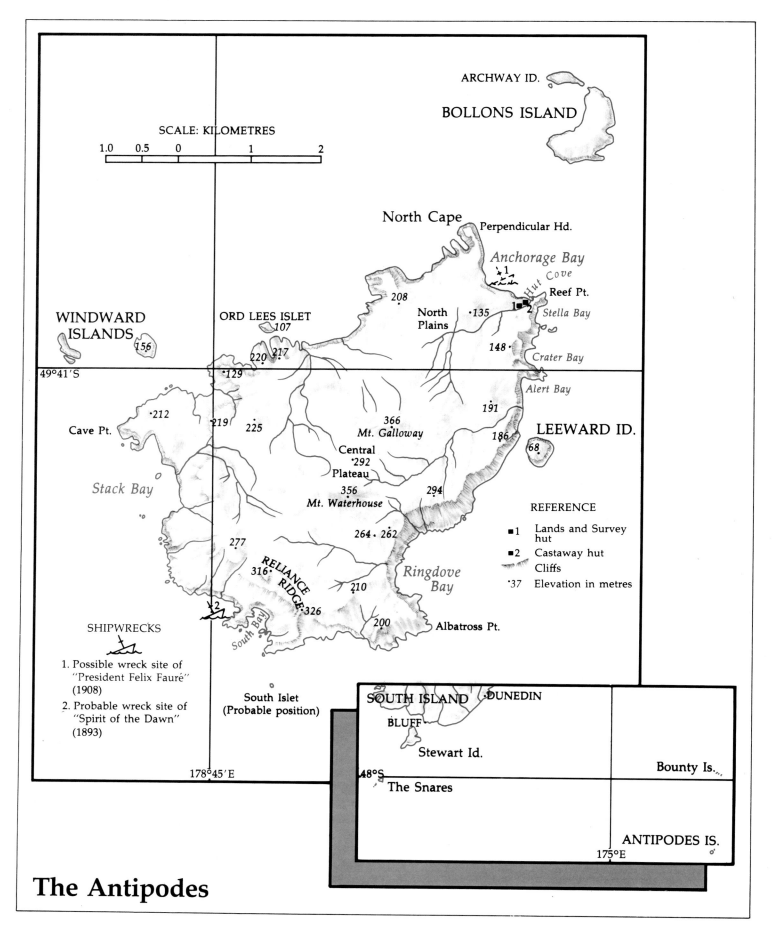

ARCHWAY ID.

BOLLONS ISLAND

SCALE: KILOMETRES

1.0   0.5   0   1   2

North Cape
Perpendicular Hd.

Anchorage Bay
Cove
1
Reef Pt.
208
North
Plains
•135
1 2
Stella Bay

WINDWARD
ISLANDS
ORD LEES ISLET
107
148•
Crater Bay
156
220• 217•

49°41′S
•129
Alert Bay

•212
191•
LEEWARD ID.
Cave Pt.
•219 225•
366
Mt. Galloway
186•
68•

Central
•292
Plateau
Stack Bay
356
294•
Mt. Waterhouse

264• 262•

277•
Ringdove
Bay

REFERENCE

■1 Lands and Survey
   hut
■2 Castaway hut
   Cliffs
•37 Elevation in metres

RELIANCE
RIDGE
316•
•326
210•
SHIPWRECKS
200•
Albatross Pt.

South Bay

1. Possible wreck site of
   "President Felix Fauré"
   (1908)
2. Probable wreck site of
   "Spirit of the Dawn"
   (1893)

South Islet
(Probable position)

SOUTH ISLAND •DUNEDIN
BLUFF

Stewart Id.

Bounty Is.

178°45′E
48°S
The Snares

175°E
ANTIPODES IS.

The Antipodes

The one marginally safe anchorage at the Snares is at Ho Ho Bay on the east coast of the main island, where a few commercial crayfishers with special permits to use the islands have moorings. But sea conditions can change rapidly, and it is by no means a reliable harbour. Between this bay and Station Point, a long narrow inlet leads in towards the small group of research huts. This inlet is navigable by launch or inflatable dinghy, and it is the only part of the coastline sheltered from ocean swells.

From the huts, designed for expeditions of four to six people, a boardwalk over black peat trodden by penguins leads for a short way into the *Olearia* forest; there, apart from the occasional marker peg in a penguin colony, signs of civilisation end. Yet the forest floor is strangely bare of leaves and twigs. This is because they have been taken underground to line the nests of the estimated six million sooty shearwaters, whose burrows riddle the peaty ground.

The hundreds of thousands of ground-burrowing sea birds on the island emphasise the extreme vulnerability of the Snares if rats should ever get ashore, and this is a problem which has caused great concern in recent years. Just as much at risk are the three species of small land birds, found nowhere else in the world — the Snares black tit, *Petroica macrocephala dannefaerdi*, the Snares fernbird, *Bowdleria punctata caudata*, and the Snares snipe, *Coenocorypha aucklandica huegeli*.

Silvereyes and redpolls are common, and grey warblers, starlings, blackbirds, and thrushes can be seen. Swallows are still rare, and a sizeable population of fantails was first recorded in 1982. But the land birds are insignificant in numbers compared with the vast population of sea birds, which includes between 60 000 and 80 000 Snares crested penguins.

The plants are typical of a small island's flora, for there are only thirty species, dominated by the *Olearia* forest and tussock meadows. The coastline, with its outlying islets and rocks, is steep and wild and rises from treacherous seas, and it is this which protected the Snares in the years from their discovery to their recognition as one of the subantarctic's most valuable sanctuaries.

The granite rocks of the Bounty Islands (map, p. 73) lie 624 kilometres east of Bluff, on latitude 47°45′ south and 179°02′ east. Their total estimated area is 135 hectares — a third the size of Disappointment Island in the Aucklands. There are three groups scattered over four kilometres. The Main Group includes the largest island, Depot Island, and then there is Centre Group and East Group. All the islands are heavily weathered and eroded. There are very few landing places in the generally heavy swell. The problem is to find an area free of the tens of thousands of penguins and mollymawks which pepper the rocks. It cannot be called ground, for there is no soil and not a trace of vegetation, other than a few lichens and algae. A thin guano, polished by rain and wind, by birds and seals, has smoothed the roughness of the granite into an enamelled surface which is extremely treacherous when wet.

The only bright colours in this world of grey, black, and white are the toffee brown, orange, and pink of rocks constantly washed by the surf, and the golden-yellow of the kelp fronds, weaving below in long, rhythmic patterns with the surge of the sea. Everywhere there is the smell of guano and a ceaseless cacaphony of wind, sea, and animals. Mollymawks come and go endlessly, and the more distant islands fade into the grey of the ocean. The horizon is lost in the murk.

When the sea birds leave them at the end of the breeding season, these are the truly desert islands of the Southern Ocean. But although by far the least hospitable of New Zealand's subantarctic islands, they were nevertheless the first to be discovered, in 1788. It was during the years of discovery and exploitation, settlement and shipwreck, and of attempts at farming which ended in failure, that New Zealand's subantarctic islands underwent their most drastic changes.

The Auckland Island teal, or flightless duck, is one of the world's rarest waterfowl. *Photo: Lynton Diggle.*

The Snares fernbird nests on the ground, and would be one of the first species to disappear if predators ever got ashore.

The Antipodes pipit, a subspecies of the New Zealand and Auckland Islands pipits, feeds off grubs and insects in the penguin colonies.

PART TWO

Plunder, Settlement, and Failure

Old farmhouse range, at Tucker Cove, Campbell Island.

7
Discovery and Exploitation

Captain Cook's outstanding circumnavigations of the world stimulated a further series of far-reaching voyages of discovery which, because of the importance of the prevailing westerly winds to navigation in the Southern Ocean, were to prove of tremendous significance to New Zealand's sub-antarctic islands.

The remote and inhospitable Bounty Islands was the first group to be discovered, a mere nine years after Captain Cook's first landing in New Zealand, and only three years after Cook, on his second expedition, had discovered and charted South Georgia and the South Sandwich Islands to the south of South America.

Captain William Bligh had been Cook's sailing master on the *Resolution* when they had found breadfruit at Tahiti. At the end of 1787 the British Government sent Bligh to the Pacific in command of HMS *Bounty* to collect valuable breadfruit trees from Tahiti and transfer them to the West Indies.

It was on his way to Tahiti, on the long and dangerous voyage that was to end in the infamous mutiny on the *Bounty*, that Bligh, on 9 September 1788,

> discovered a cluster of small rocky islands. . . . Their extent was only three and a half miles from east to west, and about half a league from north to south; their number, including the smaller ones, thirteen. I could not observe any verdure on them . . . I have named them after the ship, the Bounty Isles.[1]

Bligh had noticed "white spots like patches of snow", which were almost certainly areas of polished guano on the stark grey granite. The islands were passed by subsequent voyagers, including Captain George Vancouver, who had also sailed with Cook as a midshipman in the *Resolution*, but because of their forbidding appearance and dangerous waters no landing was attempted for another fifteen years.

Three and a half years after Bligh had left England, Vancouver was put in command of the *Discovery* — a different ship from Cook's — and sailed to survey the coast of north-western America and formally close a dispute which had flared there between Britain and Spain. His route was to be by way of the Cape of Good Hope and then Sydney, thence south of New Zealand with the prevailing westerlies and into the Pacific. He was accompanied by Lieutenant Broughton in the *Chatham*.

Hooker's sea lion pups at Sandy Bay on Enderby Island. A hair seal, this species was slaughtered for its oil.

In the early days of the 1800s, tens of thousands of New Zealand fur seals were slaughtered at the Bounty Islands, and by 1831 only five seals could be found at the height of the breeding season.

The colony and penal settlement of Sydney Cove in New South Wales, which was in effect the beginnings of modern Australia, had only been established for three and a half years, and Vancouver preferred to use Cook's favourite haven and anchorage at Dusky Sound on the south-west coast of Fiordland. After taking on water and timber for fuel and spars they left on 20 November 1791. As they were nearing Foveaux Strait a heavy sea and violent storm came up, and the two ships were separated. They did not in fact meet again until they reached Tahiti at the end of December!

Both vessels kept well south of Stewart Island, and on 23 November both stumbled separately, but on the same day, on "a cluster of seven craggy islands".[2] Vancouver, who came across them at 11 a.m., aptly named them the Snares. Broughton sailed through the narrow passage between the main island and Broughton Island at 2 p.m. and named them Knight's Island. Six days later, sailing east-north-east, he came upon the Chatham Islands, naming them after his ship.

Sealing in the Southern Ocean had started as early as 1766 at the Falkland Islands and on the coast of South America. Cook and Banks had noted seals at Dusky Bay, now more accurately known as Dusky Sound. In 1792 the first sealing gangs to reach New Zealand from Sydney started work there, but it was still some years before the trade spread south to the subantarctic islands.

On 26 March 1800 Captain Waterhouse of HMS *Reliance* was returning to England from Sydney and sighted "a desolate, Mountainous and barren Island, scarce any verdure to be seen upon it",[3] with a small island nearby. Because of their approximation to the antipodes of London, he named these islands the Penantipodes, noting that they had seals upon them.

At the Snares, Buller's mollymawks have a wide range of habitat in which to nest — bare rock, tussock-covered cliff ledges, or protected sites well within the *Olearia* forest.

The ship's surgeon was George Bass, the first European to discover Bass Strait, between Tasmania and the Australian mainland. This strait was to prove an immensely rich sealing ground for the Sydney sealers, and the foundation of a profitable trade with China, but, as it became exhausted, Bass and the Sydney schooners turned towards New Zealand's recently discovered southern islands — The Bounties, Snares, and Antipodes. Bass's adventurous life was to be cut short, his fate a mystery, but there was no stopping the trade he had so strongly encouraged.

In the opening years of the 1800s enormous quantities of sealskins were taken from the subantarctic islands, and there are some almost unbelievable stories of the hardships suffered by the sealing gangs, who were often left for long periods, and occasionally deliberately stranded if the captain of a ship found something more lucrative to divert him.

Elephant seals were slaughtered for the oil from their blubber. This large bull at Northwest Bay on Campbell Island has hauled ashore for the seasonal moult.

An American sealer under the command of Captain J. Pendleton was the first to station a sealing gang on the Antipodes, when the brig *Union of New York* left an officer and eleven men there in 1804. On returning to Sydney the *Union* immediately sailed for Fiji and disaster, for the ship was lost and its entire crew massacred. Its sealing gang was eventually rescued in 1805 after more than a year on the Antipodes by a Nantucket sealer, the *Favourite*. The gang had collected together a huge haul of almost 60 000 skins.

In the same year the brig *Venus*, commanded by William Stewart, after whom Stewart Island is said to be named, landed its captain and a sealing gang on the Antipodes. After several months they were taken off by the *Star*, which had on board the young Maori George, the son of a chief at Whangaroa. George's subsequent mistreatment by the captain of the *Boyd* led to the massacre of the crew of the *Boyd* and the burning of the ship in Whangaroa Harbour in 1809.

The Auckland Islands, which may have been known to the early Polynesians, were not discovered by Europeans until 1806. Captain Abraham Bristow, master of the *Ocean*, belonging to the British whaling company of Enderby and Co., was on his way from Tasmania to Cape Horn when he sighted land on the 18th of August:

> This island or islands, as being the first discoverer, I shall call Lord Auckland's (my friend through my father). . . . The land is of a moderate height, and from its appearance I have no doubt but it will afford a good harbour in the north end, and its greatest extent is in a N.W. and S.E. direction. This place I should suppose abounds with seals, and sorry I am that the time and the lumbered state of my ship do not allow me to examine.[4]

Bristow returned the following year in the *Sarah*, another Enderby whaler, to take formal possession of the group. He also landed several pigs to provide food for the crews of any sealing or whaling ships which might call.

There now occurred one of the most astonishing sagas of an already eventful era. A Sydney vessel, the *Santa Anna*, bound for the seal fisheries and thence to London,[5] called in at the Bay of Islands and took on board a Maori chief, Ruatara, who had already been to Sydney, and whose great ambition was to visit King George III. On arriving at the Bounty Islands, Ruatara and thirteen others were left to kill seals while the *Santa Anna* went off on further business. By the time it returned three of the men had died

Female Hooker's sea lions on Enderby Island.

from hunger, thirst, and exposure on the waterless and barren islands. The others had survived on seal meat and sea birds, and had amassed 8000 skins. Ruatara had certainly earned his passage to England. However, on reaching London he was thwarted in his wish to see the King and, already weakened by his ordeal, became seriously ill. He was befriended by the Reverend Samuel Marsden, who nursed him back to health. On their return to Sydney the chief stayed with Marsden and studied agriculture under his guidance. Finally, after further misadventures, which involved being cheated and stranded on Norfolk Island, Ruatara returned to his people. His friendship with Marsden was lifelong, and it was largely due to his influence that Marsden succeeded in his mission to the Bay of Islands, establishing Christianity there in 1814.

Sir Joseph Banks, Cook's botanist, writing in 1806, commented that

> the southern parts of New Zealand produce seals of all kinds in quantities at present almost innumerable. Their stations on rocks or in bays have remain'd unmolested since the Creation. The beach is encumber'd with their quantities, and those who visit their haunts have less trouble in killing them than the servants of the victualling office have who kill hogs in a pen with mallets.[6]

There seemed to be no limit to the ruthless harvest. The Bounty Islands, storm-lashed outcrops of grey granite and guano, isolated in the ocean, and with not a blade of vegetation, certainly lived up to their name as far as the sealers were concerned. In the first two years of sealing, some 50 000 seals were killed, at a profit of some £40,000. Numerous vessels called during the next twenty years. But by 1831, at the height of the breeding season, Captain John Biscoe could find only five fur seals. The slaughter had been indiscriminate, and the vast colonies were virtually exterminated.

It was a sealer, Captain Frederick Hasselburgh, who discovered the last and most southerly of New Zealand's subantarctic islands. Robert Campbell and Co. was a leading Sydney sealing company, anxious to find new sealing grounds as the known ones became exhausted, and it was one of this firm's ships, the *Perseverance*, which reached Campbell Island on 4 January 1810. A group of seven men was landed with supplies for several months, and the *Perseverance* sailed home. Captain Hasselburgh (whose name has many spelling variations) was about to return and take off the Campbell Island party when he was delayed by a totally unexpected event: in July 1810 he discovered Macquarie Island.

Macquarie was considered a far richer prize than Campbell Island, and by the time the Campbell gang was picked up in late October, they had been out of provisions for three or four months. The *Perseverance* stayed for several days, and before it sailed there was tragedy when its boat was overturned by

one of the sudden wind gusts for which Perseverance Harbour is notorious. Captain Hasselburgh, Elizabeth Farr (a native of Norfolk Island), and a boy apprentice were drowned. The *Perseverance* itself was lost at Campbell Island in 1828, the only ship known to have been wrecked there.

In spite of efforts to keep the discoveries of Campbell and Macquarie Islands quiet, the news got out, and there was a rush of sealing vessels from Sydney to Macquarie. One hundred thousand skins were taken in the first season, and for many years Macquarie remained a highly profitable sealing ground, supplemented by revenue from oil from its elephant seal colonies.

Every new sealing find was like a gold rush, for

> sealers were a secretive lot, leaving few accounts of their tough and bloody business. . . . Whalers could afford to swap information about likely locations for their quarry . . . but sealing was wholesale massacre ashore . . . and a newly discovered rookery was like a mine of precious metal, too easily exhausted to tell rivals about.[7]

An inquisitive New Zealand fur seal, fresh from the sea, at the Bounty Islands.

Tens of thousands of skins were also taken from the Auckland Islands, but the fur seal colonies there were often so dangerous and difficult to reach that individual cargoes seldom matched the enormous quantities taken from Macquarie, the Bounties, and the Antipodes. Even so, as late as 1823 an American schooner, the *Henry*, took off 13 000 skins. It was one of the last big hauls, for two years later the *Sally*, of Hobart, after losing six seamen by drowning, took off only 200 skins after three months' work.

The longest period for which a sealing gang was abandoned undoubtedly belongs to four escaped convicts from Norfolk Island. They had been taken aboard the *Adventure* of London as crew, and were then abandoned on the Snares for seven years.[8] On reaching the islands, the captain had told them he was short of provisions, and had given them the choice of starving aboard or chancing their luck ashore. During their long exile one became deranged, so alarming the others that they pushed him over the cliffs. They had been given a few potatoes, which they had planted, and by the time the surviving three were taken off in 1817 by Captain Coffin of the American whaler *Enterprise* they had two thirds of a hectare ready for harvesting and 1300 dried sealskins. Because of the exceptional circumstances of their ordeal they were exonerated for the death of their companion.

In the 1820s international sealing swung to new discoveries at the South Shetlands. In retrospect, Robert McNab, historian and author of *Murihiku*, the detailed account of early sealing in the subantarctic, saw the decline of New Zealand sealing as inevitable:

> The third decade of the nineteenth century saw the sealing trade reduced from one of such a magnitude that vessels could be fitted out for it and sail from Sydney seeking nothing else but a cargo of skins, to one which only supplied a portion of a cargo, the balance having to be made up with flax, spars, potatoes, whale oil and pork . . . if left alone and without legislation to protect it, no wild animal which becomes the property of its captor and which pays to catch, will survive extinction . . .[9]

In 1826, the year that saw the collapse of the sealing trade, the *Sydney Gazette* stated:

> The total annihilation of the fur seal, though insignificant when put in the balance with the moral evil, is notwithstanding, very important in a commercial point of view to these Colonies. Some years ago it was no uncommon thing for a vessel to obtain in a short trip from 80,000 to 100,000 skins. . . . [Now] here and round New Zealand, scarce hundreds or even tens are to be obtained where as many thousands were once easily procured.[10]

The early American Antarctic explorer Benjamin Morrell, calling at the Auckland Islands in 1830, wrote that

> Although the Auckland Islands once abounded with numerous herds of fur and hair-seal, the American and English seamen engaged in this business have made

Opposite: View from the sea of the large black-browed mollymawk colony at North Cape on Campbell Island.

A breeding rockhopper penguin on its nest, under the lush cover of *Anisotome latifolia*, at Castaway Bay on Disappointment Island. The number of this species is declining.

such clean work of it as scarcely to leave a breed; at all events, there was not one fur-seal to be found on the 4th of January 1830. We therefore got under way on the morning of Tuesday, the 5th, at 6 o'clock, and steered for . . . The Snares. . . . We searched them in vain for fur-seal, with which they formerly abounded. The population was extinct, cut off, root and branch, by the sealers of Van Dieman's Land, Sidney [sic], etc.[11]

Between 1840 and 1860 there was no further sealing in the subantarctic islands. Later, there would be a brief revival of sealing, with the last of the open seasons as late as 1946, but effectively it was finished.

New Zealand's subantarctic islands had been discovered, ruthlessly exploited by the international sealing countries operating in the Southern Ocean, and then abandoned: a remarkable chapter of New Zealand history opened and closed well before New Zealand became a British Colony in 1840.

The Penguin Skin Trade

There was a brief trade in penguin skins at the very end of the sealing revival.[12] It was mainly to meet a fashionable demand for ladies' muffs — open-ended fur cylinders in which to warm the hands. A large number of these skins were collected for Walter Henderson of Bluff, a merchant who, in 1880, had become part-owner of a 45 tonne sealing schooner, the *Alert*.[13]

On one of the *Alert*'s early calls to the Bounty Islands, it collected a meagre 191 sealskins, twenty-eight gallons of seal oil, and fifteen bags of penguin feathers from a gang which it had left there a month before. Soon afterwards, another vessel from Bluff, the sixty-tonne *William and Jane*, spent just under two months on the Bounties and Antipodes, and returned with 347 sealskins and 150 penguin skins.

On the *Alert*'s next expedition towards the end of 1880, the balance of seals to penguins was reversed when the ship brought a gang home with only fifty-seven sealskins, but 2990 penguin skins, fifty gallons of seal oil, and five bags of hard-won guano. The sealskins sold for 22/- each and 2750 of the penguin skins for 6d each.

Not long afterwards, the cutter *Kent* returned from the Antipodes with 3500 penguin skins. Other small boats worked the Snares and Stewart Island, bringing home cargoes which showed that by now seals had become exceedingly scarce, while the defenceless penguin colonies had become fair game. Typical cargoes were: one hair seal (a sea lion) and 3500 penguin skins;

A cache of rolled penguin skins, from the sealing days, protected by a shallow cave, at Anchorage Bay on the Antipodes. The bale stands on a platform of more rolled skins, partially buried and preserved by penguin guano.

nine sealskins at 22/- and 3452 penguin skins at 6d; twenty sealskins, 4202 penguin skins, and 160 paua shells.

Early in 1881 the *Alert* returned from the Snares with 124 sealskins, seven hair seal skins, and 2850 penguin skins, but having lost a man overboard. This virtually marked the end of the penguin skin trade, and when Henderson closed his books, his overall profit from sealing was minimal and the penguin skin account was in the red. In all he had purchased more than 15 000 penguin skins, and although the demand for muffs must have accounted for a good number, and the passing custom for butchers to display a stuffed penguin in their windows for a few more, supply had certainly exceeded demand. The cache of carefully rolled skins above the penguin colony at Anchorage Bay was never collected, and can still be found there today.

8

The Antarctic Explorers

The Russian Thaddeus Bellingshausen was the first of the Antarctic Explorers to follow the sealers and whalers into the Southern Ocean and sight the Antarctic continent at 70° south, early in 1820 and only a few days before Bransfield's discovery of the Antarctic Peninsula. Bellingshausen also made the first discoveries, within the Antarctic Circle, of Peter Island and Alexander Island, and went on to circumnavigate the continent. The names of his ships, the *Vostok* and the *Mirny*, are perpetuated in Russia's two major scientific bases in Antarctica.

Bellingshausen deeply regretted that the German botanists assigned to his expedition withdrew at the last moment, for his hopes of making discoveries in the field of natural history were dashed to the ground. He had been ordered to call at the Auckland Islands, but chose instead to go to Macquarie, where he stayed for three days. While there, he came across two Sydney gangs killing sea elephants for their oil and skins. The blubber from a single sea elephant could yield up to three barrels of oil. In the nine or ten years since the island's discovery, fur seals had become too scarce to bother with, but there was a good price for sea elephant oil and the trade was steady.

One headman, who had been on the island for six years, showed Bellingshausen how the roots and stalks of the "wild cabbage", *Stilbocarpa polaris*, could be scraped for soup and thinly sliced as a vegetable. The Russians left with large quantities aboard as a remedy against scurvy.[1]

Unfortunately, the first of the Antarctic explorers to visit New Zealand's subantarctic islands did not share Bellingshausen's empathy for science or eye for accurate observation. Benjamin Morrell's romantic view was to irritate and mislead many who followed him.

Morrell arrived at Carnley Harbour in the schooner *Antarctica* on 28 December 1829, and left the Auckland Islands on 5 January 1830, during a prolonged voyage to examine prospects for trade in the Pacific. There had been considerable illness aboard, and Mrs Morrell was among those able to recover in this astonishing haven after the storm. While Morrell gives due

Although smaller than Carnley Harbour, Port Ross was the harbour most favoured by Antarctic explorers calling at the Auckland Islands. The prominent landmark of Mount Eden, with its volcanic plug, is on the left.

The southern rata forest at Carnley Harbour, its trunks shaped by the prevailing gales, was seen with misleadingly romantic eyes by Benjamin Morrell when he visited the Auckland Islands in the schooner *Antarctica* in 1829.

acknowledgement to the western cliffs, his description of the east coast reads more like Gulliver's travels:

> The western side of this island is a perpendicular bluff iron bound coast, with deep water within 100 fathoms of the shore, while the eastern coast is principally lined with a pebbly or sandy beach, behind which are extensive level plains covered with beautiful grass and refreshing verdure, extending back about five miles and then rising into elevated hills.[2]

In reality, the coast is deeply indented, and Chambres Inlet, Norman Inlet, and the North Arm of Carnley Harbour all but cut the main island in two. There is almost no flat land, and while there are certainly beaches, there are also numerous rocky headlands and bays. Almost nowhere is access easy to the dense scrub, tussock, and the peat bogs, rocks, and stark herbfields of the interior. Morrell's misleading account continues:

> All the hills, except a few of the highest, are thickly covered with lofty trees, flourishing with such extraordinary vigour as to afford a magnificent prospect to the spectator. . . . The large trees are principally of two sorts. One of them is of the size of our large firs, and grows nearly in the same manner; its foliage is an excellent substitute for spruce in making that pleasant and wholesome beverage, spruce-beer. The other resembles our maple, and often grows to a great size, but is only fit for ship-building or fuel, being too heavy for masts or spars of any dimensions.[3]

It is hard to see the gnarled and twisted rata forest in this description, or the drab barrier of impenetrable scrub above it as "hills . . . covered with lofty trees".

Morrell must have struck a good summer, and its few balmy days must have beguiled him, but it is doubtful if sealers and whalers would have provided such a mild account of winter:

The climate is mild, temperate, and salubrious. I have been told, by men of the first respectability and talent, who have visited the island in the month of July, the dead of winter in this island, corresponding to our January, that the weather was mild as respects cold, as the mercury was never lower than 38° in the valleys, and the trees at the same time retained their verdure as if it was Midsummer.[4]

Auckland Island shags face into a storm, on Enderby Island. Beyond the island's cliffs lies the dangerous Derry Castle reef.

This, of course, they do, but just the same, all efforts to introduce deciduous trees have failed.

With intricate detail in his mind's eye, Morrell goes on to give a poetic list of the wildflowers and herbs of the island which Hooker, arriving ten years later, would have been astounded to find:

Besides the vegetables [wild celery and scurvy grass] already mentioned, there are euphorbia, crane's-bill, cud-weed, rushes, bind-weed, nightshade, nettles, thistles, virgin's-bower, vanelloe, French willow, flax, all-heal, knot-grass, brambles, eye-bright, groundsel, and a variety of others, for which I know no appelation; and many of those already mentioned differ in many respects from plants of the same family in the United States.[5]

With no knowledge of the acid peat soil or salt winds, Morrell could be excused for thinking the land highly productive. "Were the forests cleared away, very few spots would be found that could not be converted to excellent pasturage or tillage land."[6] His summary of the Auckland Islands was to have a considerable influence on Charles Enderby — all the more ironic because he was right as far as the quality of its harbours and abundance of its rainfall was concerned:

On the whole, I think that Auckland's Island is one of the finest places for a small settlement that can be found on any island in the southern hemisphere above the latitude of thirty-five. Every valuable animal would thrive here. . . . Grain, fruits, vegetables of all kinds (excepting the tropical fruits) could be made to flourish here

As on the New Zealand mainland, the first Europeans to go ashore at the Auckland Islands were charmed by the bellbird's melodious song.

with very little labour. No island on the globe, of equal dimensions, can boast so many excellent harbours, safe, and easy of access; and at the head of each is a beautiful valley, extending inland, admirably calculated for the site of a village. The whole island is well watered, and would form a delightful retreat to a few amiable families, who wish for "a dear little isle of their own".[7]

With practical men coming before and after him, Morrell's is an extraordinary interlude which shows how in a wild ocean the Auckland Islands can at times cast an illusory spell of warmth and tranquillity.

A year afterwards, John Biscoe, an Enderby Company captain like Bristow, was the first to sight a new section of the Antarctic continent. He gave it the name of Enderby Land. In January 1839 two other Enderby ships, the schooner *Eliza Scott* and the cutter *Sabrina* commanded by John Balleny, called at Campbell Island and spent seven days of foul summer weather there, with heavy rain and gales. Balleny rescued four sealers — three men and a woman — who had been abandoned by their ship, and took them off in exchange for the paltry 170 skins they had collected in four years.[8] He discovered the Balleny Islands off Northern Victoria Land, and returned to England in time to give valuable information to Sir James Clark Ross before he sailed. But the Americans and the French were to reach the Auckland Islands a few months before Ross. Altogether, 1840 was an important year in Antarctic exploration.

The United States Exploring Expedition of 1838–42, commanded by Charles Wilkes, was the first to anchor in Port Ross — or the Bay of Sarah's Bosom, as it was still called. Wilkes had charted and explored Wilkes Land on the Great Ice Barrier and was on his way to rendezvous with other ships of his expedition at the Bay of Islands in New Zealand, before continuing north into the Pacific.

With the decline of sealing, ocean whaling had increased, and America was playing a major role. Wilkes's mission was to gather navigational and other information for the industry. In addition, he was instructed to extend

the bounds of science and promote the acquisition of knowledge. Wilkes's expedition was a large one and included eleven scientists, but two of the best withdrew at the last moment, and this side of his expedition was considered disappointing. For example, acting-surgeon Holmes mentioned only six species of flowering plants collected at the Auckland Islands. However, Holmes did make considerably more accurate general observations on the island than Morrell.

> I found it very thickly covered with trees, in its less elevated parts; as few of them were of any size, I found no small difficulty in penetrating and making my way through them; in many places it was absolutely impossible. It was only after a long and fatiguing walk that I succeeded in reaching the summit of that part of the island, near which the brig was anchored, where I found the trees less numerous.[9]

In one instance, it took him an hour to travel a hundred metres!

Wilkes records that on 9 March 1840, "A whaler, under Portuguese colours, but commanded by an Englishman, arrived, and anchored in Lawrie's Cove, to await the coming of the whales!"[10] And he noted that

> these islands . . . are the resort of whalers, for the purpose of refitting and awaiting the whaling season, which occurs here in the months of April and May. Near the watering-place a commodious hut has been erected by a French whaler. Near by was another in ruins, and close to it the grave of a French sailor, whose name was inscribed on a wooden cross erected over it. Some attempts at forming a garden were observed at one of the points of Sarah's Bosom, and turnips, cabbage, and potatoes were growing finely, which, if left undisturbed, will soon cover this portion of the island.[11]

Wilkes was not to know whether the crops would mature and seed, and his supposition that introduced vegetables and seeds would spread rapidly was commonly held. Over the years, numerous abortive attempts were made to introduce European plants and trees. During Wilkes's visit, a few onions were added.

Wilkes's was a short stay. He considered the harbour an excellent place in which to refit and take on wood and water, and his men found the rocks at

For most of the year, gales and storms sweep across the Southern Ocean. Approaching the islands of the region in the days of sail was a hazardous undertaking.

The two ships of Dumont D'Urville's expedition, the *Astrolabe* and the *Zélée*, anchored off Shoe Island in Port Ross, March 1840. *Photo: Louis le Breton collection, Alexander Turnbull Library, Wellington.*

the head of Laurie Harbour covered with limpets, and small fish of many varieties were easy to catch among the kelp. The usual infestation of worms was apparently not noticed, for "The crew enjoyed themselves on chowders and fries".[12] They left on the fourth day, on 10 March.

Before reaching the Auckland Islands, Wilkes had seen Dumont D'Urville's two ships, the *Astrolabe* and the *Zélée*, off the Great Ice Barrier of Antarctica. There, D'Urville had discovered Adelie Land. Sailing north, he had arrived at the Aucklands on the same day as Wilkes, but had continued round them, down the west coast and back up the east. He did not finally anchor in Port Ross until 12 March, two days after Wilkes's expedition had sailed for New Zealand and the Bay of Islands.

Although D'Urville only stayed eight days, his investigations were more thorough than Wilkes's, and he had caustic comments to make in the third person on what he called Morrell's lack of veracity and scruple:

> In spite of the glowing descriptions that Morrell gave of the vast forests of the Auckland Islands, the navigator finds nothing in the depths of the valleys but a few miserable trees, twisted and stunted.[13]

D'Urville's scientists used a large whalers' hut on the shore near Shoe Island, built in 1837 by the crew of the French whaling ship *Nancy*. Astronomical observations and weather readings were taken, and a good collection of seaweeds was made. A message there told them that a vessel they had seen two days earlier was the *Porpoise*, of Wilkes's expedition.

In *The Voyage of the Astrolabe*, D'Urville tells of a remarkable incident which illustrates the importance of Port Ross to the early whaling ships:

> Close at hand there was a fairly high point from which a little red flag was flying and this . . . excited our curiosity sufficiently to make it one of the first places to be visited. We soon saw that the spot had been chosen to serve as a last resting-place for two or three sailors, belonging no doubt to whaling vessels. One of the graves was surmounted by a little wooden cross, and the earth seemed to have been recently dug. This was the grave of M. Lefrancois, the owner or captain of a

Dumont D'Urville's expedition at the Bay of Sarah's Bosom (later named Port Ross), March 1840. *Photo: Louis le Breton collection, Alexander Turnbull Library, Wellington.*

whaling vessel, who had committed suicide on the island, having been driven to despair because a new method which he had invented for harpooning whales had not proved a success. . . . M. Lefrancois had conceived the idea of shooting the harpoons from a gun. Like all inventors, he was very enthusiastic over his new discovery and he wanted to make the first attempt himself. . . . [When it failed] life became an intolerable burden to him and he resorted to these deserted islands to carry out his fatal decision.[14]

Years later, the British Admiralty description of New Zealand's outlying islands summed this up as a cruel fate for an inventor whose idea was to be so successfully used through to modern times.

Because of its strong scientific and geographical aims, Sir James Clark Ross's British Antarctic Expedition was by far the most significant of the three major expeditions of the 1840s. Ross was at the Auckland Islands from 20 November until 12 December, and at Campbell Island from 13 to 17 December, before making his famous voyage south, in which he made major contributions to the knowledge of terrestrial magnetism in high latitudes, and discovered Victoria Land, the Ross Sea, and the two volcanoes of Mt Erebus and Mt Terror, which he named after his ships.

Due to the depth of the peaty soil, Ross had the greatest difficulty setting up his observatory with its magnetometers and instruments, which was the main purpose of his visit to the Aucklands. A further problem which had to be overcome was the highly magnetic state of the rocks. Dea's Head and Shoe Island, with their columnar basalt structures, were highly magnetic, and with some exasperation Ross concluded that the whole land mass was "one great magnet".[15]

Meteorological readings were taken for temperature, barometric pressure, winds, and weather. Hooker and David Lyall, who were both only twenty-two years of age at the time, collected botanical specimens, including eighty flowering plants and 200 species of seaweeds, mosses, and lesser plants. Dr McCormick made a large collection of insects, and shot teal, merganser, bellbirds, and tuis — "the beautiful 'tooe' bird of New Zealand".[16] On Enderby Island he

> caught two old albatrosses, sitting together among the long grass flanked by bushes; they were doubtless about selecting a nesting-place. These birds are now in my own collection. . . . [He also] found snipe in the long grass, which were very difficult to flush . . . rising close under the feet, rendering it a somewhat difficult matter to secure specimens without having them shattered to pieces.[17]

Ross introduced several animals and plants:

> In order to increase the stock of useful animals, I directed a ram and two ewes . . . to be landed on the western side of the harbour; and a ram and two ewes brought by the Terror were taken several miles inland to the southward. Besides these were landed from our private stores some pigs, poultry, and rabbits . . . together with a quantity of cabbage, turnip, mustard and cress, radish, and other seeds. . . . Some seeds of each kind were sown in the small place we had cleared; and a great many gooseberry and currant bushes, and raspberry and strawberry plants . . . were distributed over various parts of the island by Dr. Hooker. . . . The hens had formed nests in well concealed situations, and had laid several eggs before we left the place.[18]

Campbell Island was of less importance, and they made only a short stay. Joseph Hooker, in making the first collection of plants from the island, noted that sixty-six flowering plants were taken, of which fourteen were not seen in the Aucklands: "thus in two degrees of latitude, thirty-four species had disappeared from the Flora of this longitude, and been replaced by at least twenty other plants".[19] Campbell Island's flora differed more widely than that of the Aucklands from New Zealand. In the Auckland group only a seventh of the plants were common to other antarctic regions, whereas at Campbell Island fully a quarter were found in similar longitudes round the Southern Ocean.

Like D'Urville and Wilkes before him, Ross was greatly impressed by the magnificent harbour of Sarah's Bosom:

> I was so struck with the many advantages this place possesses for a penal settlement, over every other I had heard named, to which to remove convicts from the now free colonies of New South Wales, New Zealand, and Van Diemen's Land, that I addressed a letter on the subject to Sir John Franklin on my return to Hobart Town, recommending its adoption. This letter was forwarded to the Secretary of State for the Colonies; but I believe Chatham Island, as being seated in a milder climate, has been preferred, although I am not aware of any other advantages it possesses; whilst the want of good harbours will be found a great drawback, and the two tribes of New Zealanders from Port Nicholson, who took possession of it in 1835, after eating the half of the aborigines they found there, and making slaves of the other half, will prove a difficult people to dispossess of the land they have gained by conquest.[20]

Unknown to Ross, further unrest at the Chathams would affect the Auckland Islands by the time the book of his voyage was published in 1847. It is surprising that Ross did not visit Carnley Harbour, although he knew of it. He may have felt that Port Ross with its sheltered coves and bays offered everything that was needed, for he considered it

> well calculated for the location of an establishment for the prosecution of the whale fishery: many black and several sperm whales came into the harbour whilst we were there; and from such a situation the fishery might be persued with very great advantage. I am rejoiced to hear that the enterprising merchant, Charles Enderby, Esq., is making application to the government for a grant of the Islands for that purpose.[21]

With such favourable recommendations reaching England, it seemed almost inevitable that the early Antarctic explorers should be followed by people intent on settling the islands.

Hooker's *Flora Antarctica*

Sir Joseph Hooker's *Flora Antarctica* was the first major scientific work to be published on the subantarctic and antarctic regions. Within a few months of his return to England he was at work on it, with the Government's financial support. The unpublished botanical collections of Banks and Solander from Cook's voyages were made available, as were Charles Darwin's from the voyage of the *Beagle*. (It was to Joseph Hooker that Darwin first outlined his theory on the origin of species, and Hooker who persuaded Darwin to make his controversial views public in 1858.)

Hooker's great work, *Botany of the Antarctic Voyage*, has three separate parts: *Flora Antarctica*, *Flora Novae-Zelandiae*, and *Flora Tasmaniae*. Each part is complete in itself. In drawing it up, Joseph Hooker was helped by his father, Sir William Hooker, whom he succeeded as director of Kew Gardens.

Flora Antarctica is the most celebrated of the three works, and falls into two parts: Part One comprises the Auckland Islands, Campbell Island, and Macquarie, and Part Two the South American sector of the subantarctic, including Tierra del Fuego, South Georgia, the South Shetlands, the Kerguelen Islands, and the Falkland Islands.

The first part was the most notable, because the material had been collected by Hooker himself, and because so little was known of the Auckland and Campbell Islands. Yet Hooker had felt sure he would make a wealth of new discoveries here, for he wrote in Sir James Clark Ross's account of their voyages:

> Perhaps no place in the course of our projected voyage in the southern ocean

Myosotis capitata, one of the many detailed plates in Hooker's *Flora Antarctica*. "It is upon the hills that the more beautiful plants abound . . . Amongst those of humbler stature, several European genera occur . . . [including] a Forget-me-not with flowers much larger than those of any English species." *Photo: Conon Fraser, courtesy National Museum.*

A superb colour plate from Hooker's *Flora Antarctica* reveals even the somewhat drab *Dracophyllum* as a plant of intricate detail. *Photo: Conon Fraser, courtesy National Museum.*

promised more novelty than Auckland Islands. Situated in the midst of a boisterous ocean, in a very high latitude for that hemisphere, and far removed from any tract of land but the islands of New Zealand, it proved, as was expected, to contain, amongst many new species, some of peculiar interest.[22]

Hooker was particularly struck by the grandeur of the magnificent giant herbs such as *Pleurophyllum speciosum* and *Chrysobactron rossii*, or *Bulbinella*, but he did not overlook the beauty of humbler plants such as the forget-me-not *Myosotis capitata*. He considered the botany of the Auckland Islands unrivalled:

> Eighty flowering plants were found, a small number, but consisting of species more remarkable for their beauty and novelty than the flora of any other country can show, no less than fifty-six being hitherto undescribed, and one half of the whole peculiar to this group, or Campbell Island, as far as is at present known. . . . the vegetation is characteristic of New Zealand, but contains many new forms typical of the antarctic regions.[23]

9
The Enderby Settlement

The opinion of an explorer as distinguished as Sir James Clark Ross carried enormous weight with the British Government, particularly when it became concerned at the decline of the nation's whaling industry in northern Arctic waters. At the time, increasing numbers of American whalers were moving down into the subantarctic. The United States had between 600 and 700 vessels manned by some 18 000 seamen, and its industry was eight times the size of Britain's. Yet the seas to the south of New Zealand and the Auckland Islands remained unexploited, and it was Ross's opinion that "In the whole range of the vast Southern Ocean, no spot could be found combining so completely the essential requisites for a fixed whaling station."[1]

Ross had backed Charles Enderby, a director of the prominent British whaling company, from the start of his plans to establish a whaling base and settlement on the Auckland Islands. It was widely considered an excellent proposal, and it was, after all, a whaling ship belonging to the same historic firm which had discovered the islands. William Gladstone, Britain's Prime Minister, was on its Board of Directors. National pride and prestige were involved, and it seemed almost Enderby's due that he was soon able to announce, "Her Majesty's Government has been graciously pleased to grant these islands to . . . [Enderby and Company] on very advantageous terms for the purposes of the whale fishery, as a station at which to discharge the cargoes and refit vessels."[2]

Not only was Enderby to be the Company's resident Commissioner at the settlement, but also he was to be appointed Lieutenant-Governor of the Auckland Islands, directly responsible to the Crown through the British Colonial Office. The Governors of Australia, Tasmania, and New Zealand were instructed to assist him in every possible way, as New Zealand's boundaries were not extended south to include the Auckland Islands until 1863.

Southern rata flowering on a rare calm morning at Erebus Cove, Port Ross, on the site of the Enderby Settlement. Just in from the shore, a benched road and faint house excavations can still be made out.

John Mahoney's grave began as that of an unknown castaway. After his identity became known, the original wooden board was replaced with this painted marble headstone — the name spelt Mahony — by the crew of the provincial paddle steamer SS *Southland*, in 1865.

Although Charles Enderby had not yet set foot on it, the colony was already complete in his mind, with

> mechanics and labourers employed in laying out roads, constructing wharves, storehouses, houses, cottages, &c.; together with . . . boiling out the oil, discharging the cargoes of the ships, storing, . . . coopering the oil, cleansing the whalebone . . . repairing, when necessary, the hull, masts, rigging, and sails of the whaling ships, (etc, etc.)[3]

Convinced that settlement at the Auckland Islands would have fewer difficulties and more obvious advantages than emigration to Australia, he wrote in his persuasive and enthusiastic prospectus:

> The Auckland Islands are subject to high winds and much rain, but they are exceedingly healthy; they are covered with wood and have a very rich virgin soil, capable of feeding on one acre of land as many sheep as can be fed on six acres in Australia; the land is equally suitable for feeding cattle, horses, &c., it is also capable of growing all such products as are usually grown in England. . . . There is scarcely a spot which is not within five miles of the east coast or bays. . . . Such a situation must be of incalculable advantage to a settler, since, however distant he may take up his residence from the site of the town, he will have facilities of communication without the heavy expense of constructing or keeping up roads. . . . He will also be free from aboriginals or wild animals, there being none on the island.[4]

Because this was to be the nucleus of a permanent colony as well as a commercial venture, the emphasis was on young married settlers who had among them a wide range of trades and professions.

With much publicity and influential backing, a subsidiary company, the Southern Whale Fishing Company, was formed, and in August 1849 three small whaling vessels left England. The first of them sighted the western cliffs of the main Auckland Island on 2 December, and two days later reached Ross's Rendezvous Harbour, or the Bay of Sarah's Bosom, which Enderby had renamed Port Ross "in compliment to our distinguished navigator".[5]

The first shock for the settlers was to find about seventy Maori people already there. They had arrived not long after Ross's departure from the Aucklands, as a result of inter-tribal fighting in the Chatham Islands. They may also have feared reprisals for the massacre of the crew of the *Jean Bart*, a French merchant vessel unfortunate enough to be at the Chathams in 1839. The Auckland Islands, chosen because one of their chiefs had been on a sealing expedition there, was probably the furthest south Polynesians had ever ventured, and they were living in miserable conditions. They were extremely pleased to see the colonists. In turn, their skill at hunting and coaxing vegetables to grow would come to be heavily relied upon. The two chiefs, Matioro and Manatere, were sworn in as constables, and did much to maintain harmonious relations between the Maori and the settlers.

The next shock was to find swamp and scrub in place of woods and grassland, but in spite of this the planning and building of the settlement went ahead quickly at Erebus Cove, with clearing of the rata forest and the assembly of the eighteen prefabricated buildings brought out on the ships. There was a large house for the Lieutenant Governor, cottages for the families, and a barrack building for the single men, as well as a workshop, stores, and a small chapel. On New Year's Day, 1850, the settlement was formally named Hardwicke, in honour of the Earl of Hardwicke, the Governor of the Southern Whale Fishery Company.

April and May marked the beginning of the first shore-based whaling season, when the whales were expected to come into the bays and shallow waters to calf. But in spite of sightings no whales were captured, and the whaling vessels which were sent out on long and hazardous ocean voyages did little better. Few of the foreign whaling vessels which had been expected to use Port Ross for refitting and taking on fresh vegetables and meat materi-

Historical Features of Port Ross

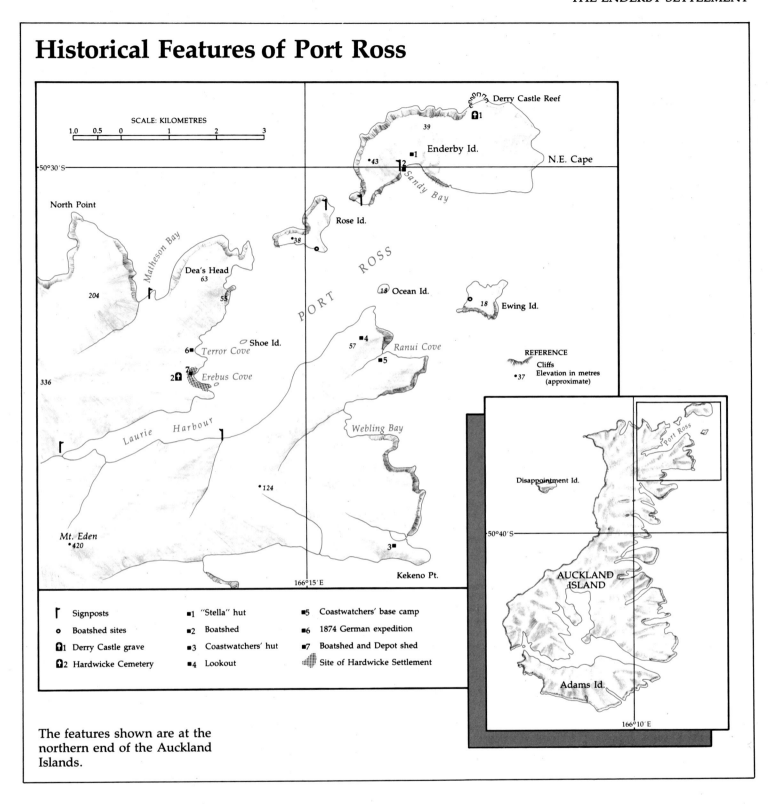

SCALE: KILOMETRES

Derry Castle Reef

Enderby Id.

N.E. Cape

Sandy Bay

North Point

Rose Id.

Matheson Bay

Dea's Head
63

PORT ROSS

Ocean Id.

Ewing Id.

204

55

Shoe Id.

REFERENCE

Cliffs

Elevation in metres
(approximate)

6 Terror Cove

57

Ranui Cove

336

2 Erebus Cove

5

124

Laurie Harbour

Webling Bay

Disappointment Id.

Mt. Eden
420

3

Kekeno Pt.

166°15′E

AUCKLAND
ISLAND

Port Ross

Adams Id.

166°10′E

Symbol	Feature	Symbol	Feature	Symbol	Feature
⌐	Signposts	■1	"Stella" hut	■5	Coastwatchers' base camp
∘	Boatshed sites	■2	Boatshed	■6	1874 German expedition
⌂1	Derry Castle grave	■3	Coastwatchers' hut	■7	Boatshed and Depot shed
⌂2	Hardwicke Cemetery	■4	Lookout	▦	Site of Hardwicke Settlement

The features shown are at the
northern end of the Auckland
Islands.

alised, and the weather deteriorated into the prevailing dismal climate of the
subantarctic.

During the year several colonists left for Sydney, but Enderby remained
perpetually optimistic. The colonists dubbed him "law maker and law
breaker", and he soon came into conflict with his Assistant Commissioner,
William Mackworth, who was in charge of the administration and practical

The township of Hardwicke at Port Ross, Auckland Isles, *circa* 1850, by an unknown artist, at the time of the Enderby Settlement. *Photo: National Library of Australia.*

running of the colony. Enderby was a blind idealist, and Mackworth a practical realist, who at one stage actually relieved his superior of his office!

It seemed that the peak of whaling in the Southern Ocean had left numbers more severely depleted than anyone had imagined. Modern whaling with large factory ships was still to come, and Enderby's plan for using small vessels operating from a permanent base was not working.

In November 1850 Sir George Grey arrived from New Zealand, ostensibly to pay a friendly visit. But his real purpose was to have a first-hand look at the colony's affairs. He left sceptical of conditions and the colony's prospects. No doubt he heard of an incident Mackworth recorded in his private diary on 14 October 1850:

> 12 o'clock at night — one of the most appalling attempts at murder and suicide has just been made by Miss Hallett sister of chief medical officer. It appears that this young Lady after firing through a door panel at her Brother with intent to kill (he providentially escaping) leisurely reloaded the gun and shot herself while endeavours were being made to force the door. Was on the spot immediately afterwards — the side of this unfortunate person's head fearfully lacerated, the skull has not been fractured — hopes are entertained for her recovery.[6]

A fortnight later Mackworth noted:

> The Lieutenant Governor has informed me that on being assured by Mr Hallett *that such an act, as that committed by his Sister on the night of the 14th instant, will not occur again*; he has signified to that Gentleman that no notice will be taken of the occurrences of that night.[7]

Had it not been for Mackworth's efforts to control the sailors from visiting ships and the numerous problems ashore, the colony might not have lasted

Shoe Island, with its remarkable basalt lava formation, was used as a prison for the Enderby Settlement, with a barrel as shelter for the prisoner.

as long as it did. He organised a system of wages and pay — using the colony's own currency! — and set up a regular school and Sunday school, besides taking Divine Service every Sunday. But even his undoubted determination failed at times:

> Sun 25 May 1851: Incessant rain. Read Divine Service. I am in very low spirits, nothing to cheer or encourage one in this dismal banishment. My health too has suffered much latterly from anxiety of mind and exposure to the weather.[8]

In New Zealand, rumours of the colony's troubles had begun to circulate, and Bishop Selwyn, intending to visit the most southerly outpost of his diocese, referred to it in a letter to a colleague in England as "the principality of Enderby, the Antarctic Prince of Whales"![9]

During 1851, the company's whaling fleet was increased to eight ships. A schooner, the *Black Dog*, was purchased to bring stores from Australian and New Zealand ports. Food had to be imported: native plants, used to the salt-laden winds and gales, thrived, but the exotic crops and vegetables failed because of the acid peat soil and low soil temperatures. Besides this, constant improvements had to be made to the buildings at Hardwicke. The steadily mounting cost of the colony and lack of revenue from whale oil and whale products such as whalebone were causing increasing concern back in London.

By now, there was constant unrest at the colony. Mackworth wrote on 13 May 1851 of "the damning fountain of crime from the issue of spirituous liquors",[10] and noted that his "order to destroy all the spirits on board the *Sir James Ross* has been carried out".[11] In spite of this, he observed on 14 June, "*Sir J. Ross* ready for sea — one general scene of intoxication afloat and on shore".[12]

Shoe Island was used as a prison, and a dismal penance it must have been. Mackworth, in sending seven men there for refusal of duty, commented that "the difficulty of supporting discipline in this Port is extreme".[13] The root of the problem was typified by an occasion when "the Medical officer nearly drowned near the jetty — he was taken out of the water so violent through intoxication that confinement for a short while was necessary".[14]

At the end of 1851 two Special Commissioners, Mr George Dundas, M.P., and Thomas Preston, the Company Secretary, arrived from London and relieved Charles Enderby, for the second time, of his post as Commissioner.

Enderby Island, photographed while looking towards Auckland Island. The climate here is noticeably sunnier than on the main island, and Sandy Bay was used by the Enderby settlers for picnics and recreation, and by families in need of a prescribed break from the stresses of the colony.

At first, Enderby swore that he would do his utmost to ruin the company and would shoot anyone who attempted to remove him from his official residence, but after five days he complied. The Company's servants were told of the intention to close down the settlement, and Mackworth, as Acting Commissioner, wrote to Enderby:

> Sir, I am instructed to inform you . . . that a passage to Wellington, New Zealand, will be provided for you in the Southern Whale Fishery Company's Schooner "Black Dog" which will proceed thither as soon as she can be ready for sea. A passage will also be provided for you from Wellington to England in the event of your desiring it.[15]

Enderby still held his title of Lieutenant Governor, and on reaching Wellington, tried to have the Special Commissioners arrested. After failing in this, he carried out a prolonged legal battle with the Colonial Office in London, until he was finally defeated, and returned to England and obscurity.

In May 1852 HMS *Fantome* had arrived to prevent possible trouble during the breaking up of what must surely be the shortest lived of all British colonies. At the time, with the 123 men of the *Fantome*'s crew and forty seamen of the smaller vessels in port, there were 306 people at Port Ross. R. E. Malone, the assistant surgeon on the *Fantome*, recorded that

> A battery of four old guns saluted us on arrival; the powder being damp, the discharge kept fizzing and puffing down the bank. . . . We passed a most miserable time. It hardly ever ceased blowing a gale, and the rain was incessant, with very few days excepted.[16]

Of the efforts at cultivation, he wrote:

> The farms, and there are several, are everywhere failures; nothing grows to any size, although every care seems to have been taken. The potato and vegetable gardens are fenced round with stakes; and every fourteen feet inside with the same, to keep the wind off, looking like sheep pens, but all to no purpose. The potatoes are about an inch and a half in diameter, and bad; and the turnips run down like miserable radishes. . . . The Maories [sic], at a small pah [sic] of theirs at Ocean Point, grew the best cabbages and turnips, but they were good for nothing.[17]

About this time the *Hardwicke* returned to port from a four months' cruise, with hardly any whale oil, one man dead, four in irons, and the whole crew ill with scurvy. The ship had been three weeks beating off the island, unable to get in to the safety of Port Ross. The settlement's ships had even been as far as Macquarie Island for sea elephant oil. They had had some success there, killing more than 150 animals for fourteen tons of oil, but because of high seas had been forced to leave the oil behind.

During the final weeks of the settlement, the only whale to be caught in the harbour was killed, causing a last stir of excitement, and Malone gives a vivid account of the event:

> being well lanced and exhausted, he sank, and we buoyed him. Two days after he rose, and all the boats in the place, including ours, towed him to the "Fancy" whaler, six miles. Here he was secured alongside, the whole body being secured with hawsers and chains round the fins and tail from the fore and main yards. . . . One of the whale captains got in the chains, and, with a long-handled kind of sharp-edged spade, made the first, or, as they called it, the bride-cut. . . . The escape of foul air was so great, and the stench so unbearable, that I was sick for some time, and the noise was like the rush of steam from the boiler of a steam-engine when the steam is eased off. After this piece was got in, other pieces were dealt with in the same way, till the whole of the outside covering, or fat, of the whale, was got on board. . . . It was a young cow-whale come in to calve, about 45 feet long, and yielded five tuns of oil and some whalebone. The whalebone, the article of commerce that our civilised ladies envelop their chests with, answers the purpose of the gills of a fish, as well as a strainer for the mouth. In this whale it was in long ribs of about eight feet long, [and] in some whales there are as many as four hundred of these. . . . This was the first and only whale ever taken in the islands, notwithstanding all the expectations and the numbers seen in the bay; and it was quite a holiday in the settlement, every one, even the women, some of them with children at the breast, came to look at the beast. They did not remain long, however: it was a disgusting sight, and the stench was intolerable.[18]

The Hardwicke cemetery, a short way inland from Erebus Cove, at Port Ross. Most of the graves are those of shipwrecked mariners, added some fifteen years or so later. The recent fencing was erected to keep out sea lions and wild pigs.

Women in the Subantarctic

On board the three small whalers which brought the first colonists to the Enderby Settlement were sixteen women and fourteen children. Others, both wives and single women like Miss McKennie who arrived on the *Black Dog* and was married the following day, came out later; and by the time the settlement came to an end there were twenty-two women and thirty-four children. The Maori population then was twenty men, seventeen women, and ten children. Prefabricated houses were brought out from England, and R. E. Malone, the assistant-surgeon on HMS *Fantome*, noted to his surprise that "although there is constant rain and wind, and most unpleasant weather, yet the climate is extremely healthy, as the thriving appearance of the men, women, and children . . . fully testify".[21]

It was not an easy life. Early on, William Mackworth had to "appoint a small force of special Constables (Married men) to protect their wives from disturbance and insult while in the Batchelors [sic] Quarters",[22] and later in the year "a body of men waited on me and complained that they and their families were in a miserable state from want of sufficient food, alluding principally to the limited quantity of flour."[23] There were also frequent shortages of vegetables and meat.

The notably better climate and sheltered sandy beach of Enderby Island permitted outings for families and those in need of a change. In July 1851 Mackworth "sent a man (Cripps) to Enderby Island with his family for change of air and propose allowing all the men with their families to spend a week there in turn".[24] In May 1852 he

> had the pleasure of accompanying Mrs Munce, Mrs Barton and families and also Captain Glennys and some of the *Fantome*'s Officers, to Sandy Bay where a constitutional run on the sand, as well as dinner was indulged in — all returned in good spirits before dark.[25]

But such pleasures were relatively few.

There are very few records of women on the subantarctic islands before the Enderby Settlement. Occasionally, there would be a woman on board a sealing vessel, like Elizabeth Farr who was drowned at Perseverance Harbour, or one might be landed with a sealing gang. Ross noted at Port Ross "the ruins of a small hut . . . which I have since learnt formed for several years the wretched habitation of a deserter from an English whale ship and a New Zealand woman"[26] — and a Mrs Cook spent the 1911 shore whaling season on Campbell Island with her husband.

Best known was the legendary "Lady of the Heather", allegedly the illegitimate daughter of Bonnie Prince Charlie, but in fact the fabrication of the journalist Robert Carrick. His tale inspired William Lawson's romantic novel *The Lady of the Heather*, published in 1945.

Fourteen years after the Enderby Settlement, Mary Ann Jewell survived the shipwreck of the *General Grant* with her seaman husband; and the *Illustrated London News* of 24 December 1887 tells of a man and woman living in isolation at Port Ross. They were Mr and Mrs Nelson, caretakers for Dr Monkton's farming venture. Years later, in 1927, William Herbert Guthrie-Smith's daughter Barbara accompanied him as his photographer aboard the *Hinemoa* in the final year of the servicing of the castaway depots.

In general, opportunities for women to visit or work on the subantarctic islands were limited. They still are today. At present women cannot travel on naval ships, with the very occasional exception of HMNZS *Monowai*. They have, however, served on the meteorological staff of Campbell Island; and the RV *Acheron*, skippered by Alex and Colleen Black, has made numerous trips to the subantarctic islands, often with women as passengers or members of the crew.

As co-owner with her husband of the RV *Acheron* from 1971–1985, Colleen Black, a tutor in biology at the University of Otago, has been to the Auckland Islands, Campbell Island, and the Snares on numerous occasions. In 1981 she became the first woman in New Zealand, and is still the only one to date, to hold a Deep Sea Fishing Boat Skipper's ticket. *Photo: Alex Black.*

This poignant memorial in the Enderby Settlement graveyard to Isabel Younger's death at the age of three months on 20 November 1855 gives a misleading impression of conditions on the Auckland Islands. In the two years and nine months that the colony lasted, two infant deaths, five weddings, and sixteen births were registered.

Southern skuas, scavengers like the giant petrel, squabble over a prize, which could be the regurgitations of a sea lion, at Sandy Bay on Enderby Island.

Recent gold discoveries in Australia made many impatient to leave the scene of such hardship and failure. The world was moving fast; Victorian England had been through the railway building boom of the 1840s, and in New Zealand, after the arrival of the First Four Ships at Lyttleton in 1850, settlement was spreading rapidly through the South Island. The Maori on Enderby Island appealed in vain to Sir George Grey to be taken off with the rest of the colonists, and must have felt abandoned and cheated when the settlement's buildings were dismantled, and the company ships and HMS *Fantome* sailed for Sydney on 5 August 1852. Malone was glad to leave "these miserable islands",[19] and Mackworth records that "the satisfaction I feel at this moment is beyond description. My miserable life at Port Ross will never be forgotten."[20]

Most of the colonists settled in Australia, and a few returned to England. By the time they got there, Enderby's historic firm had gone into liquidation.

In 1856, the Chatham Island Maori chartered a ship to take their kinfolk back to the Chathams. It was the final end to a disastrous attempt at Maori and European occupation. Defeated by the climate, the isolation, and the soil, the would-be colonists abandoned the islands to the wildness of the surrounding ocean.

An artist's impression of the wreck of
the *General Grant* on the Auckland
Islands, from the *Illustrated London
News* of 18 April 1868. *Photo:
Illustrated London News collection,
Alexander Turnbull Library, Wellington.*

10
The Shipwreck Era

During the years of sail, the subantarctic islands, and the poorly charted Auckland Islands in particular, came to be much feared by seafarers using the Great Circle trading route from Australia and the prevailing winds of the Roaring Forties to travel to Europe by way of Cape Horn. Charles Enderby had planned to service whaling vessels, but this trading route was something he could not have foreseen: he had been just twelve years too soon for this regular, growing commerce with Australia.

The Auckland Islands lay in the direct path of shipping, and between 1864 and 1907 were the cause of eight known wrecks and two probable ones. Several ships lost without trace may have foundered on them, thinking they were passing safely to the north; and if the charts had been correct, it is likely that both the *Derry Castle* and the *Dundonald* would have avoided them.

The first Auckland Islands shipwreck, however, had nothing to do with mist-enshrouded rockbound coasts looming out of the wild ocean, for it took place well within the normally sheltered reaches of Carnley Harbour. The *Grafton*, a small Sydney schooner, had been chartered by F. E. Raynal, a French adventurer who had been goldmining in Australia and now wanted to search for rumoured deposits of argentiferous tin on Campbell Island.

No signs of tin were found, and Raynal decided to look for seals on the Auckland Islands on the way home, to help offset the cost of the expedition. On entering Carnley Harbour in January 1864 he saw numerous seals, which were probably Hooker's sea lions, as fur seals had been nearly exterminated by this time.

> It was evident that they inhabited the island in scores. This fact inspired all of us with pleasure, and we resolved to stay for a few days only — just long enough to fill our casks with oil and salt some skins — then to return as quickly as possible to Sydney . . . and again revisit the island, accompanied by twenty-five or thirty men, to organise a settlement, and hunt these animals on an extended scale.[1]

Before they could begin sealing, however, the *Grafton* was driven aground and irreparably damaged by a heavy storm during the night. All five men managed to reach the shore safely, on the east side of North Arm, opposite a promontory they named Musgrave Peninsula after the *Grafton*'s captain. The

Remains of the wreck of the *Grafton*, first known shipwreck on the Auckland Islands, at Epigwaitt, Carnley Harbour. The wreck occurred in 1864.

ship's dinghy was saved, and they were more fortunate than later castaways on the open coast in that they were able to salvage from the wreck sails, provisions, and materials to build a hut.

The young American Thomas Musgrave and Raynal were both exceptionally resourceful. Their hut, which Musgrave called "Epigwaitt", a North American Indian word meaning "dwelling by the water", had a stone fireplace and chimney, two small windows salvaged from the ship, a wooden floor, thatch and canvas roof, and benches and tables. Both kept diaries, and when their small bottle of ink ran out they used seal's blood.

While exploring Figure-of-Eight Island, the main sea lion colony in Carnley Harbour, Musgrave records that they came across a place where an earlier party had camped.

> They had evidently been seal hunting, as we found a number of bricks which had been used for their try works. . . . Perhaps a whaler had come in for wood and water, and, finding the seals so numerous, had taken a few. At any rate, it gave us some comfort to see these signs of previous visitors, and renewed our hopes of release from bondage.[2]

But as the first winter passed they realised that their friends in Sydney must have given them up for lost. They decided to try and enlarge the dinghy and attempt to reach New Zealand. Raynal built a forge, with sealskin bellows, and laboriously manufactured tools, nails, and bolts from rusted iron taken from the *Grafton*. It took the others all their time to find wood for fuel, and forage for food, which with the departure of the seals had become extremely scarce.

Eventually, the boat was finished. Two of the *Grafton*'s crew had to be left behind while Musgrave, Raynal, and the fifth castaway sailed for New

Zealand. They had no chart or compass, and within a few hours of leaving were caught in a gale which lasted for the five days it took them to reach Port Adventure on Stewart Island.

Unsuccessful appeals were made to both the Southland Provincial Government and the central Government of New Zealand to send a ship to rescue the two men still on the Aucklands, but, fortunately, enough money was raised locally for Captain Cross, to whose house they had first been taken, to sail back with Musgrave in his schooner the *Flying Scud*.

On the way home, one year and eight months after being shipwrecked, they called in at Port Ross, where Musgrave was surprised to find how little was left of the Enderby Settlement. While there, they found the decomposing body of a man in a ruined shack. He had died within the last few months, apparently from starvation. They buried him in the cemetery, with the word "unknown" scratched on a piece of slate. After some confusion, it was later assumed that this was the body of John Mahoney, second mate of the *Invercauld*, which had been wrecked in even less fortunate circumstances while the *Grafton* castaways were at Epigwaitt.

The *Invercauld*, bound for Valparaiso, had struck a reef at the northern end of the western cliffs of the main Auckland Island during a storm, on the night of 10 May 1864, and was in fragments within minutes. Nineteen of its crew of twenty-five managed to get ashore, in a small cove at the base of towering cliffs. They had a box of matches, found enough wreckage to build a makeshift hut, and salvaged two pounds of sodden biscuits and three pounds of pork. Several of the crew were wounded, and all were suffering from cold and exposure. They managed to scale the cliffs, but four of them died on the journey to Port Ross, less than ten kilometres distant.

Photograph by William Dougall, in 1888, of seamen at the provision depot for shipwrecked mariners at Tucker Point, on Campbell Island. No trace of the depot remains today. *Photo: N. Judd collection, Alexander Turnbull Library, Wellington.*

111

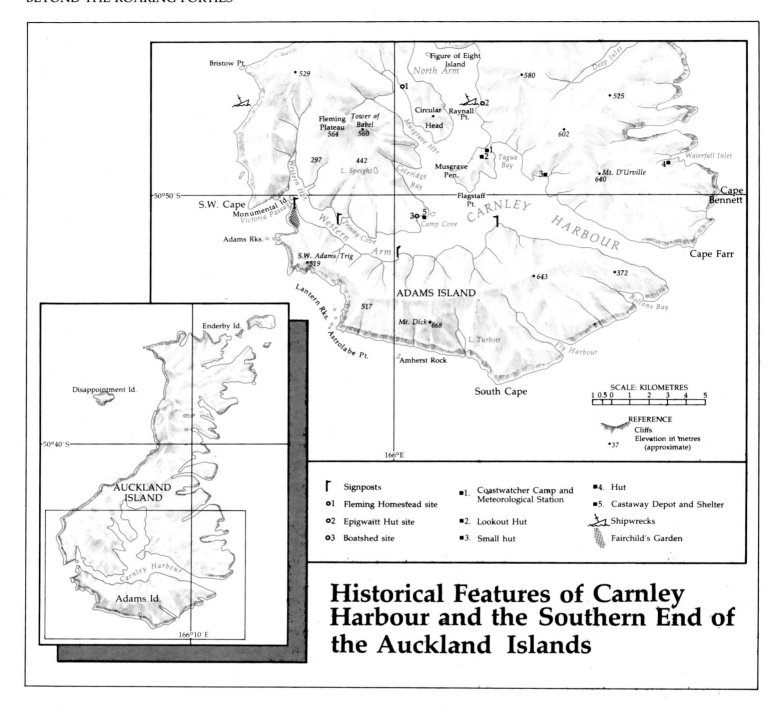

Historical Features of Carnley Harbour and the Southern End of the Auckland Islands

Lacking Musgrave's leadership or Raynal's practical skill the survivors soon split into two or more groups, and after three months only Captain Dalgarno, the first mate, and a seaman remained alive. (After separating, Dalgarno's party never saw any of the others again.) They made a canoe of rata branches and sea lion skins, in which they crossed to Enderby Island, where they were able to live off the roots of giant herbs and to hunt and kill rabbits. After a year, the three survivors were rescued by a Spanish brig, the *Julian*, which had put into Port Ross in the futile hope of being able to repair serious leaks at the Hardwicke settlement.

A third wreck in 1864 was that of the *Minerva* of Leith. Little is known of this ship, apart from the inscription found on a barrel in a scrub hut by the castaways of the *General Grant*, which recorded that four of its crew were rescued in March 1865, after being wrecked the previous May.

Captain Hopper and seamen from a government steamer at the castaway provision depot at the Bounty Islands. An old cooking pot and a few pieces of timber wedged here and there amongst the rocks on Depot Island are all that remain. *Photo: Alexander Turnbull Library, Wellington.*

On Thomas Musgrave's further urging, and as a result of the wrecks of the *Grafton* and the *Invercauld*, the state governments of Victoria, New South Wales, and Queensland, and the Southland Provincial Government, now recognised the problem of shipwrecks on the subantarctic islands as a direct responsibility, although it was not until 1877 that the central Government of New Zealand undertook the servicing of castaway depots and the search for survivors on a regular basis.

In October 1865 Captain Musgrave was asked to return to the Auckland Islands from Melbourne, not on the terms of his original proposal to search for castaways, but as a cabin passenger on the steamship *Victoria*.

> While thanking you for your handsome offer, voluntarily made, to head an expedition . . . for which service you asked no consideration whatsoever, this Government cannot permit you to make this sacrifice, knowing, as it does, that you are without means, and have a wife and family entirely dependent on your exertions for support. Firstly, therefore, you have been requested to obtain a suitable outfit (to an assumed cost of £20); and secondly, the Government will provide you with the sum of £25, to serve as a remittance to your family for their present necessities, and also undertake to pay you a further sum of £25 on your return from the proposed voyage, to enable you to rejoin your family after a prolonged absence of two or three years.[3]

Under the command of Captain Norman, HMCS (Her Majesty's Colonial Steam-Sloop) *Victoria* visited all New Zealand's subantarctic islands except for the Snares. Animals were landed as food for castaways, and guns fired at regular intervals to attract the attention of anyone ashore. At Erebus Cove the sawn, flat face of a large rata was carved with the inscription H.M.C.S. VICTORIA Norman In Search of Shipwrecked People Oct 13th, 1865, and the names of several of the crew were included beneath. The tree, lopped of its upper branches, was painted black and white, and was a prominent feature until the loss of branches and the vigorous growth of surrounding trees obscured it. An attempt has been made to preserve what is left of it under an open corrugated-roofed A-frame structure, but while most of the carving can still be made out, the *Victoria* tree is certainly not an inspiring relic of the past.

Steam was slowly arriving at sea, but it still took second place to sail. The American built *General Grant* was a fine, three-masted barque of more than a thousand tonnes. She was on her way from Melbourne to London in 1866,

As the months passed, the survivors of the *General Grant* decided to send out a series of wooden "messengers" with sails. The third one was almost ready to be dispatched when the survivors were rescued. Neither of the first two messengers was ever found. *Photo: Conon Fraser, courtesy Southland Museum.*

with twenty-five crew, fifty-eight passengers, some of them from the gold-fields, and a cargo of wool, hides, timber, and a shipment of eighty kilogrammes of gold from the Bank of New South Wales, when she encountered the Auckland Islands. The wind died away to a dead calm, and the barque slowly drifted in towards the western cliffs at a place where they rose sheer for 460 metres from the sea. The ship's boats could have been lowered, but the captain kept waiting for a breeze to take them away from the cliffs, and the danger was not realised until it was too late. The breeze never came, and during the night the *General Grant* drifted into a cavern. Here, the foremast struck the roof as the ship rose on a surge, driving the mast's foot through the hull. The belated breeze had arrived, and rapidly grew to a gale. The sea roughened, and the decks were awash by the time the third boat was launched, only to capsize with forty people on board. Sixty-eight people died in the bitterly cold sea, and only fourteen men and one woman — a stewardess, Mary Ann Jewell, who had the courage to jump when told to do so — survived. They rowed for twelve hours to reach Disappointment Island, where they spent two days and nights before completing the hazardous journey to Port Ross.

During the eighteen months which followed the survivors overcame incredible hardships. Irishman James Teer was a natural leader and the strongest factor in their survival. He was also the only one with a box of matches. (It is incredible that the *Grafton*'s castaways also had a single box, and the *Dundonald*'s survivors just one match.) Several damp matches were wasted, and Teer insisted on drying the last one in his hair until it was ready. "From that one match we obtained a fire which by constant care we never allowed to go out."[4]

The survivors foraged for timber and useful articles from the old Hardwicke settlement and derelict whaling and sealing huts, and Teer became cobbler and tailor, using albatross bones as needles, flax for thread, and sealskin and rabbit fur for shoes and clothing.

As the months passed without rescue Chief Officer Bart Brown suggested following Musgrave's example and sailing to New Zealand for assistance. They decked in one of the open boats with sealskins, and with makeshift sails Brown and three others set off in January 1867. One of those who saw them go wrote later that "Both parties appreciated the danger and the mutual dependence of their fates. Tears trickled down the faces of all, and a silent handshake was their adieu."[5]

The awesome west coast of the main Auckland Island, where the *General Grant*, or possibly the *Anjou*, was wrecked, and the remains still lie. The remains were discovered on an expedition led by Commander Grattan in 1975, and an unsuccessful attempt to salvage gold and prove the ship's identity was made in 1976. The ship drifted into the cave which can be seen at the base of the huge cliffs, and which pierces the promontory to the far side.

Without chart or compass, the four men sailed off on a course of east-north-east — a disastrous decision that would take them not to New Zealand, but out into the vast and empty South Pacific. They were never heard of again.

The others went through ten months of increasing tension and despair. After a while they moved to Enderby Island, where they could keep a constant lookout and have large bonfires ready to light. They farmed pigs and goats they had caught and tamed, and grew potatoes. On the day they at last sighted a sail their fires proved useless because the wind flattened the smoke against the ground. But two days later they were finally rescued by Captain Paddy Gilroy of the *Amherst*, who had come down on a sealing expedition. The remaining ten castaways of the *General Grant*'s original complement of eighty-three had been marooned for eighteen months, only two months less than the survivors of the *Grafton*.

Two months later the Southland Provincial Government sent the *Amherst* with Henry Armstrong J.P. on a thorough search of the islands, in the slim hope that Brown and his crew might have tried to return, or been carried by a storm onto one of them.

On the Snares, the *Amherst*'s crew set up a large marker, with bottles at its base, containing a message, matches, dressed flax cord, and fishhooks. The *Amherst* then went on to Enderby Island in the Aucklands, where the first official castaway depot was established at Sandy Bay. One of the huts built by the *General Grant*'s castaways was used. The hut, reported Armstrong,

> is in capital repair, and only required a little extra fastening to the thatch, which was given to it. The case No. 1, containing clothing, blankets, compass, matches, tools, &c., was placed in a good position, and on it I wrote — "The curse of the widow and fatherless light upon the man who breaks open this box, whilst he has a ship at his back."[6]

A letter included details of food supplies and animals liberated as food. A board was fixed under the eaves, carved with the words "Depot of necessaries for castaways. Landed from the brig *Amherst*, Feb. 1, 1868. By order of the Government of Southland."

At Erebus Cove, a fourteen-metre signal mast was erected at the site of the old settlement flagstaff, with a large white triangle as a marker and a small shed at its base. A letter, a case of supplies, and a small box of books were placed in the shed. Armstrong noted that English trees planted by Captain Norman of the *Victoria* were already looking sickly. Further depots were established at Norman Inlet and Carnley Harbour, where Musgrave's hut at Epigwaitt was given minor repairs and stocked with provisions. Signposts with the distance to the depot were left on Musgrave Peninsula and at the entrance to the harbour.

Another depot was set up at Perseverance Harbour on Campbell Island, and signposts left at strategic points during a thorough search of the island. A marker and bottles were then left at the Antipodes, as they had been at the Snares. A gale prevented a landing at the Bounty Islands,

> but we saw every rock distinctly with the naked eye, and had there been anything as large as a goat moving on them we must have perceived it. Neither man nor beast could exist on the Bounty's [sic], and had I known their nature, I would not have deemed it necessary to visit them.[7]

There had been no sign of the four lost men from the *General Grant*, and, "It must be now beyond a question that the poor fellows perished in their boat at sea."[8]

Armstrong's report concluded by drawing attention to the 1851 chart, which had the Auckland Islands situated thirty-five miles south of their true position, and by pointing out the necessity of "informing the shipping world . . . of this glaring error".[9]

In 1877 the servicing of castaway depots was at long last taken on by the central Government of New Zealand on a regular basis — a service which continued until 1927. More substantial buildings replaced those at Norman Inlet and Erebus Cove, the latter being used by the crews of the *Derry Castle* and the *Compadre*.

The *Derry Castle*, an iron barque bound from Geelong to Falmouth with a cargo of wheat, was wrecked on the night of 21 March 1887 on the reef which bears its name, on the northern point of Enderby Island — an extreme misfortune, as the ship would have passed the Aucklands safely had it been only another hundred metres or so further north. Of the ship's twenty-three men only eight managed to get to shore alive. The rest were battered to death or swept out to sea. The survivors built tussock huts near the A-frame depot at Sandy Bay, which is still standing today but was too small for the survivors to use as accommodation. Later, they constructed a crude punt out of planking

Until its collapse in the 1980s this castaway supply depot at Camp Cove was one of the most historic buildings on the islands. Castaways of the *Compadre* used it, as did the survivors of the *Anjou* in 1905.

from the ruins of the *General Grant*'s castaways' hut, in order to reach the main island and the Erebus Cove depot.

The *Compadre*, another iron barque, of 800 tonnes, was on its way from Calcutta to Chile. It was deliberately beached at North Harbour in March 1891 because its cargo was on fire. The crew got ashore safely, and eventually managed to find the depot at Port Ross. Although one of them became separated on the way and was never seen again, the others lived at the depot in reasonable comfort for three months until rescued by a sealer, the *Janet Ramsay*.

The *Awarua*, a sealing vessel chartered by the central Government, built the A-frame depot at Camp Cove in Carnley Harbour during the first year of regular servicing, to replace Musgrave's old hut. For many years this depot was one of the most historic buildings on the islands, with the names of survivors and ships carved into its wooden weatherboards. Struck by a falling rata, it is now in an advanced state of decay. Some of the *Compadre*'s crew used the depot, as did the survivors of the French barque *Anjou*, en route from Sydney to Falmouth in 1905. The survivors of the *Anjou* managed to reach the depot without loss of life after the total wreck of their ship on the notorious western coast, and were rescued after three months by the government steamer *Hinemoa*.

Two wrecks which took place on the Antipodes, near the end of the shipwreck era, were those of the *Spirit of the Dawn* and the *Président Felix Fauré*. The *Spirit of the Dawn*, a 716 tonne barque on its way from Rangoon to Chile, struck the south-west coast of the main Antipodes island in thick fog, on 4 September 1893, and sank before its boats could be lowered. The captain and four of the crew drowned, but the remaining eleven officers and men had

Detail of carving on a broken weatherboard.

The wild coast of the north-west corner of Disappointment Island. The *Dundonald* was wrecked in the bay into which the sea is surging, in 1907.

climbed into the rigging, and managed to get ashore in one of the boats, after drifting several kilometres from the island in the fog.

The next morning the survivors found the boat had been swept away. Two of them went off to explore and got half way round the island before giving up because of cold and exposure. One account has it that they were frightened by one of the cattle beasts landed as food for castaways. In the weeks that followed they never ventured from the southern part of the island again. They lived in a shelter of turfs stacked against an overhanging cliff, and ate raw penguins, penguin eggs, and edible roots, probably of *Stilbocarpa polaris*.

The castaways twice saw ships, but their flagstaff was not sighted until the arrival of the *Hinemoa* eighty-seven days after their ship sank. The *Hinemoa* had been on the point of leaving the island, having checked the depot which had replaced the *Amherst*'s original markers and bottles, and its crew was amazed that the *Spirit of the Dawn*'s castaways had not found it, as it was only four or five hours walk from their shelter. As well as clothing and provisions, the depot had a rifle with which they could have shot the sheep and cattle which had been landed for that very purpose.

In 1908 a large, four-masted French barque, the *Président Felix Fauré*, was driven well south by storms and ran onto a reef, probably near Anchorage Bay, again in heavy fog. Its crew of twenty-two got into one lifeboat, and reached the shore safely, although the boat with its stores and provisions was smashed to pieces and lost. According to one account the survivors had landed right below the castaway depot, where they spent the first night standing, crowded into a hut designed for six. They lived on albatrosses, penguins, and shellfish. At one stage they caught a calf, but the bull, cow, and sheep left by the *Hinemoa* had died, and only their remains were found. These castaways had to endure a particularly cold sixty days, with rain, hail, and snow on all but four of them, before they were rescued by HMS *Pegasus*.

The *Président Felix Fauré* was the last of the shipwrecks, but the story of the *Dundonald*, a year before, made world headlines, and was the last of the wrecks on the Auckland Islands. The hardships endured by its castaways, and their ingenuity in adversity, rivalled those of the *General Grant* and the *Grafton*.

The *Dundonald* was a four-masted barque bound from Sydney to London with a crew of twenty-eight and a cargo of 30 000 bags of wheat. On 6 March 1907 she was wrecked in rough seas on the steep north-west coast of Disappointment Island. Sixteen of her crew managed to scramble ashore as her masts grated against the cliffs, but the rest perished. Charles Eyre recalled their first dawn:

> a group of shivering, bleeding castaways standing on the edge of those black cliffs in the grey light of the morning, whilst below us the waves dashed, and the masts of our poor ship stuck up like gravestones marking where she lay. . . . I cannot describe the cold . . . we trembled with it so that we could not keep still. . . . Most of us, too, had very little clothing and the majority of us had kicked off our boots . . .[10]

They supposed that they were on the main island, where they knew there was a depot, but soon found that it was separated from them by over nine kilometres of rough, open sea. Disappointment Island, so aptly named, had only a few patches of low scrub and was bleak and exposed to the weather. Its peat soil was permanently waterlogged. For the first few days they ate raw mollymawks, until one of them found a vestas match and they were able to light fires, which they kept constantly tended. They added *Stilbocarpa polaris* roots to their meagre diet. On the twelfth day the mate, Jabez Peters, died of his wounds and the cold. They salvaged his clothes and buried him in a shallow grave under the tussock.

Huts built of *Hebe* branches and tussock grass, used by the survivors of the wreck of the *Dundonald*, on Disappointment Island. *Photo: Alexander Turnbull Library, Wellington.*

Sealskin moccasins made by survivors of the wreck of the *Dundonald*. *Photo: Conon Fraser, courtesy Canterbury Museum.*

Rescued castaways of the *Dundonald*, with the frame of the coracle they built to cross from Disappointment Island to the main Auckland Island, on the deck of the government steamer *Hinemoa*. *Photo: Bollons collection, Alexander Turnbull Library, Wellington*.

Towards the end of a long winter it became evident that the mollymawk chicks would soon be leaving the island, and that their main source of food would be gone. The few seals had become extremely wary and difficult to kill. In desperation they hit on the idea of building a coracle in which they could reach the main island and the depot. Their first attempt failed when the three who had made the crossing were unable to scale the cliffs and were forced to return.

On a second attempt, two months later, the coracle was wrecked, and its crew was forced to find a way up the cliffs or perish. After four days, weak and starving, they finally came across a finger-post at the head of Laurie Harbour, and were encouraged to press on to the depot at Erebus Cove. After recovering, they returned in the depot's whaleboat, unrecognisable in three-piece worsted suits, to rescue their companions.

The following weeks were spent building a jetty and preparing a flagstaff and roughly embroidered "Welcome" flag for the rescue they now knew would come; but it was still a great day when the government steamer was sighted on 15 November.

> We hoist our flag, and give three cheers for the Hinemoa, which is replied to by those on board. The Captain and four men come ashore in the boat. They are surprised to learn that we have been seven months on Disappointment Island and five weeks at the depot. The captain tells us this is only his second place of call, and as he has forty scientific men on board, and having to go further south, decided, with the second mate, that we should stay here until he attended to the southern depots. He said he would be back in a fortnight's time. . . . He was kind enough to give us some stores, and hoped that we would content ourselves until his return. This has been a great day of rejoicing.[11]

Before the *Hinemoa* finally left, the mate was brought to Port Ross and reburied in the cemetery, and photographs were taken as a record of the castaways' ordeal on Disappointment Island.

The wrecks of the *Dundonald* and the *Président Felix Fauré* marked the end of another stage in the remarkably rich history of these now remote and isolated islands. Sail was giving way to steam, and with the opening of the Panama Canal in 1914 the islands were no longer on one of the world's major shipping routes. The shipwreck era had been an extraordinary period of misfortune, courage, and endurance.

A wooden signal, fixed two metres above the ground to the old Hardwicke settlement flagstaff, during a servicing round of castaway depots. The inscription reads: "HMS Blanche Painted and Refitted Beacons, Examine Replenish Necessaries. March 1869 and July 1870."

11
Farming and Whaling

From the earliest years of exploration in the subantarctic, domestic animals had been landed on the region's islands as food for sealing gangs and castaways. While some animals died out or lingered on in small numbers, others adapted better, indicating that while conditions were marginal, farming might still be a possibility in some parts of the subantarctic.

Pigs have proved among the hardiest of survivors. They were liberated by Abraham Bristow at Erebus Cove on the main Auckland Island when he returned to take formal possession of the islands a year after discovering them in 1807. By 1840 Sir James Clark Ross, adding some pigs of his own, reported these animals "very numerous", and they have been plentiful ever since, with their tracks everywhere from the coast and rata forest up to the open, exposed high country.

Goats have not fared so well. The first four — three females and a male — were landed by Norman and Musgrave from the *Victoria* in 1865. From Erebus Cove they spread to nearby Laurie Harbour and north to an area north and west of Dea's Head, and until the mild summer of 1985 remained confined to these areas. On Enderby Island, where conditions might appear to be better, and cattle have maintained consistent numbers on the open sward, ten goats landed from the *Victoria* at the same time as those on the mainland had died out by 1888 — but this was after two shipwrecks and several other visits to the island by expeditions and sealers.

Two or three goats were left on nearby Ewing Island in Port Ross in 1895, and their descendants were seen in 1904, but that was the last report. Yet on neighbouring Ocean Island, which is considerably smaller, a number of goats liberated in 1886 had apparently become numerous by 1903, and the island abounded in goats by 1907. They continued to thrive on it until they were shot out, as food and for environmental purposes by the Cape Expeditioners in the 1940s.

Perhaps because climate and conditions were that much less favourable further south, goats did not survive so well at Carnley Harbour. There were no further sightings or reports of animals liberated at Musgrave Peninsula in 1865, on Figure-of-Eight Island in 1890, or at Epigwaitt in 1891. A small number of goats released on Adams Island in 1885 died out without any

Sheep at Northwest Bay. These animals have proved remarkably hardy, resistant to disease, and of genetic interest — important reasons for their reprieve.

123

noticeable effect on the environment, and for some reason the same thing happened to goats introduced to the Snares in 1900.

In view of the success of Campbell Island's feral sheep, which increased in large numbers some years after being abandoned at the end of the farming venture, it is surprising that both pigs and goats failed to survive on the island. Repeated attempts were made to establish them, from the *Amherst*'s search for castaways in 1868 onwards. In that year goats — "2 billies and 3 nannies" — and pigs — "2 boars, 3 sows"[1] — were put ashore, and the practice was continued by the *Victoria* and other ships on all the groups except, for obvious reasons, the Bounties. Cattle, sheep, and goats were regularly landed on the Antipodes. But this group, with its main island smaller and with even less shelter than Campbell Island, was clearly too hostile an environment, and according to Captain Bollons of the *Hinemoa*, goats and other animals regularly left by the government steamers on their half-yearly visits soon died out.[2]

With the failure of the Enderby Settlement, and Musgrave's warnings about the deceptive richness of the waterlogged peat soil, which he concluded would produce only native vegetation, it is hard to imagine how anyone could have even considered farming worth the risk and effort in the isolation and bleak climate of the subantarctic.

The first attempt was admittedly half-hearted. A Mr Young and a Mr Ford applied for a lease of the Auckland Islands in 1861, but as the islands did not belong to New Zealand until two years later their request was referred to the Colonial Office in London, and nothing more was heard of them.

The second attempt to farm the Aucklands was made by Dr F. A. Monkton of Invercargill. In 1874 he sent a Mr and Mrs Nelson with some sheep to Port Ross, to await his arrival with a cargo of cattle. He intended to settle there with them, but bad weather soon after he had set sail forced him to take shelter at Stewart Island, and the cattle had to be let ashore to forage. After several days of storm it was impossible to muster them when the time came to leave, and Dr Monkton had to abandon them.

Sheep and stores were sent to the Nelsons later in the year, and in 1875. In October 1875 a Mr W. Watts was instructed to take over as farm manager. The sealing vessel *Awarua* was to bring back the Nelsons, who were suspected of raiding the castaways' provision depots, but they refused to co-operate.[3] They were not totally isolated, for in their three years at Port Ross they met members of the German Transit of Venus Expedition in 1874, had visits from the *Awarua*, and made contact with the diver of an expedition which came with the *Gazelle* in search of the *General Grant*'s gold. But it was a lonely life, and a naval correspondent of the *Illustrated London News*, calling on them in 1877, recorded that

> This poor couple had collected a number of seal-skins. They had been nine months without being visited, and had eaten most of the provisions placed on the island for shipwrecked people. They refused to come away; but on a later visit to the island, it was found that they had been removed by a schooner sent to fetch them. . . . Their house was the only habitation on these lonely islands . . .[4]

The Nelsons had in fact departed on the *Gazelle*, in 1877, at about the time Monkton forfeited his lease.

Another twenty years elapsed before the next farming venture on the Auckland Islands, and in the meanwhile the Government was wary of granting further leases on either the Aucklands or Campbell Island, in spite of a number of applications.

In 1891 an official report by Mr John Hay, District Surveyor for the Southland Provincial Government, which now administered the islands, stated:

> The formation of the Auckland Island is, no doubt, all that one could desire for sheep-country — beautifully rounded, rocky hills and spurs, attaining an altitude of from 1,500 ft to 2,000 ft, with a north-easterly aspect; but, as it has such a scarcity of nutritive grasses, and also an undoubtedly excessive rainfall, I fear,

Two of the three iron trypots at North East Harbour, in which the whale blubber was rendered down into oil. Walls, pits, foundations of buildings, bricks, iron, and ringbolts set into rocks can still be seen. The base was abandoned in 1914.

with all these drawbacks in the way, the country is not suitable or adapted for sheep-farming. . . . I might mention that a Mr Knight, a settler from Akaroa, accompanied me on my stay on the island, and with the object in view of taking up a run if he found the country suitable. His opinion of its adaptability for sheep-farming exactly coincided with mine.[5]

Three years later, a conflicting report was presented to Parliament by James Joyce, M.P. for Lyttelton. He was of the opinion that "the pasturage on Campbell Island is excellent"; while "for pastoral purposes the Auckland Islands rank high". And he concluded:

While it is not likely that grain, with the exception perhaps of oats and rye, would ripen satisfactorily, there can be no doubt that the ordinary vegetables of the garden could be easily grown. . . . It would be an error, however, to convey the impression that the islands are suitable for settlement on a small scale. By whomsoever they are taken up, a considerable amount of capital will have, in the first instance, to be expended. Large storage room for wool, and freezing works, would be essential features.[6]

Captain Tucker, on verandah, and shepherds, with their dogs, at the farmhouse at Tucker Cove on Campbell Island. Note the cat, probably an ancestor of those which run wild on the island today. *Photo: Kerr collection, Alexander Turnbull Library, Wellington.*

He further added:

> The Snares Islands were scarcely within the scope of my instructions, but I may be permitted to say that they are neither barren nor unsuitable for occupation. When the proposed lighthouse is erected, it will be possible to run on the two main islands, on which there is abundant firewood and grass, some 1,500 or 2,000 sheep, the produce of which will render them, so to speak, self-supporting.[7]

It was fortunate for the unique environment of the Snares that the lighthouse was never established and Joyce's recommendation for sheep farming never acted upon. However, the Government was persuaded to ignore Hay's report and offer, for lease by Public Auction, Run No. 511, comprising Campbell Island and three farming runs on the Auckland Islands, with a fourth comprising Enderby and Rose Islands in the following year, 1895. That same year the Commissioner of Crown Lands also offered, with remarkable precision, "Run No. 513, being the Bounty Islands, containing 335 acres 2 roods; term, twenty-one years",[8] evidence of how rapidly the privations suffered there by the sealing gangs had been forgotten. When it was pointed out that there was not a twig of scrub or a blade of grass upon the Bounties, the lease was quickly withdrawn.

W. J. Moffett was the only person to take up his lease on the Auckland Islands. He landed nine cattle and twenty sheep on Enderby Island in 1895. Writing to the Minister of Marine of his intention to add "large quantities more" to these he complained that

> the presence of the sea-lion (an inferior kind of seal) is in the highest degree detrimental to the depasturing of stock. That particular species of seal which is absolutely of no ascertained market value, has literally overrun the more accessible, and, consequently, the best, grazing grounds . . .[9]

The Campbell Island lease was taken up by J. Gordon of Gisborne, who had been on Joyce's survey. A practical farmer, he wrote, "I like this island much better than the Aucklands . . . less rain, less scrub, good soil."[10]

In 1895 he released between 300 and 400 sheep on the island, and built a house, woolshed, and store at what is now Tucker Cove on the shores of Perseverance Harbour. The station began well, with a mild winter and a good shearing season, but the bleak isolation of the island and difficulty of finding shepherds made it impossible to continue, and Gordon's sheep had to be left untended for three years. In 1900 he sold up to Captain W. H. Tucker of Gisborne, but returned to Campbell Island as Tucker's manager. During the following months three lots of a thousand Leicester-Merino and Lincoln-

Merino-cross sheep were successfully freighted down from Bluff, and two substantial consignments of wool brought back to New Zealand. But distance and loneliness remained the greatest drawback in persuading men to work so far from home. Gordon resigned in 1903, and Captain Tucker, deciding that hardy Scots might fare better than some New Zealanders, took the imaginative course of advertising in the Shetland Islands.

The Shetlands, 200 kilometres north of the Scottish mainland, had supported remote agricultural, fishing, and pastoral communities for centuries, in climatic conditions little different from those of Campbell Island. However, there was no other habitation on Campbell Island, and it was more than three times further from the nearest mainland. Although Shetlanders were to maintain intermittent associations with Campbell Island for many years, the isolation soon proved too much for the four shepherds who arrived in 1904.

By this time most people would have given up, but Captain Tucker now approached a group of Tory Channel whalers from Cook Strait, led by John Heberley and Jack Norton. Captain Tucker proposed they should hunt whales in the winter shore-whaling season and tend and shear his sheep during the rest of the year. Catches had been falling off in New Zealand waters, and eleven whalers accepted his offer.

Shore whaling at Campbell Island lasted from 1909 until 1916, when the whole of Norton's party enlisted for the war. The first years were the most profitable. In their opening season from their station at Northwest Bay, they caught thirteen right whales, and eighteen more over the following two seasons.

In 1911 another shore-whaling party, led by H. F. Cook of Whangamumu in the Bay of Islands, arrived and set up a station at the head of North East

Feral sheep on Campbell Island are the remnant of farm stock which once roamed the island. The sheep are now confined by the most recent fenceline, built in 1984, to a small western section.

127

Three men, probably belonging to Heberley and Norton's party at Northwest Bay, about to cut the blubber from a right whale. *Photo: Alexander Turnbull Library, Wellington.*

Jack Norton and king penguin in their Sunday best. *Photo: N. Judd collection, Alexander Turnbull Library, Wellington.*

Harbour, the remnants of which can still be seen today. Whereas the Nortons were only interested in hunting for the sake of whalebone, admittedly worth more than £1,000 a ton, Cook's party had trypots for rending down the blubber, and was better equipped, with a twenty-eight metre chaser of eleven knots armed with a harpoon gun, and a fifty-nine tonne schooner, the *Huanui*. In 1911 they caught thirteen whales, and in 1912, seventeen, but the next two seasons were poor, and they left Campbell Island after the winter season of 1914. As catches failed, the Nortons turned to sealing, for which the Government issued licences, but the steep access to the rookeries made it dangerous and unpleasant work.

Captain Tucker's lease expired in 1916, and although he was successful in having it renewed, it was at an increased rental. As the Nortons had pulled out, he decided to sell the farm to two Dunedin men, Messrs Matthewson and Murray. Matthewson, with a change of partner and the addition of two more to form a syndicate, worked the farm until 1926. At the time he took it on it was at its peak, with 6800 sheep shorn, 1600 lambs, and a year's wool clip of 131 bales.[11] However, rising wages, freight charges, ship charters, and the failure of an attempt to start up whaling again turned profits over the next few years into a growing annual loss. Sheep numbers had fallen, partly due to the export of 1300 in 1917 to pay off debts. Shipping and the weather were equally unreliable.

During Matthewson's last two years, the factory ship of a fleet of Norwegian whaling chasers dropped off shearers on the way down to the Antarctic in November and picked up the men and the wool clip on the way back to New Zealand in March. When this arrangement broke down, the Government was persuaded to charter the *Tutanekai* at a price the syndicate could ill afford. John and Arthur Warren were aboard with three other men and eight dogs when the deal fell through, and they successfully bid for the syndicate's lease. A few months later the *Tutanekai* made the last government trip to service the old castaway depot on the island, and the Warrens and their shepherds were on their own.

By 1930, with the approach of the Great Depression, wool prices could not meet even the cost of charter, and no vessels called at Campbell Island that year. In March 1931 relatives of the Warrens, who had not been off the island for four and a half years, and of Mr Alex Spence, who was with them, urged the Government to send relief. The Government disclaimed responsibility,

The promontory at the head of North East Harbour on Campbell Island was used as a shore-whaling base by H. F. Cook's party from the Bay of Islands. Access was from the sea, the bog and vegetation inland being almost impenetrable.

but the *Tamatea* was at last dispatched, on a winter voyage that took three weeks through gales, snow, and stormy seas.

For the last three months, the men marooned on Campbell Island had lived on tea, mutton, and occasional fish and shag meat. Supplies of condensed milk had been finished more than a year before. They had had no bread or vegetables for eight months. There was no kerosene left for their lamps, and sheep tallow was being used for candles and raw hide for boots. However, the *Otago Daily Times* report of 4 August 1931 concluded that

> In narrating their experiences the men made no complaint of the loneliness of their life. Darning and mending occupied a large proportion of their spare time, and for the remainder there was no lack of reading matter. In addition, they possessed a gramophone and some 80 records. The only pack of cards which they possessed were used until their values could no longer be recognised. . . . The news of the economic depression came as a severe blow to the party, for it was realised that the return for their two years' work would be greatly reduced.[12]

This was in fact the end of thirty-six years of farming on Campbell Island. Four thousand sheep and between twenty and thirty cattle were left behind on the island. Years later, in the 1950s, when wool prices were high, a number of proposals were made to go down and shear them, but nothing was done, and only one ship is known to have called at Campbell Island between 1931 and the outbreak of the Second World War.

Farming on the Aucklands never reached the scale or tenuous profitability of the sheep farming and whaling ventures on Campbell Island. In 1900 George Fleming, a Southland farmer, took over all four Auckland Island leases, built a homestead and sheds at Circular Head in Carnley Harbour, and landed some 2000 sheep. But the sheep died off within a few years, and in 1910 all his leases, with the exception of Adams Island, were re-let to the Moffett family.

1910 was a significant year: it was effectively the end of farming on the Auckland Islands, and also the year that Adams Island was declared the subantarctic's first Flora and Fauna Reserve. Later, in 1934, when the Moffetts' lease expired, the whole Auckland Island group was gazetted as a protected reserve. These developments marked the start of a new and enlightened policy which recognised the unique environmental value of New Zealand's subantarctic islands to science and the world.

12
People and Change

The handful of truly unspoilt subantarctic islands are those which have been too small, remote, or dangerous to exploit in the past: the sheer-sided offshore stacks such as Jacquemart Island in the Campbell group and Leeward Island in the Antipodes, or some of the steeper Bounty Islands, are examples. Jacquemart Island was not landed on until December 1980 when, in marginal weather, two New Zealand botanists, Martin Foggo and Colin Muerk, persuaded the United States icebreaker *Glacier* to drop them on to its summit by helicopter for one and a half hours of hurried study.[1] Such operations are always hazardous, and in 1985 HMNZS *Monowai* refused to grant scientists a similar landing on Leeward Island for fear of not being able to fly them off again. If the wind, already at forty knots, had risen, it would have been impossible for them to have climbed down to the sea to be taken off by boat.

Although Disappointment Island was lived on for seven months by the castaways of the *Dundonald*, it has no introduced plants or animals, its tussock was not burned, and it is the most pristine of New Zealand's more substantial subantarctic islands. Dundas Island (in spite of being near Port Ross) and Bollons Island at the Antipodes are similarly unspoilt. It would be hard to modify the stark Bounty Islands, although even they carry a few clues of people having been there in the past: Depot Island still has a few broken planks from the castaway depot wedged among its angular rocks and a few iron relics down by the shore; and on some of the group are survey markers and short pipes concreted into the rock, from HMNZS *Monowai*'s mapping operations in 1985.

Apart from these few islands, there are virtually no places people have reached which they have not changed or affected to some extent, and those subantarctic islands which are euphemistically termed "unmodified", such as the Snares, and Adams Island in the Aucklands, appear to have retained or regained their original ecosystems, and effectively healed themselves from past tampering, because of their dominant natural vegetation.

The most persistent impact by people on the Snares, the Antipodes, and Adams Island was made during the shipwreck era, although sheep were

Clearance by burning, for farming, has killed large areas of rata scrub on Rose Island in Port Ross. This is very noticeable in the foreground and on the land to the far left. Rabbits keep the sward open, but the natural tussock cover is beginning to regenerate over much of the island.

131

Two Hooker's sea lion pups investigate a deadly bog hole, into which a third pup has already fallen and drowned. In a particularly severe case, eighty-eight pups were found dead in a large hole, well away from the sea. *Photo: Simon Mitchell.*

landed on Adams Island by Fleming,[2] and the two-thirds of a hectare of potatoes grown by the sealers marooned on the Snares early in the nineteenth century could allegedly still be traced in the 1930s, when the tubers had, according to the *Southland Times*, "run riot all over the neighbourhood".[3] There is certainly no trace of them today, and in recent times the Snares had a total of only two adventive plants, *Poa annua* grass and *Stellaria media* chickweed.

Henry Armstrong, who was the official representative for the province of Southland on the brig *Amherst* when it set up the first depots on the subantarctic islands in 1868, records going ashore at the Snares, with a disregard for the environment which would be unacceptable nowadays.

> Our progress was painfully slow, the entire surface being literally honeycombed with mutton-bird holes, into which the foot sank deeply at every step, the inmates thereof betokening their dissatisfaction at our presence by giving vent to a half-choked querulous cry. The penguins (ludicrous birds) in hundreds drawn up in rank and file, stood to oppose us on our march, and it required not a little vigorous kicking to force our way through them. We fired the grass on the open, and made a considerable smoke, but during our stay of four hours we had no evidence whatever to show that any one was or had been living on the island, and feeling satisfied that had there been any castaways present we must have seen them, or traces of them, we returned to our boat.[4]

A similar procedure was carried out on the main island at the Antipodes.

> When close to the Island, we fired our gun, and lowering a boat, I went ashore with an officer, effecting a landing very easily under the lee (east side), although a considerable sea was running outside. Firing the grass as we went, we made for a hill in the centre of the island, which we climbed, and from its summit carefully scanned the whole surface around. We saw nothing but the tussock waving in the wind, the albatross sitting quietly on their nests, and a few parroquets [sic] flitting about. We remained four hours here; the men spread out in different directions, and then returned to the boat with the conviction that no human beings (with the exception of ourselves) were present on the island.[5]

Setting the tussock alight to alert castaways was regularly carried out. The Earl of Glasgow, who as Governor of New Zealand was with Captain Fairchild on the *Hinemoa* in 1895, wrote in his memoirs that "A fire which was lighted by the egg party two days ago on Adams Island was still burning, and at dark was a beautiful sight."[6] As with Disappointment Island, there is no record of Bollons Island in the Antipodes having been fired, but the tussock-covered slope of its volcanic rim would have been easy enough to check from the sea.

Tagged sea lion pups exploring a large rabbit hole at the back of Sandy Bay beach. Pups enjoy the closeness, but get jammed and cannot reverse out. Burrows are responsible for the death of up to ten percent of pups each year.

Firing undoubtedly affected unmodified environments. On Campbell Island, the burning of dry snowgrass resulted in an increase of *Dracophyllum* scrub and a change in the balance of native grasses and herbs because *Dracophyllum*, *Poa litorosa*, and *Bulbinella* are more resistant to fire. Firing was also carried out to encourage introduced grasses to spread, as on Enderby Island, or to make progress easier. Some of Ross's officers, exploring towards higher country, set fire to the scrub behind Erebus Cove, and the blaze rapidly spread in all directions, fanned by the wind. The scene from the ships at night was described as "one of great magnificence and beauty. It was nevertheless a thoughtless prank, and might have been productive of great mischief, besides destroying so much valuable wood."[7]

Because of their harbours or sheltered shores, Campbell Island, the main Auckland Island, Enderby Island, and Rose Island in Port Ross have suffered most from the animals and plants introduced as food for sealers, colonists, and castaways.

Planting European trees, sowing vegetable seeds, and releasing domestic animals was a deliberate policy carried out by government vessels such as the *Victoria*, *Amherst*, *Stella*, and *Hinemoa* throughout the castaway servicing years. In October 1865 Thomas Musgrave, with Captain Norman of the *Victoria*, was pleased to see "some beautiful English grass, clover, sorrel, the common daisy, and dandelion, and here and there a maorie [sic] cabbage on Enderby Island",[8] where the *Victoria* landed ten goats and twelve rabbits. At

The close sward on Enderby Island includes fine introduced grass and a primitive liverwort. The pebbles have been regurgitated by sea lions, which swallow them during their search for food.

Erebus Cove the crew dug the ground, sowed seeds, and planted English trees. Four goats sent by the Acclimatisation Society were landed, but Norman was deterred from releasing rabbits and fowls because a dog had been sighted. In 1868 "two woodhens (wingless species) of opposite sexes"[9] were turned into the scrub on Enderby Island from the *Amherst*, and it was noted that the English grasses and goats were thriving.

The goats landed on Adams Island from the *Hinemoa*, which had a long association with the subantarctic islands and made many such liberations, soon disappeared, as did three goats and six or seven sheep left on the Antipodes by the *Stella* in 1888. Grass seed was sown there, and gums, firs, wattles, and Scotch broom planted, although none survived.

Animals and plants had been brought to the islands from Abraham Bristow's day onwards. On Sir James Clark Ross's expedition, Joseph Hooker, outstanding botanist though he was, planted gooseberry, currant, raspberry, and strawberry plants to provide food for castaways; no doubt if he could return today, he would be enormously relieved to find that not one of his plants has survived.

On Campbell Island, the more open terrain and lack of heavy coastal trees and dense scrub presented less of a barrier to pastoral development, and English grasses, weeds, and perennials established more easily, while the cooler climate slowed the regeneration of native vegetation on cleared land. Not only was pasture "improved" by the firing of tussock, cutting of scrub, and grazing of sheep, but the sheep found many of the spectacular giant herbs of the subantarctic such as *Pleurophyllum speciosum* and *Stilbocarpa polaris* highly palatable.

Oak, ash and elm, gums, firs, wattle, broom, and even heather were all planted — the latter no doubt for sentimental reasons, possibly by the Shetlanders — but the larger trees soon died out, and only traces of heather were left by 1953. The only surviving tree on Campbell Island, if one discounts the native *Dracophyllum* scrub, is the sole spruce at Camp Cove.

Campbell Island, which is severely modified, has about eighty introduced plants, although only a dozen or so are well established. Others, such as grasses and chickweeds, are confined to sites of human disturbance, around huts and along tracks. Gorse, broom, and lotus — a low-growing, creeping variety — have all turned up from time to time, and constitute the most serious threat to the generally dominant native vegetation.

Plants and weeds, brought as seeds clinging to clothing or lodged in crevices in the soles of boots, tend to occur where people have landed, camped, or carried stores and equipment ashore. While most soon perish in the acid peat soil and chill climate of the subantarctic, some are vigorous enough to cause conservationists concern. *Olearia lyallii*, the giant tree daisy with numerous lightweight seeds, which is native to Stewart Island and the Snares, where it constitutes the predominant wooded cover of a large part of the island, is thought to have been accidentally introduced to Port Ross by sealers early in the nineteenth century, or at the time of the Hardwicke settlement. It has established itself strongly at the southern end of Erebus Cove, on the site of the old Enderby settlement, and covers considerably more of Ewing Island than the southern rata. There is some controversy as to whether or not it is replacing the original rata forest, and recommendations have been made to prevent it colonising other parts of Port Ross and the Auckland Islands.[10]

Flax — *Phormium tenax* — another plant belonging to the same broad New Zealand biogeographical region as *Olearia lyallii*, was brought by the Maori fugitives from the Chatham Islands. It was important in marking the sites of their gardens, and is one of the few introduced plants which has survived, although it is confined to such places as Erebus Cove and Tandy Inlet.

Most European plants have died out within a few years. When Captain Norman rescued the *Grafton* survivors in 1865, he planted trees and sowed seeds at the head of Carnley Harbour and on Adams Island, as well as oak, ash, and pine trees at Port Ross. Henry Armstrong, visiting these places in the *Amherst* three years later, noted that most of the trees were still "alive, but looking sickly".[11]

Animals introduced to the subantarctic have generally adapted better than vegetables and plants. It is hard to imagine why sheep and goats should have died off in such a favourable environment as Adams Island; however, as in recorded instances elsewhere, they may well have been killed off for the very purpose for which they were liberated. Sometimes, as with the goats on the main Auckland Island, they were prevented from spreading by a boundary of dense scrub which limited their open, preferred grazing; or, as in the case of the cattle on Campbell Island, they remained confined in numbers and range because of marginal conditions and the presence of necessary minerals in just that one particular part of the island. But, generally, pigs, sheep, cattle, and rabbits have done well. The "very numerous" pigs noted by Ross at the time fed chiefly on *Stilbocarpa polaris*, "one of the most beautiful and singular of the vegetable productions of the island",[12] and on *Pleurophyllum criniferum*,

> a very common and striking plant, often covering a great extent of ground, and according to Dr Hooker, forming the larger proportion of the food of the hogs which now run wild upon the main island of this group. It is indeed so abundant in the marshy spots, that these animals frequently live entirely amongst it, particularly where it grows near the margins of the woods, where they form broad tracks through the patches, grubbing up the roots to a great extent, and by trampling down the soft stems and leaves, make soft and warm places for them, to litter in.[13]

A few years later, Charles Enderby reported "a vast number of pigs" on the two islands of Auckland and Enderby. "I have seen (when standing on the cliffs of the latter) as many as one hundred at a time feeding on [seaweed on] the rocks beneath."[14]

Pigs were not too difficult to catch on Enderby Island — the *General Grant* survivors hunted them with an iron hook and noose fixed to the end of a three-metre pole — and they are now confined to the main Auckland Island. They have by this time almost eliminated the giant herbs such as *Pleurophyllum*, *Stilbocarpa*, and *Anisotome* from the entire island, except for the steepest country and cliff ledges. By rooting up nests and eating eggs and

The feral goats on the main Auckland Island, introduced as food for castaways, have been found to be larger than those on the New Zealand mainland. Recent findings indicate they may have considerable potential as mohair breeding stock.

A wild pig, surprised by a stealthy approach from the sea, breaks for cover at Terror Cove, Port Ross.

135

Above: More than a century ago, rabbits of a French breed, Argenté de Champagne — also known as French blues — were released on Enderby Island as a source of food. There are now some 4000 of them, many of which live in the sand dune country and close-cropped sward behind Sandy Bay.

Right: Calves, resting among the fired remnants of rata scrub on Enderby Island. Clearance for farming and the presence of cattle and rabbits have considerably altered the island's original environment. *Photo: Simon Mitchell.*

young, they have also combined with cats to all but wipe out the ground-burrowing prions and petrels, and have even been found with the remains of yellow-eyed penguins and shags in their stomachs. In the last thirty years the number of pigs seems to have stabilised at a reduced but constant population of about a thousand, which remains in a tenuous balance with the severely impoverished flora.

When sheep farming was abandoned on Campbell Island in 1931, the number of sheep left there to run wild fell steadily from about 4000 to 1000 in 1961, and it was assumed they would eventually die out. But within a few years the trend reversed, possibly through some genetic change or the survival and resurgence of the fittest, and by 1969 numbers had increased to 3000.

The Department of Lands and Survey decided to fence the island in half and eliminate sheep to the north of the fenceline in 1970, and more recently to further confine the sheep with a second fence to less than a quarter of the island. As a result, it now looks as if the changes made to Campbell Island may not be as serious as people at first thought. The palatable megaherbs,

which were severely knocked back or eliminated by grazing, have regenerated with an unexpected rapidity, suggesting that in spite of earlier misgivings the greatly modified native vegetation could return to something approaching its original state.

Enderby and Rose Islands in Port Ross have also been heavily affected by introduced animals and farming. The small population of cattle had died out on Rose Island by 1920, and the native tussock has been slowly growing back since then and reducing the areas of pastoral sward. As a consequence, the rabbits on the island, too few to keep the sward open, are in turn steadily declining in number.

Enderby Island, with more sunshine and a better soil than the main Auckland Island, has hundreds of rabbits and some forty head of cattle. The cattle are survivors of the animals landed by W. J. Moffett in 1895, and have remained constant in numbers for years, browsing over the large areas of open sward and sheltering from winds and storms in the gaunt and stunted remnants of the rata forest.

Moffett and others set fire to the scrub and rata from time to time to increase the grazing areas. The natural progression of tussock to scrub to rata at the forest edge was destroyed, allowing the wind to penetrate. Trampling cattle and browsing rabbits then prevented seedlings from growing, with the result that the trees on the edge of the forest died. Large areas of Enderby Island resemble a war-scarred landscape, with lifeless trunks and barren branches standing or lying uprooted on the sward. They give the impression that the island is irreparably ruined. However, there are places where healthy rata forest has spread onto the sward, and this is particularly noticeable at the back of Sandy Bay, where the *Stella* castaway depot once stood well out in the open, but is now several metres into the forest, with only the

A small blow-out in peat soil due to grazing by sheep, where trampling has cut into the ground and made it vulnerable to removal by the wind. More severe examples occur on exposed and open country.

The Norway rat and feral cats have wiped out most of the smaller sea birds on Campbell Island. Rats are also thought to be one of the main causes for the severe decline in the number of rockhopper penguins on the island. They are the greatest single threat to the wildlife of New Zealand's subantarctic. *Photo: Graeme Taylor*.

top of its mast visible above the canopy of trees. Much as with the pigs on the main Auckland Island, the situation on Enderby is one of an uneasy and impoverished equilibrium.

With the activities of sealers, colonists, and farmers came rats, cats, mice, and dogs. It is quite astonishing that there are no rats on the Auckland Islands, but the more voracious ship rat, which is the predominant rat of the Middle East, did not reach the New Zealand mainland until the 1870s. The rat on Campbell Island is the brown Norway rat, less aggressive, but still an environmental disaster. The Norway rats are numerous, widespread, and with cats have wiped out almost all the ground-burrowing petrels and prions, which are defenceless against them. These predators are probably on Campbell to stay, unless worldwide research on new biological methods of control is eventually successful.

Cats and mice have been on the main Auckland Island since the 1920s, and mice on Enderby Island since the time of the Enderby settlement. Mice are also common on the main Antipodes Island, where they were carried ashore with stores and fodder in the sealing days. Mice appear to have a negligible effect on the environment, but cats have done far more damage to bird life on Campbell Island and the main Auckland Island than either rats or pigs. According to Sir Charles Fleming, who was one of the World War II coast-watchers there, they are the main predators of smaller petrels on Auckland Island, and are probably responsible for the extinction of the merganser, the rail, the introduced wekas, and the Auckland Island snipe and shore plover.[15]

In 1840, Sir James Clark Ross recorded that "The party employed cutting fire-wood found a cat's nest with two kittens in it, still blind; they were of course destroyed, but the old cat escaped."[16] Musgrave, while a castaway at Carnley Harbour, wrote in his diary, "About six weeks ago we caught a young cat of the common domestic species . . . She soon cleared the house of mice, with which we were dreadfully infested."[17] Laurie Pollock, one of the Cape Expeditioners, was to note in his diary that these wild cats were still capable of domestication. "The embers from clearing up were still hot this morning and Ginger (one of our cats) was lying at the edge of the timbers enjoying the warmth oblivious to the pelting rain and hail."[18]

Dogs did not fare so well. Charles Enderby reported that "There are a number of dogs on Auckland Island (now in a wild state) lost by the New Zealanders."[19] They must have bred, because two dogs were seen by the castaways of the *Grafton*, "one a fine shepherd's dog, white and black, with a long plume-like tail; the other, of smaller size, seemed a cross between a bulldog and a mastiff." However, they "darted off into the jungle, where it was impossible to follow them".[20]

Dogs, possibly the same animals, were seen by some of the *General Grant* survivors who went down to Carnley Harbour. A bulldog with torn ears and several others approached their hut. The last sightings of dogs occurred in the 1880s on Auckland and Enderby Islands, and in the early 1900s on the main Auckland Island.

The story of people's early activities on the subantarctic islands is, environmentally, one of mistaken zeal, error, and tragic accident. Yet these islands are still, fortuitously, of enormous ecological importance to the world. Within the widely varying groups there are still unmodified islands, still places which have shrugged off the sometimes fleeting impact of people and resisted change. The Bounties and Antipodes are virtually unscathed; Disappointment Island, Adams Island, and the Snares have no introduced animals or rodents, and as much as anywhere else on Earth have evolved undisturbed since their creation. Such places are exceedingly rare and valuable natural laboratories for the scientists of a new generation, which seeks not to change or exploit, as was so frequently the case in the past, but to study and understand.

Hatch's Penguin Oil Works

Joseph Hatch of Invercargill, who as F. J. Hatch had applied for one of the early leases on the Auckland Islands, was to gain a grim and lasting place in the history of the subantarctic as a result of his operations on Australia's Macquarie Island. These operations not only exploited men, but wrought severe changes to both flora and fauna.

Hatch had begun work on Macquarie Island by boiling down the oil of elephant seals and king penguins — oil used in cosmetics, margarine, and even for fuelling ships. But there were problems in transporting the heavy seal blubber to his works at the north end of the island and in rending down the king penguins efficiently, and Hatch therefore turned his efforts to the vast rookery of smaller but more accessible royal penguins at the Nuggets, where he built his main boiling-down works.

The main penguin season began in February, when the year-old young or "fats" came out of the sea to moult. Adult birds returning to the sea after nesting were allowed to do so, as they in turn would fatten before coming ashore to moult in March, when they, too, could be slaughtered.

The Nuggets colony was only one of several on Macquarie Island, but it was vast, and was estimated from photographs to cover four hectares, with a population of half a million birds. To counter public protest, Hatch claimed that after twenty-five years of operation the rookery was in fact larger than when he started. He was called a liar, but subsequent research has shown that he was almost certainly right.[21]

At the height of the season the men worked in two twelve-hour shifts, and were able to process more than 2700 birds a day. The penguins were clubbed to death as they filed up a narrow creek to the huge rookery inland, and taken to the "Hall of Smells", where they were loaded into the top of large "digesters". After twelve hours of cooking the oil would rise to the top, and would then be run off, cooled, and stored in casks.

Coal to fire the boilers arrived in barrels, which were rafted ashore. As soon as they grounded, the heavy barrels would begin to sink and had to be manhandled out of the surf before

A sailor from the New Zealand frigate *Tutira* examines the remains of Joseph Hatch's penguin-oil works at the Nuggets on Macquarie Island, during a visit in 1949 with stores and mail for the island's weather station staff. *Photo: New Zealand National Film Unit.*

they became immovable. It was exhausting work, and several times men were badly injured in the turbulent water. Food was landed in the same way, and was frequently ruined by seawater. It had to be paid for just the same, out of the men's pay. More than once gangs received a mere few pounds or shillings for months of hard toil and isolation, and one gang actually ended up owing Hatch money in return for their labours!

Conditions were appalling, but Joseph Hatch can at least be credited for living and working with one of his gangs for five months. At the beginning of a season the huts would be overrun with rats, which were quite fearless and had to be driven from the chaff mattresses. On one occasion a man fell into a digester and was severely scalded, and there were never adequate medical supplies on the island.

Although Macquarie Island belonged to the Tasmanian Government, Hatch's gangs and the ships which serviced them were from New Zealand, and it was the New Zealand Government which responded in times of privation or disaster. Because of the lack of a harbour and the dangerous seas, this happened several times. The

Kakanui, sent by the Government in 1890 to relieve seven men, two boys, and a woman who were believed to be short of provisions, took off all but the married couple and was then lost without trace. The *Hinemoa* included Macquarie Island in a search for any survivors of the *Kakanui* in its usual round of the depots on New Zealand's subantarctic islands. Hatch's schooner the *Gratitude* was beached and wrecked at the Nuggets in 1898, and its crew stranded for three months until they were rescued by the New Zealand Government vessel *Tutanekai*. The *Jessie Nicol* was wrecked in 1910, and the *Clyde* in 1911. Several times Hatch had to charter the *Hinemoa* from the Government, to land provisions or take off men and casks of oil.

In 1911 a scientific party associated with Sir Douglas Mawson's Australasian Antarctic Expedition was landed on Macquarie Island, and remained there four years. In 1919, Mawson added his concern to public opposition against the slaughter of royal penguins at the Nuggets, and it was largely due to his influence that Macquarie Island was declared a sanctuary in 1920.[22]

After nearly thirty years, a gruesome and bizarre industry came to an end.

PART THREE

The Scientists

Members of the German Transit of Venus Expedition at Terror Cove, Auckland Islands, in 1874. *Photo: Monash University, Australia.*

13 The Early Scientists

Although a live Antipodes green parakeet had reached the London Zoo from the farthest corner of the Earth by 1831,[1] the scientific investigation of New Zealand's subantarctic islands did not begin in earnest until the three Antarctic expeditions of Dumont D'Urville, Charles Wilkes, and Sir James Clark Ross in 1840.

During D'Urville's eight-day stay at Port Ross, a disappointingly small number of ferns and flowering plants was collected by his biologists Jacques Hombron and Honoré Jacquinot, although they did better with seaweeds, mosses, and liverworts, flora of particular interest to D'Urville.

The American expedition led by Charles Wilkes was considered poorly equipped, in spite of having eleven scientists aboard and specific instructions to "extend the bounds of science, and promote the acquisition of knowledge".[2] During his short visit, acting-surgeon Holmes, standing in for a qualified botanist, described the peat soil of the Auckland Islands as of "considerable richness",[3] and noted that the giant herbs, of which several were collected, resembled tropical plants in their lush growth.

Sir James Clark Ross's British Antarctic Expedition was fortunate to have first class botanists in Joseph Hooker and his assistant Dr David Lyall. Dr Robert M'Cormick, with the help of Dr John Robertson, surgeons of HMS *Erebus* and HMS *Terror* respectively, made the zoological and geological collections. There is often a notorious time lag in the publication of the results of scientific expeditions, and Ross's was no exception: some of the final zoological descriptions of insects, crustacea, and molluscs were not published until 1874[4] — thirty-four years after the event! Hooker's was the outstanding contribution: for example, in his eleven days at Port Ross and five days at Campbell Island he collected 102 different species of flowering plants — about two thirds of the present known flora of the Auckland and Campbell Islands — as well as sixty-six mosses, eighty-four liverworts, forty-nine seaweeds, and numerous other specimens of ferns and lichens.[5]

The general observations of these early scientists are useful because they show how greatly some places have changed through settlement and

Remnants of an instrument plinth at the back of a narrow strip of grass near the beach at Terror Cove. The tablet on the ground bears the engraved inscription, in English: "German Expedition, 1874."

Commemoration medal of the French Transit of Venus Expedition to Campbell Island in 1874, from the Institute de France. *Photo: Conon Fraser, courtesy National Museum.*

farming. Dr M'Cormick described the land behind Sandy Bay on Enderby Island as

> a hollow, filled with long grass, growing in a rich boggy soil in such rank luxuriance as to be up to the hips, and flanked by a sand-hill clad to the summit by the same kind of grass, having the whole skirted by a thicket of trees and bushes.[6]

Today, it is the shortest imaginable sward of mosses, liverworts, and fine grass, closely grazed by wild cattle and hundreds of rabbits, while beyond the eroded sandhill the thicket of trees has become an open scattering of long-since burnt or stunted and ailing rata. The original luxuriance is gone.

A lull, equivalent to the thirty-four years delay in the final publication of M'Cormick's findings, followed the scientific impact of the French, Americans, and British in 1840, although the islands were by no means forgotten, with the foundation of the Enderby Settlement in 1849 and the series of shipwrecks which began with the *Grafton* and the *Invercauld* in 1864. Useful comments and recommendations about the subantarctic islands were made by Thomas Musgrave and Captain Norman of the *Victoria* in 1865, and by Henry Armstrong after his voyage on the *Amherst* in 1868, but New Zealand scientists had not yet found ways of getting to the subantarctic, their earliest requests for passages being turned down. So in 1874 it was Germany, and France once again, which sent the next expeditions to these remote islands.

The occasion was the transit of the planet Venus across the face of the sun. The phenomenon, last observed in 1769, had been the motivation for Captain Cook's first voyage to Tahiti, from which, after his astronomical observations, he had gone on to search for the elusive "Southern Continent", and had found and circumnavigated "the land discovered by Tasman and now called New Zealand".[7]

Astronomers, simultaneously watching the Transit of Venus from various parts of the world, had, on that occasion, been able to work out for the first time the approximate distance of the earth from the sun. It was hoped that the 1874 Transit of Venus would enable these earlier, optically imprecise calculations to be determined more accurately. Such transits are extremely rare: the next would be in 1882, and the one after that in the year 2004. Five expeditions were sent to the Southern Ocean: the Americans, British, and Germans to the Kerguelen Islands, a German expedition to the Auckland Islands, and the French to Campbell Island.

Very little remains of the French expedition site at Venus Cove, next to Garden Cove, on the furthest arm of Perseverance Harbour from the sea. Campbell Island's predominantly overcast weather meant they had only glimpses of Venus against the sun and had little success in observing the event for which they had come so many thousands of kilometres. Dr Henry Filhol, as surgeon and naturalist, did, however, manage to add to the knowledge of Campbell Island's flora, fauna, and geology in his observations, published eleven years later, in 1885.

During their three and a half month stay a technician named Duris died of typhoid and was buried on the promontory, at Garden Cove, originally chosen for the observations. The expedition leader Bouquet de la Grye's report reads:

> The spot is the most beautiful part of the road-steads, if this term is at all applicable at Campbell Island. . . . Thank God, the remains of Duris will not require a Geologist to distinguish them from those of a seal. A large gravestone with an inscription will cover him, and a wrought-iron cross, a keepsake from his engine-room comrades, will bear witness that Christians have been here.[8]

Unfortunately, although photographs exist of the fine cross over Duris's grave, both the grave site and the cross are now lost. The cross was last seen in 1931, and in 1985 attempts to find it with a metal detector failed.

The French had missed a previous opportunity to investigate the natural history of Campbell Island when, in 1820, the explorer Louis de Freycinet had passed close to the island in difficult seas and poor visibility, and had

Three members of the German
Transit of Venus Scientific Expedition
of 1874. The plinth on which their
apparatus was mounted still stands at
Terror Cove (see page 142). *Photo:
Monash University, Australia.*

been dissuaded from landing by tales of "savages" and "tigers" ashore![9]

The 1874 visit was not of great scientific importance, but the French will always be associated with Campbell Island for the places they named — for example, Vire Point for their ship; Courrejolles Peninsula after their photographer; Jacquemart Island after the Captain of the *Vire*; Duris Point; Mounts Dumas, Paris, Azimuth, Fizeau, and Filhol; Faye Ridge; and Dent Island, which is shaped like a tooth.

The German expedition to the Auckland Islands, arriving in the bark *Alexandrine*, set up its base at Terror Cove in Port Ross, at the place chosen by Ross for his observatory. During their long stay, from 15 October until 6 March, through the "gales, heavy showers, hail and snow . . . and constant rain" of the subantarctic summer, the weather was "the most wretched imaginable".[10] Clearing the scrub and assembling the buildings, the photographic laboratory, magnetic observatory, and iron observation towers involved "extreme hardship", and because of the appalling weather and difficult terrain the group was largely confined to its base and had very little free time for pleasure or exploration, beyond occasional visits to the islands in Port Ross, and in particular Enderby Island. Meteorological and tidal

Red rata in flower at Terror Cove, where the German expedition of 1874 was based.

readings were taken, but the insects recorded and few plants collected by Krone and Dr Schur were of little importance.

The expedition's report on the main purpose of their visit illustrates the fine line between failure and success experienced by the scientists.

> The outcome now only depended on the weather and in this respect the hopes were not high; for until now only sad and discouraging experiences had been our lot. Nearly every day the weather was cloudy and rainy; only seldom was the sun shining in full brightness and it could not be expected that the 9th of December would be an exception from this general rule. The morning began grey and cloudy, the barometer had dropped, thick fog hung over the island. Because it was calm for once there was little chance of clearing up. However everything went well beyond expectation; at 1 o'clock Venus was supposed to pass by the sun, at 12 o'clock a gentle wind sprang up, which cleared the fog and broke the clouds in front of the sun just before the phenomenon occurred. Although the start of the transit of Venus could not be observed clearly the conditions were generally as favourable as could be desired. The astronomers obtained six complete sets of 16 angles on the heliometer and several observations of the inside and outside contact from the ending of the transit; the photographers took 115 pictures, 95 with dry and 20 with wet plates. During the whole event the sky was generally only clear in the region of the sun and just a quarter of an hour after the transit of Venus everything was covered in clouds again.[11]

The Germans' final task was to record the exact position of the observation point. This involved a journey to check their chronometer at Bluff and interminable waits for favourable weather conditions, which extended their stay for a further three months. The American Transit of Venus Expedition's relief ship called to see whether they were all right, as nothing had been heard of them for so long. The Germans finally departed, "reconciled to their many hardships and privations by the joyful knowledge of their success".[12]

Unfortunately, the various 1874 calculations were to prove little better than those of 1769, and it was to be many years before the sun's distance from the earth would be accurately calculated by a far less protracted and onerous method.

Soon after these visits, the servicing of castaway depots on the islands was taken over on a regular basis by the New Zealand Government, although it was several years before scientists began to take advantage of the government steamers' rounds, glad of even a few hurried hours ashore. John Buchanan, assistant to James Hector, F.R.S., Director of the Colonial Museum, was one of the first, travelling to Campbell Island on the *Stella* in 1883. He made useful sketches of the landscape and was able to collect herbarium specimens, although many plants were lost on the homeward voyage. Sir James himself, knighted in 1887, visited the subantarctic islands on the *Hinemoa* in 1895, with the Earl of Glasgow, Governor of New Zealand.

New Zealand scientists also visited Macquarie Island. Professor John Scott, in 1880, and Augustus Hamilton, in 1894, both from the staff of Otago University, made the first extensive botanical and zoological collections from the island. They travelled, respectively, in Joseph Hatch's schooners the *Jessie Nichol* and the *Gratitude*, and at considerable personal risk, for on the *Gratitude*'s return voyage most of Hamilton's specimens and three members of the crew were swept away by heavy seas.

The Austrian Andreas Reischek, who worked in New Zealand for twelve years, was the first naturalist to land on the Snares, in 1888. Like many of the so-called zoologists of the time, Reischek was also a commercial collector, and his report in *Transactions of the New Zealand Institute* echoes the zeal with which he shot large numbers of now rare birds on the mainland:

> Each of our party had his work to do. The captain and the sailors turned out two goats; Mr Dugald, the photographer, took views; Mr Hibs had to sow tree- and grass-seeds. . . . Thousands of penguins were on the rocks, standing like regiments of soldiers. It was amusing to see Captain Fairchild, who delights in such sport, tumbling them into sacks, to be taken on board for museum purposes.[13]

Reischek then travelled on in the *Stella* to the Auckland Islands, where

> I was delighted to be once more among my feathered friends, and spent some hours watching their movements and procuring specimens. . . . I also saw six mergansers, and shot two of them; the others concealed themselves among the rocks.[14]

The Auckland Island merganser, *Mergus australis*, Australasia's only sea duck, is now extinct. Reischek's reputation would almost seem to have preceded him, for at Campbell Island

> One of the young birds which I saw on shore, when I approached it, walked to meet me, opened its bill, and disgorged a mass of oily matter over me, as if poured from a spout. Its smell was so bad that I had to throw away the clothes I had on. . . . [However] I caught some of the young birds and brought them alive to Wellington; but when I looked for them there I was told by the sailors that they had gone overboard.[15]

Reischek's attitude was not unusual for his day. Even as late as 1926, Rollo Beck, a leading member of the Whitney South Sea Expedition of the prestigious American Museum of Natural History, records that early one morning, on the main Antipodes Island, he shot fifty-one birds, "which is the most I ever shot before breakfast".[16]

Scientific interest in the subantarctic continued with an important visit in 1890 by the eminent New Zealand botanist Thomas Kirk, accompanied by Judge Frederick Chapman. Both men were passengers on the *Hinemoa* with Captain Fairchild. As the second scientist to land on the Snares, Kirk made the first botanical collection, of flowering plants and ferns. He also made the first botanical collection at the Antipodes. It was on this round of islands that

A bottle, inscribed with the name of Wilhelm Schur, the astronomer for the German expedition, found at Terror Cove by members of the Auckland Islands Expedition 1972–73. *Photo: Conon Fraser, courtesy National Museum.*

147

Members of the Philosophical Institute of Canterbury's Expedition of 1907. The expedition was a scientific milestone for the subantarctic islands. *Photo: Subantarctic Expedition album, Alexander Turnbull Library, Wellington.*

the beautiful flowering slope of Fairchild's Garden on Adams Island was named.

The southern cruises of the government steamers became fashionable as holidays with a scientific flavour for Governors General. The Earl of Glasgow was followed in 1900 by the Earl of Ranfurly, accompanied by Professor Hutton. Birds were collected for the British Museum. Then in February 1907, two of the leading scientists on the Philosophical Institute of Canterbury's expedition later that year, Professor Benham and Mr Waite, were invited to accompany Lord Plunket on the *Tutanekai*.

Overseas interest also continued. Port Ross was still valuable as a staging place for Antarctic expeditions. In 1890 C. E. Borchgrevinck made a brief stay on his way back to England in the *Southern Cross*, after spending the first winter on the Antarctic Continent. Then in 1904 Captain Robert Falcon Scott's ship *Discovery* met its relief ships the *Terra Nova* and *Morning* there,

The fort-like promontory of the Courrejolles Peninsula, named after the photographer of the French Transit of Venus Expedition.

before continuing on to New Zealand. The naturalist and ornithologist Dr Edward Wilson found Port Ross a wonderful relief from the vast white continent:

> Tues 15 March. Turned out 6.30 am to see the green land. What a rest! And what a beautiful sight! The whole island is clothed with bright green and russet scrub to the water's edge, and what bright yellows and reds and whites and blacks there were on the beach. It was a lovely sight and we all enjoyed it to the full in the sunshine. . . . Ah! the sight of the green scrub and the warm breezes carrying shadows over it all as over a wheat field, the joy of the warm air and the novelty of some blue-bottle flies that found their way on board and were soon buzzing round the ward-room. We seemed to have plunged all at once back into life again out of the Antarctic.[17]

In 1912 Sir Douglas Mawson's Australasian Exploring Expedition spent two weeks nosing round the inlets of the Auckland Islands in the *Aurora*, but it was June, the weather was poor, and so very little was achieved.

The first major scientific expedition from New Zealand to its subantarctic islands took place between Scott and Mawson's visits, in November 1907. The purpose of the Philosophical Institute of Canterbury's Expedition was to extend the magnetic survey of New Zealand and study the structure, rocks, animals, and plants of the islands, and it did so with impressive thoroughness. The reports and observations of the twenty-two scientists involved were edited by Charles Chilton, Professor of Biology at Canterbury University, in two very substantial volumes entitled *The Subantarctic Islands of New Zealand* and published in 1909. The Hon. Robert McNab, author of *Murihiku*, was the Minister of Lands who gave enthusiastic backing to the expedition and wrote the historical introduction to the volumes.

One party of twelve scientists and their assistants from the Philosophical Institute's expedition was landed at Carnley Harbour in the Auckland Islands after calling at Port Ross — where they found the survivors of the *Dundonald* and took Charles Eyre from among them to act as the cook on Campbell Island — and a second party of ten scientists and their helpers was left at Campbell Island. The government steamer *Hinemoa* then collected them after it had made its annual round of inspection of the Antipodes and

Dr Leonard Cockayne studying a large subantarctic tussock grass, *Poa litorosa*, on Ewing Island. *Photo: Subantarctic Expedition album, Alexander Turnbull Library, Wellington.*

Bounty Islands. The Snares were visited on the outward journey, and Disappointment Island was investigated by scientists for the first time before the expedition left the Auckland Islands on the homeward journey.

The two parties included leading scientists of the day, such as Professor (later Sir William) Benham, F.R.S., and E. R. Waite, zoologists; Dr Leonard Cockayne, botanist; B. C. Aston, soil scientist; G. V. Hudson, entomologist; and Professor Chilton, zoologist, who did a masterful job in summarising their conclusions. The work of Dr Cockayne, who had made a previous round of the subantarctic islands in 1903, and of Aston and Waite in adding to a wider knowledge and popular understanding of the general character and terrain of the islands, has been mentioned in previous chapters.

T. F. Cheeseman, curator of the Auckland Museum and New Zealand's leading systematic botanist, was to have been with the Campbell Island party, but objected to being sent where he felt "there was the least chance of doing useful work",[18] and withdrew from the expedition. However, he was

The main Auckland Island seen from Disappointment Island, which is of great interest to scientists because of its pristine condition. In the left foreground is the yellow, umbelliferous flower-head of *Stilbocarpa polaris*; then the daisy-like flowers of *Pleurophyllum speciosum*; the fronded leaves of *Anisotome latifolia*; and the large tussock grass *Chionochloa antarctica*.

later persuaded to contribute to the published results, and his brilliant and detailed analysis of our subantarctic islands' affinities with those of other nations in the Southern Ocean is described by Dr Eric Godley as "a classic for Southern hemisphere botany".[19] Cheeseman's hypotheses of former land links with New Zealand, and more importantly of a once warmer Antarctica's land links with South America and several of the subantarctic island groups, are particularly fascinating in that they were propounded in the days before the present accepted theories of continental drift and plate tectonics. While owing much to Sir Joseph Hooker's earlier conclusions, his work added enormously to the significance of the 1907 expedition.

1927 marked the end of the regular servicing of castaway depots by government steamers. The Hawkes Bay farmer and naturalist H. Guthrie-Smith, author of *Tutira: the story of a New Zealand sheep station* and *Sorrows and Joys of a New Zealand Naturalist*, the Canterbury ornithologist Edgar F. Stead, and the botanists Dr W. R. B. Oliver and Dr Einar du Reitz were on that final trip of

A distant view of the chasm shown on page 153 today, from the opposite, western side. Heavy rock falls have filled the gap so that the sea no longer separates the rock stack from adjoining Adams Island.

the SS *Tutanekai* with Captain Bollons. From this year onwards, and for a long time, it was to be much harder for scientists to visit the subantarctic islands.

Dr Oliver, like Wilson of the *Discovery*, was struck by the summer beauty of Port Ross.

> The colouring of the growth is surprisingly gorgeous, far more indeed, than is that of the New Zealand bush on the mainland, which colouring is sombre by comparison. The force of the winds is so great that the tops of the plants are nipped off, and the vegetation has a close-cropped appearance, and yet its colouring is exceedingly beautiful in its dense masses . . . varying from the fresh green of the haumakaroa (*Nothopanax simplex*) to the deep red of certain forms of rata. Entering the forest one finds the larger trunks prostrate, an evident effect of the constant winds. Trunks and branches bear mats of moss, liverworts and filmy ferns . . .[20]

Guthrie-Smith, however, was more concerned with the degradation of the subantarctic, when, in 1936, he wrote of Campbell Island:

> The ravening energy of the Anglo-Saxon breed, its ferocious rat-like pertinacity has accomplished the ruin of a Fauna and Flora unique in the world . . . What a poor, curtailed, mutilated, sterile world we threaten our descendants with! Man and the rat sharing it — fit mates in many ways — in their desperate, deplorable, gnawing energy, in their ruthless destruction of every obstacle.[21]

His words could almost be seen as a prelude to a wider war that was imminent: not of people against the environment, but of people against each other.

Watercolour by B. Lane of sheer cliffs and a great chasm on the south coast of Adams Island, entitled "Auckland Islands, 31 Dec 1878". *Photo: Alexander Turnbull Library, Wellington.*

14
The "Cape Expedition"

Late in August 1939, only a few days before the start of the Second World War, the German cargo steamer *Erlangen* slipped quietly out of Dunedin. A telegram had warned that war was imminent, and there had been no time to take on fuel. A course was set for the next port of call in Australia, but under cover of darkness, with the ship blacked out, Captain Alfred Grams turned for the Auckland Islands, to lie low and see what would happen next. En route he received a further telegram, directing him to a neutral port within the next few days. The nearest was almost 8000 kilometres away, in South America, and the *Erlangen* had coal for only five days steaming. There was nowhere else to go but the Aucklands.

The *Erlangen* reached Carnley Harbour four days before war was declared on 3 September, and the steamer's crew was greatly relieved to notice its wooded shores. At the head of North Arm, the furthest inlet from the sea, the *Erlangen*'s Chinese crew, who had thrown in their lot with their German officers, began to cut out two to three hectares of the iron-hard, stunted rata forest as fuel for the boilers. Captain Grams later wrote that "the wood was so incredibly hard that our axes bounced off it with almost no effect. Moreover it was so twisted that splitting it was impossible."[1] The ship's engineers made saws from winch guards, and these were continually sharpened. Working ten-hour shifts, they cut and loaded 235 tonnes of the 400 they had estimated they would need. Makeshift sails would have to compensate for the shortfall.

Although the crew found mussels and killed "wild geese" — probably shags — they were short of provisions and could not afford to stay longer than five weeks. During that time, only bad weather prevented the cruiser HMS *Leander* from entering Carnley Harbour and finding them. *Leander* returned in November, but that was after the *Erlangen* had gone. A year later a search by the *Achilles*, following a hunch that Carnley Harbour might have been used by the enemy, failed to find the promontory of rata forest cleared by the *Erlangen*'s crew.

With tarpaulins rigged to its masts and derricks, the *Erlangen* was able to limp across the South Pacific Ocean to Ancud in Chile, a distance of 4826

The old Second World War coastwatching headquarters at Campbell Island was used as the first "met" station until 1957 when the present station was opened at Beeman Cove.

nautical miles, 1507 of them under sail alone. By the time the steamer got there, all the wooden fittings in the ship, including bunks, furniture, and cabin bulkheads, had gone into the boilers. It had been an astonishing feat of ingenuity and nautical skill. After travelling round Cape Horn to Argentina, the *Erlangen* started on the final dangerous leg of the journey back to Germany, but was intercepted by HMS *Newcastle*. To avoid capture of his ship Grams ordered his crew to set it on fire and to open the sea cocks. He and his German officers, however, were interned for the rest of the war.

The strategic importance of the Auckland and Campbell Islands as likely bases for enemy warships was realised early on in the war. In August 1940 the *Turakina* had been sunk by a German raider in the Tasman Sea. The *Holmwood*, on its way back from the Chathams, was sunk on 25 November 1940, and the *Rangitane* sunk off the New Zealand coast two days later. New Zealand prisoners from the *Turakina* were kept below decks, but reported that they had been taken south into a noticeably colder climate, and had glimpsed the snow- and tussock-covered hills of what must have been either the Auckland Islands or Campbell Island.[2] These islands, with their large sheltered harbours, could have been used for mounting attacks against Australia or New Zealand. Japan had not yet entered the war, but the Germans were active in the Pacific and Indian Oceans, and a decision was made to establish small coastwatching parties of three men at Port Ross and four at Carnley Harbour on the Auckland Islands, and four at Perseverance Harbour on Campbell Island. These men could then immediately radio back reports on enemy shipping. Base camps and lookout huts were to be well concealed, and the men would pose as fishermen if captured. The twin-engined ketch *Ranui*, under the command of Captain Webling — and later the Lindsays — would act as a mobile link between the groups, and would be based at Waterfall Inlet on the east coast of the main Auckland Island.

The code name given to the operation was the "Cape Expedition". The first-year volunteers sailed from Wellington on 5 March 1941 on the schooner *Tagua*, without knowing their destination — only that the assignment could be dangerous, and that they would be on their own for a year. Although there were so few of them, they needed an enormous amount of equipment and supplies: dinghies; Orion ranges for cooking and cast-iron stoves for heating; a .22 rifle and a .45 Colt revolver at each base, expressly for killing pigs, goats, or sheep for meat; bedding and furniture, books and medical stores, and cold- and wet-weather clothing.

Because of the uncertain future, the Cape Expeditioners had rations for three years, and because of the isolation and climate, luxuries such as chocolate, tobacco, and rum were included. Their prefabricated buildings were designed for the Antarctic, and had double plywood walls and double-glazed windows. Although Antarctica is dry and the subantarctic region wet, the building proved very adequate during the years the men were there. Electric light was from twelve-volt batteries charged by generators or wind-driven chargers, and they had kerosene lamps in reserve. "Nothing was forgotten, from egg-beaters to flat irons, from camouflage paint to hair clippers."[3]

It was while searching for a site for their emergency station that the Carnley party came across the evidence of the *Erlangen*'s visit. "Cape" personnel believe that Captain Grams may have over-dramatised his difficulties. They cross-cut many cords of rata, and found that if straight-grained trunks were selected, the wood split relatively easily.

Coastwatching hours were from dawn until dark. In the winter this was from eight until four, but in the summer the watches, which were varied to allow for scientific work or recreation, began at half past two in the morning and finished after ten at night. Two months after they went down, a German raider, the *Atlantis*, sighted the Auckland Islands on the horizon, but was not seen by those on shore. Japan entered the war in December 1941, and the number of men in the second year was increased to five at each station to cope

Left: The World War II coastwatching station at Tagua Bay, Carnley Harbour, is fast falling into disrepair.

Below: Mussels, at Figure-of-Eight Island in Carnley Harbour, of the sort that were gathered by the sackful to supplement the *Erlangen*'s meagre supplies on its long wartime voyage across the South Pacific to Chile.

with the long summer watches and increased responsibility. Radio communications to New Zealand, although coded, were no doubt intercepted, but the enemy still appeared to know nothing about the parties deployed on the subantarctic islands. As Ron Balham, stationed at Ranui Cove in 1943, reasoned:

> If the Japs knew that there were five guys at the top end of the Aucklands, for example, armed with a ·45 Colt and a ·22 rifle, they wouldn't have been very deterred, so it was very comforting to get to the lookout at dawn and see that there weren't any Jap ships in the harbour. From those lookouts where we spent many hundreds of hours we actually spotted only two ships in five years, and they turned out to be American Liberty ships. But nevertheless we had to keep up this dawn to dusk watch.[4]

Although each party had a leader, everyone shared duties and took turns to cook. Even after December 1942, when they were given military rank because of the fate of civilians summarily executed in the Pacific, the Master of the *Ranui*, who was nominally in overall charge, was a private like the rest of them. They had no identifying badges, and with their unconventional special duty passes took some delight in bewildering the military police when they returned home.

Despite the isolation, the Cape Expeditioners enjoyed the life. Ron Balham recalls:

> We produced a magazine. We had sports tournaments with trophies and prizes. We had things like debating, dancing lessons on Thursday night, and a full scale dance on Saturday night when we drank our weekly supply of rum. . . . We had fancy dress balls — it sounds weird today, but it wasn't — and Christmas with Santa Claus, and on any occasion when there was a birthday or something to celebrate there'd be an elaborate menu and the cook was expected to prepare something very special for that day.[5]

The "something special" was not always successful: a midwinter's day feast on Campbell Island in 1944 featured "Roast Epomophora" — an albatross which had been chloroformed and proved to be inedible.

As the direct threat of enemy action against the islands decreased, especially after the Battle of the Coral Sea, opportunities improved for undertaking scientific observations during time off from coastwatching duties. The Cape Expeditioners had been chosen throughout for their ability to cope with isolation and their interest in an outdoor life, and all contributed to observations of the mammals, birds, insects, and flora of the islands.

One of the first scientists posted to Carnley Harbour in the second year, 1942–43, was the young geologist C. A. (later Sir Charles) Fleming. He was to become chief palaeontologist of the Department of Scientific and Industrial Research, and a broad-based yet in-depth scientist with a prodigious output of publications in biology and the earth sciences.

Other Cape Expeditioners were also to become eminent in their particular fields: J. H. Sorensen, naturalist, ornithologist, and author of *Wild Life in the Subantarctic*, was at Campbell Island from 1942–44; Dr W. H. Dawbin, now of the University of Sydney, a world authority on dolphins and whales, and on the physiology of the tuatara, was at Carnley Harbour in 1943, the same year that Dr R. A. (later Sir Robert) Falla was leader at Port Ross; E. G. Turbott, who pioneered census work on bush birds, and became Director of the Auckland Institute and Museum, was at Port Ross the following year; and Dr Ron H. Balham, who became Reader in Zoology at Victoria University, was at Port Ross in 1943 and at Campbell Island in 1944, where Dr Robin L. Oliver, geologist and son of Dr W. R. B. Oliver, was also stationed. Their reports and papers, and those of other scientists who drew on the Cape Expeditioners' work, ranged from auroral research to ornithology, botany, and entomology, and were later published by the DSIR as the *Scientific Results of Cape Expedition Bulletins 1941–45*.

An intriguing incident, in which lay members of the Cape Expedition advanced scientific knowledge, concerned the controversy over a new genus

View of Ewing Island from the coastwatching lookout above Ranui Cove, Port Ross.

and species of flightless duck on Campbell Island, — the teal *Anas aucklandica nesiotis* — first described by a Canadian zoologist, J. H. Fleming, in 1937. Edgar Stead, writing in *Transactions of the Royal Society of New Zealand* in 1937 on "The Supposed Flightless Duck from Campbell Island", had strongly discredited Fleming's claim. Stead dismissed the possibility of a new species, and claimed that Reischek's failure to see one of these ducks, although he had been told of them, was strong evidence against the existence of the bird, and that "mistakes in labelling birds are by no means uncommon . . . and a slip of the tongue by Captain Fairchild may unintentionally have given the impression that the bird came from Campbell Island".[6] He added that Mr Bethune, the engineer on the *Stella* and a keen collector of birds and eggs, had also never heard of such a duck.

Unconvinced that Stead was right, Dr Falla, in 1944, asked Laurie Pollock and Ron Balham to find one of the ducks for him when they went to Campbell Island. Pollock's logbook of 28 May records:

Left at 12.10 pm for penguin rookery below Dumas. Made good time, but found the penguins had gone to sea. Returned via North West Bay. Surprised to see two flightless ducks between NW Bay and Windlass Bay, and although (Balham and I) tried for an hour with stones to secure specimen did not have any luck. Arrived back in dark.
29th May. Managed to shoot [a flightless duck].
30th. Put Flightless Duck in pickle after weighing and measuring.[7]

The maligned J. H. Fleming died a fortnight before the specimen arrived back in New Zealand — although he would have had to wait until the 1980s for an indication that his duck was at best a subspecies of the flightless teal of the Auckland Islands.

Cape Expeditioners were posted to the subantarctic for a year, and had little communication with the outside world, apart from their radio. *Photo: Laurie Pollock.*

Like many others, R. F. Wilson, of the first Campbell Island party in 1941, kept a personal diary, and these extracts show how his observations built up into a detailed and valuable record.

Sunday 5.10.41. Saw a baby elephant (seal) born this morning so now I can keep track of him. Out in the boat today and the bay is full of very small jelly fish about the size of the end of a pencil. Took a specimen.

Tuesday 14.10.41. Went up on Mt St Col to have a look at the albatross today. Blowing a gale and had the pleasure of watching one attempting to fly. He was right on the ridge in a wind of force 8. He would stand with his wings stretched and then jump into the air and actually stay aloft by flapping for a period of 5 seconds and then alight in the same place . . .

20.10.41. Visited Garden Cove. There are now 25 calves excluding 3 dead ones, and 33 cows all under the supervision of one cranky old bull. Some of the babies are now just balls of blubber with two eyes.

28.10.41. The albatross chicks are gradually taking wing now. The chick mentioned on 14.10.41 was today flying up and down his own particular piece of ridge but making no attempt to leave the island. Seemed to be enjoying himself . . .

1.11.41. Older albatrosses are all courting in pairs now so they will soon be laying again. The albatross chicks which I ringed have just left. . . . Bull elephants very busy now serving the cows . . .

25.11.41. Sea elephants still on beach. Very few cows here now, as they seem to have left the island . . .

1.12.41. Went to the back of Mt Dumas. Penguins still sitting on eggs. No chicks as yet. Royal Albatross eggs now in about 50% of nests.[8]

The fourth-year (1944–45) parties were taken south in January by the *Ranui* and the *New Golden Hind*, which had replaced the *Tagua* as relief ship. A documentary film of the voyage and servicing of the bases, *50° South*, was made by Peter Whitchurch, mate of the *New Golden Hind*, as a record of the Expedition's work.

The Tagua base at Carnley Harbour was closed down four months later. The coastwatching role was winding down, and the work of the Cape Expedition now became increasingly scientific. The topographical survey and mapping of the Auckland Islands and provisional mapping of Campbell Island by the three-man survey party which had joined the expedition was a major achievement in the two years until the end of the war.

Allan Eden, author of *Islands of Despair*, a very readable account of the Cape Expedition and the subantarctic islands, was in charge of the surveying. The three surveyors were occasionally joined by other members of the expedition, and all did a remarkable job, under persistently difficult conditions, of putting right a long history of errors.

The first chart of the Auckland Islands had been made by Abraham Bristow in 1806. On that map, the northern end of the islands and Laurie's Harbour — which then referred to the whole of Port Ross — was greatly exaggerated in scale, while Carnley Harbour, though fairly detailed, was shown as smaller than Port Ross. Disappointment Island is named on this early chart, for a reason no longer clear, but which occurred long before the disappointment suffered by the castaways of the *Dundonald*.

In 1840, D'Urville doubted the existence of Adams Island on previous maps, which showed "a channel separating this alleged island from the main landmass".[9] In the same year, Sir James Clark Ross made a remarkably accurate map of the Auckland Islands, but because it was not included in his published journals it went largely unnoticed, even though it was used by Enderby in his prospectus for a settlement.

Thomas Musgrave's sketch map of 1864, published with his diaries, was a surprisingly retrograde effort and vastly exaggerated the southern end of the islands, reducing Port Ross to no more than the northern apex of a triangle which had its base as Adams Island. Although Port Ross grew considerably in size in his sketch of a year later, published with the journals of HMCS *Victoria*, the southern end of the Auckland Islands still remained far too prominent. A chart prepared by HMS *Blanche* in 1870 is very similar to Musgrave's later map, and was again nowhere near as accurate as Ross's, even though it incorporated features from his surveys.

Mapping became of increasing importance in the final years of the Cape Expedition. The necessity for getting onto high ground to set up base lines and an accurate triangulation for topographical mapping was the greatest drawback to Allan Eden's wartime work, for the tops were frequently

Young royal albatrosses form a sociable "gamming" group on exposed and lonely Campbell Island, near Col Ridge. In the background is Northwest Bay.

Abraham Bristow's "Sketch of Lord Auckland's Groupe", 1806.

Interior of the wartime coastwatching station at Tagua Bay.

blanketed in cloud for days and weeks on end. Above the impenetrable scrub, through which tracks had to be slashed, the surveying party found the winds cruelly cold on any but the mildest days:

> The plateau consisted entirely of bogs, which fortunately were firmly frozen and therefore easily crossed. My observations at the trig occupied four hours, as the snowstorms were frequent. Since we were thoroughly wet and the temperature was below freezing point our clothing soon froze rigid, and we were rather relieved when the job was finished.[10]

The frequent bad weather did, however, give Eden the chance to catch up on painstaking calculations:

> I was engaged on the rather laborious adjustment of the triangulation. I had no calculating machine, and the computation by logarithmic tables was very tedious, some of the individual adjustments requiring up to sixty hours' work each. As George completed sections of topographical work they were plotted onto the final plan, so that we could see the map of the islands gradually taking shape.[11]

Aerial photography would have helped the work enormously, and an RNZAF Catalina was on standby for six weeks, with drums of aviation fuel waiting for it to refuel at Carnley Harbour. But in spite of several attempts the weather never cleared. In fact, a complete set of aerial photographs of the Auckland Islands was not finally obtained until late in 1984, when an Orion aircraft of the RNZAF was able to complete the work in cloudless conditions.

There were, of course, times when the weather was better, and the work had its unexpected rewards. Graham Turbott recalls accompanying the survey party on a clear day on Adams Island:

> We went onto every high point of that island . . . and I had the privilege of looking for the first time at a lake which occupies the floor of a valley in the middle of the south coast and cannot be seen from the sea. I think it was just chance that I was the first in the party to come over the rise; and I looked down and I said "There's a lake!" — and Lake Turbott it is![12]

In 1942, Les Clifton made a basic survey and map of Campbell Island, using limited equipment. He found the French map of 1874 reasonably accurate, with the biggest errors in the north-east part of the island. Two years later, Allan Eden and Clifton were able to check his work and correct some minor errors. Eden also verified Campbell Island's geographical position as being very close to the latitude given by Ross and the French, but about three kilometres east of the previous longitude on the British Admiralty chart. Clifton's map of Campbell Island was to remain the only one available for the next forty years.

Today, the base camps and lookouts of the Cape Expedition, although still standing, are fast deteriorating with the weather. Dr Ron Balham, who went as a meteorologist but later became a zoologist, is well qualified to judge conditions there.

> It was a shocking climate — after all it was overcast 95 percent of the time, the wind velocity was frequently Force 6 on the scale, and the cloud cover about 95 percent, the humidity about 95 percent, so it really was a shocking climate, and no wonder the Enderby settlement was such a fizzer — but the greyness and the tempestuous climate really appealed to me, and the wildlife, of course, is quite fantastic. To hear a sooty albatross in the mist on Campbell was quite marvellous.[13]

Les Clifton summed up his war history report of the Cape Expedition as follows:

> The Department . . . never expected volunteers who had served one year to return for a second and even a third. Some of them did. The easy-going life appealed to them and, after a while, they grew even to feel a sort of affection for their grim surroundings — the grey, wind-swept ocean and the stark cliffs that echoed the cries of the sea birds and the thunder of the surf.[14]

Clifton, who was killed in an aircraft accident in New Zealand, was brought back for the final time, in 1951. His grave stands at the north end of the meteorological station, on a bluff overlooking Perseverance Harbour.

Sir Robert Falla: Gentleman Naturalist

Born at Palmerston North in 1901, Sir Robert Falla was one of the last of a generation of naturalists and broad-based scientific observers in the 1920s and 1930s such as Dr Leonard Cockayne and H. Guthrie-Smith. Scientists working in the subantarctic today often tend to be more specialised.

In 1929 and 1930 Robert Falla was the assistant zoologist and ornithologist on Sir Douglas Mawson's British, Australian, and New Zealand Antarctic Research Expedition to Enderby Land and the coastal waters of the Antarctic Continent, and the subantarctic's Kerguelen, Crozet, Heard, and Macquarie Islands. His report on the birds studied during Mawson's expeditions gained him his doctorate in 1937 — the year he became director of the Canterbury Museum in Christchurch.

On the outbreak of the Second World War Dr Falla was consulted about plans to establish the coastwatching stations of the "Cape Expedition", and it was on his suggestion that scientists and naturalists were included among the men posted to the Campbell and Auckland Islands. He was leader of the third-year (1943–44) party, during which time he visited Campbell Island on a memorable voyage.

During a night watch with Laurie Pollock, in such heavy seas that everyone aboard was seasick, "Doc" Falla staggered to the side and lost his dentures in the scuppers, which were awash at his feet. Groping in the icy water, he somehow found his teeth and struggled back to the wheelhouse to find that he had also picked up a small fish. It was duly preserved and later identified as *Bovichtus pyschrolutes*, the first such find in the hundred years since the *Erebus* and *Terror* expedition had collected the first specimen of this rare fish some three degrees further north. Dr Falla later commented to Laurie Pollock that history does not record whether Sir James Clark Ross captured the holotype in his teeth or his beard!

After the war, in 1947, Robert Falla became Director of the National Museum in Wellington, and in the summer of that year led the first of

Sir Robert Falla among Salvin's mollymawks and erect-crested penguins, on his last visit to the Bounty Islands, November 1978. *Photo: Evening Post, Wellington.*

many scientific expeditions to the subantarctic, in Alex Black's vessels the *Alert* and its successor the *Acheron*. This expedition, sponsored by the New Zealand Government and the American Museum of Natural History, was to the Snares, to which Falla had paid a brief visit in 1944 when returning from his year on the Auckland Islands. The 1947 expedition, in staying on the Snares for thirteen days, was the first party of scientists to spend more than a few hours on the group.

In 1950 Dr Falla completed his tally of New Zealand's subantarctic islands by leading a privately sponsored expedition, again in the *Alert*, to the Antipodes and Bounty Islands. "Doc" Falla thus visited the subantarctic on numerous occasions. He was a great champion for the protection of the natural environment, and was the first Chairman of the Nature Conservation Council. Knighted in 1973, he paid his last call to the subantarctic on HMNZS *Waikato*, at the age of seventy-seven, when he landed on the Bounty, Antipodes, Campbell, and Auckland Islands, and flew by helicopter over his old coastwatching sites at Port Ross. He died three months later, on 23 February 1979.[15]

15
Campbell Island Weather Station

When the Second World War ended and the coastwatching parties were brought home in 1945, it was decided to keep the base camp at Tucker Cove manned for meteorological observations and ionosphere research. The value of regular "Met" reports from Campbell Island had been proved during the war, and there was also an international demand for strategic stations on islands such as Campbell and Macquarie, and on France's Kerguelen and Crozet Islands, in the otherwise empty but vastly important weather region of the Southern Ocean.

By 1947 it became clear that Campbell Island's old coastwatching headquarters, deliberately built some distance from the harbour to avoid detection, not only was too small and in poor repair, but was in the wrong place for a modern meteorological and scientific base. However, it was not until 1953 that the present site at Beeman Cove was decided on. Work on the jetty started in 1954, and the new station was completed in 1957 in time for the island's important role in the International Geophysical Year.

The I.G.Y. lasted from July 1957 to the end of 1958. It was a vast, worldwide research programme, carried out by sixty-four nations, into the earth sciences, which included weather, the ionosphere and aurora, oceanography, magnetism, earthquakes, gravity, solar radiation, and radio and cosmic rays. The I.G.Y. was to provide the stimulus for the establishment of many of the present international bases on the Antarctic Continent, and was a milestone in international scientific co-operation. Such co-operation has remained a hallmark of Antarctic research.

The Campbell Island weather station has a staff of twelve, which is relieved each year. The officer in charge is also the postmaster and usually the medical officer. There are five meteorologists, who maintain a twenty-four hour watch, two telecommunications technicians, a mechanic, whose main responsibility is the generator room, two electronics technicians, and a cook.

Besides the standard meteorological instruments, an ionosonde measures changes in the ionosphere for forecasting radio conditions, a riometer the absorption of radio waves in the ionosphere, and an All-sky camera auroral activity. Earthquakes, tides, and variations in the earth's magnetic field are also recorded.

During the frequent gales, williwaws — sudden gusts of wind up to 240 kilometres an hour — funnel down Perseverance Harbour with battering force, lifting the surface off the sea. *Photo: Kim Westerskov.*

Campbell Island meteorological station, from the slopes of Beeman Hill. The accommodation building is at the left. The white dome houses the weather balloon tracking equipment.

Daily radio contact is kept with New Zealand, 700 kilometres to the north.

Communication with New Zealand is by radio telephone. Although there is no guarantee of mail from home, at least two deliveries are made each year by RNZAF Orions. One precious air drop took several weeks to find in the thick scrub on the slopes of Beeman Hill! Outgoing mail is less frequent, and depends on the Navy. Because of its unique postmark, Campbell Island quite often gets packages of pre-addressed letters from philatelic agents anxious to make a quick profit out of one of the world's most remote post offices.

The staff at Campbell Island are generally young and in their twenties. Most find the year a memorable experience, and some, like the Cape Expeditioners of the past, return there, particularly if they are interested in tramping, photography, and the island's wildlife. Events in the world become unimportant. Grant Harper, a zoology student who was there in 1984, observed that

> Campbell Island must be one of the few places left where you can be totally alone. Out at Bull Rock there was nothing but you, the weather, and the island. No telephones, no planes, no ships, cars, absolutely nothing, apart from the hut, that had anything to do with people. Apart from the few bods away at base, nothing. How many people have spent three to four days *that* alone? It was a precious experience."[1]

Mark Crompton, officer in charge during the 1983–84 season, is one of those who has returned more than once. He celebrated his twenty-first birthday the day after arriving for the first time as a meteorological observer in 1969, and was there every year until 1977, apart from a fifteen-month tour of duty on Raoul Island. After a break of six years farming on Banks Peninsula in the South Island, he returned to Campbell for the 1983–84 season, then went to the Chatham Islands in 1984–85, and Raoul again in 1985–86.

Because of the isolation, the leader's role is particularly important, and much depends on his skill at settling disputes fairly and impartially, and combining the informal life-style of the base with the efficient running of its daily duties and chores.

The view from Col Ridge as a winter squall sweeps in towards the Courrejolles Peninsula. *Photo: Ramari Stewart.*

Expedition members quickly adapt to the climate. In 1984 it was typical that nobody caught a cold, and a sunny 10°C day would see people out in shorts and T-shirts. But Campbell Island averages only 635 hours of sunshine a year,[2] compared with 2019 for Wellington, 2440 for Sydney, and 1514 for London.[3] Low stratus cloud and mist are common, and as many as four fronts can pass over the island within twenty-four hours. Although rainfall is moderate, it falls on 325 days of the year.[4] Anything with a wind under fifteen knots is regarded as a calm day. Strong winds are frequent, averaging 30 to 40 knots (gale force 8 on the Beaufort Scale is 24 to 40 knots), and gusts can reach up to 130 knots or 240 kilometres an hour, which is off the Beaufort Scale.[5] Sir James Clark Ross described the squalls in Perseverance Harbour as of "astonishing force" and "a remarkable characteristic phenomenon of all the islands in about this latitude".[6] Not for nothing is the region referred to as the Roaring Forties.

Dismal weather was undoubtedly one of the main reasons for the failure of the Enderby Settlement. William Mackworth wrote in his diary for 10 January 1850: "Our greatest enemy in this undertaking is the weather. Gales of wind and perpetual rain."[7]

As on Macquarie Island, which in January can experience "generally fine and sometimes very hot weather for a few days, with now and then an occasional burst from south east or south west with hail",[8] summer conditions are highly untypical of the greater part of the year, and can deteriorate rapidly.

The subantarctic climate is cloudy, windy, and bleak, with high humidity and frequent rain. On the Auckland Islands summer temperatures vary between 10° and 16°C and winter temperatures between 4° and 10°C.[9] Campbell Island has a lesser range, and a mean annual temperature of 6°C. In earlier years, icebergs were occasionally sighted in winter. Both islands have light, impermanent snow on about forty days of the year, although the falls

An elephant seal rears up to look out from its mud wallow, near Tucker Cove. Abandoned wallows, hidden by vegetation, can be a hazard for meteorological station staff. Occasionally, wallows can become so deep that animals are unable to leave them.

are more frequent and heavier on the high country. In 1941 Allan Eden noted only forty-four days when the cloud base was above 660 metres.[10]

The Snares tend to be north of the belt of cyclonic storms which circulate round the Southern Ocean, but are still exposed to strong westerly winds and frequent gales. The mean temperature for 1972, a typical year, was 10.8°C, and the sky is generally overcast.[11] However, low cloud and mist are not as common as on the islands to the south.

Information for the Antipodes is slight, but it seems that the average temperature is comparable to the Auckland Islands, and the high humidity similar to Campbell Island and the Snares, although cloud and rainfall are considerably less. Visiting scientists have in fact been surprised at the dryness of the islands and the lack of clearly defined streams. Winds also tend to be lighter.

On fine nights, the aurora australis may be seen, an atmospheric pheno-menon caused by charged particles from the sun bombarding the atmosphere and coming under the influence of the earth's magnetic field. Such displays are most frequent in high latitudes, where the lines of magnetic force converge.

Emerging from their hut late one cold winter evening, the survivors of the *Grafton*, on the Auckland Islands,

> saw before us a most magnificent spectacle. It was a Southern aurora in all its pomp of splendour . . . the stars paled before the sheaves of fire of different colours which rose from the horizon, and sprang towards the zenith, swift as lightnings, but succeeding one another without intermission. In the south, the aurora was permanent: it was a grand semicircle inclosing a ghostly radiance, whence in every direction darted forth the serpentine fires.[12]

Charles Wilkes's United States Exploring Expedition of 1838–42 saw the aurora closer to the latitude of Campbell Island, on 29 February 1840:

> the whole southern hemisphere was covered with arches of a beautiful straw colour, from which streamers radiated, both upwards and downwards, of almost a lustrous white; numbers of concentric arches would occasionally show themselves, of a width of a few feet, uniting to form a complete canopy for a moment, and then vanish. The arches extended from east-south-east to west-north-west; the display continued for over two hours; the stars were seen above them. Previous to, and during its continu-ance, the thermometer indicated a change of four degrees, and the wind shifted to the southward.[13]

The All-sky camera on the roof of "Aurora House", a shed on the lower slopes of Beeman Hill above the main hostel buildings, records similar auroral displays on clear nights.

Ramari Stewart, a member of the 1982–83 staff of Campbell Island, engaged in behavioural study of Hooker's sea lions. *Photo: Ramari Stewart.*

The weather station staff, when they are not carrying out general maintenance, help in a variety of scientific research programmes. Approximately 3000 birds are banded each expedition year for the Wildlife Service — mainly royal and sooty albatross and mollymawk chicks. In some years, up to 8000 have been banded. Regularly, on his day off and regardless of the weather, Mark Crompton checked, throughout the 1983–84 season, maximum and minimum air and soil temperatures and rainfall at sea level, at 275 metres, and at 550 metres near the summit, on the slopes of Mt Honey, as part of a study of the effect of climate at different altitudes on the production growth rates of tussock and certain plants.

Ramari Stewart, a member of the 1982–83 expedition and a naturalist with several years experience of studying dolphins and killer whales, spent most of her spare time carrying out a detailed census and behavioural study of right whales, elephant seals, and sea lions, as part of a programme started in 1975 by the Research Division of the Ministry of Agriculture and Fisheries. She told me:

Campbell Island's one of the few places you can observe the rare southern right whale, not only in numbers, but over a period of time. Unlike many whales that roam the oceans in social groups it's normally a solitary species, but when they congregate for mating you can see groups of three and even four together.

I'll never forget the first time I saw them. It was truly amazing, to see such large, gentle giants rolling around close inshore amongst all the other residents — the sea lions and penguins. The immature whales often played with the sea lion pups. It's not unusual to see young toothed animals such as sea lions playing with objects, but I didn't expect to see a young baleen whale doing it. One of them, a young bull, developed the habit of towing pieces of kelp about, so I nicknamed him "Seaweed". He would cruise off and find a length of weed somewhere in the Bay, and then deliberately seek out a group of pups who would immediately respond to his approach. The whale only needed to swim a slow circle to excite them, and they'd go after the seaweed trailing from his jaws. Each week the relationship strengthened, and new and more spectacular games developed. Occasionally the pups would actually climb onto a whale's back. They

169

The station maintains a twenty-four hour watch on surface weather conditions, and makes twice-daily reports of atmospheric conditions up to a height of 25 000 metres.

particularly enjoyed straddling "Seaweed's" tail, and then he'd lift it and tilt it and up to three of them at a time would slide off into the water. This activity would be repeated over and over again.

This sort of thing was absolutely fascinating, and my census included recording whales' distinctive individual markings — such as colour patterning and the different characteristics of the bonnets, or excrescences, round their heads. This helped to confirm numbers, and I was able to positively identify twenty-eight whales plus two small yearling calves, one of them an albino, which'd be rare.

Of course I had numerous experiences with sea lions. I was at Northwest Bay on one occasion, sitting in the tussock. It had actually got dark, but for once it was a pleasant evening, and I was listening to the whales bellowing and blowing close inshore, and could see them in the moonlight, when I heard this sea lion toddling along. It sniffed me and then carried on, but shortly afterwards returned and decided that I was the only bed-mate for the night. So it snuggled down beside me and went to sleep! But I won't tell you what it did in my gumboots![14]

King penguins, which breed on many islands round the subantarctic, sometimes reach the Auckland, Antipodes, and Campbell Islands as stragglers from Macquarie Island. This sub-adult bird, which has not yet acquired its vibrant orange neck colouring, has reached Tucker Cove on Campbell Island, and will stay ashore until it has finished moulting.

This incident seemed an extreme example of Ramari Stewart's facility to get involved in her subject!

Hooker's sea lion behaviour tends to be different on Campbell Island. There are no harems, a high number of bachelor bulls, and comparatively few cows. The tendency is for pups to be born in secluded places inland, sometimes at heights of from 200 to 500 metres. As the result of a tagging programme, it was noticed that a number of the pups born at Northwest Bay were being brought over Col Ridge by their mothers, to learn to swim in the safety of Perseverance Harbour. The hostel held no fears, and sea lions would even try to open doors. Once a young bull smashed a window and climbed inside. Ramari Stewart remembers:

> We had one cow determined to pup under the building somewhere, and eventually near Christmas she actually had her pup under the kitchen section of the hostel. After ten days she left for the first time, and this presented a problem because she was able to slip back under the building, but the large bulls that congregated around couldn't — so people had to run the gauntlet coming and going.
>
> When the pup was about ten weeks old, I noticed that the mother was calling for quite lengthy periods, with no response from her pup. So I checked all the places where he might have fallen down, and some time later found him dead.
>
> The mother called around the hostel for another two and a half weeks. She kept that up day and night. It got on some people's nerves. It was a mournful sound, a little bit like a heifer mooing, and to hear it on the wind — it was really sad.[15]

This story seemed very much to reflect the Campbell Island experience. As Mark Crompton put it,

> Campbell Island has a mystery and a magnetism that gets deeper the more time you spend there. As much as any other place, now, it's just about home. It's like the Outer Hebrides of Scotland must be, or the Shetland Islands. The wildness, the winter storm, and the heavy seas crashing in — it's a romantic's view I suppose, but I'd always go back.[16]

171

16
Scientists Today

These days, apart from the meteorological staff on Campbell Island, scientists have the most frequent contact with New Zealand's subantarctic islands. Sometimes, as in the days of the government steamers, it is still only possible for them to snatch a few hours on land, taking advantage of a rough trip down on a relief or supply vessel to Campbell Island or, in recent years, aboard a naval frigate patrolling the Exclusive Economic Zone; but at times people have managed to spend several days or even weeks ashore, and carry out programmes of more worthwhile duration.

After the considerable impact of scientists during the coastwatching years, particularly in the latter months when the threat of war to the islands had diminished, there was a brief spell of activity, and then a post-war lull in regular contact with the islands set in.

The first expedition after the war, and the first party to stay for more than a day on the Snares, was a combined visit to the group by Robert Cushman Murphy of the American Museum of Natural History, and several New Zealand scientists, including two former Cape Expeditioners — Dr Robert Falla as leader, and Dr Charles Fleming. The party went on Alex Black's ship the *Alert*, and stayed from 24 November until 6 December 1947.

In 1948 Dr Lancelot Richdale, a world authority on the royal albatross and yellow-eyed penguin, camped for more than a month in the old castaway hut on the Snares — now part of the biological station — and in the same year a group of physicists visted the Snares, the Aucklands, and Campbell Island to make magnetic observations.

In 1950, Dr Falla led a privately sponsored expedition to the Antipodes, which included Dr R. K. Dell of the Dominion Museum and E. G. Turbott of the Auckland Institute and Museum. They chartered the *Alert* and were there for six days.

Then came the lull. For Campbell Island it was little more than a slackening of activity, but for other islands it was considerable. The Aucklands had a pause of nine years between the end of the war and the first two expeditions in 1954, while the Snares were not visited again until 1961. The first post-war visits to the Antipodes and Bounty Islands were made by the Oceanographic Institute in 1962.

The Danish research vessel *Galathea*, accompanied by the ubiquitous Dr Falla and John Moreland of the National Museum, visited Campbell Island in 1951 to collect specimens of marine mammals and birds. In 1958 Dr Alfred

Martin Cawthorn, expert on the Hooker's sea lion, rarest of the world's five species, weighs a narcoticised bull animal on a special portable machine he has developed and patented. *Photo: Simon Mitchell.*

One of the many colonies of Snares crested penguins, in a typically muddy clearing in the *Olearia* forest, on the Snares. The pole is part of a study programme being carried out by the University of Canterbury.

Bailey of the Denver Museum of Natural History was on Campbell Island for six weeks, accompanied by New Zealander Dr Kaj Westerskov of the Wildlife Service, to make a collection of flora and fauna. The results of this expedition were published in Bailey's *Subantarctic Campbell Island*, co-authored with J. H. Sorensen.

The next expedition to Campbell was in 1961 when a party of zoologists and botanists, led by Dr Eric Godley, spent a month studying the problem of the island's feral sheep. Their recommendation, as an alternative to exterminating the sheep, was that a fenceline be built to divide the island, and that the sheep be shot out from one side. Rowley Taylor of the Ecology Division, Department of Scientific and Industrial Research (DSIR), and Brian Bell of the Wildlife Service spent three weeks on the island in 1969, and found that sheep numbers had increased by two thousand. A swift decision was made to build the suggested fenceline, and this was done in 1970.

Other expeditions to Campbell Island — and this does not set out to be an exhaustive list of expeditions — included a Wildlife Service expedition the following summer, led by Don Merton, and a major expedition in 1975–76.

The 1975–76 Campbell Island Expedition covered a wide range of sciences, and it is important to go into some detail on the people and work involved in this and other expeditions, to illustrate the scope and thoroughness of scientific research on New Zealand's subantarctic islands. Norm Judd, a ranger from the Department of Lands and Survey and the expedition's leader, had a particular interest in the island's historical sites. Among the other nineteen members were Iain Campbell of the Soil Bureau, DSIR, who investigated the nature of the peat soil and problems of erosion; Dr David Given of the Botany Division, DSIR; Colin Meurk, at that time from the University of Otago, who studied the flora, and plant ecology; Dr Frank Climo of the National Museum, who studied land snails and the intertidal zone; Peter Johns, of the University of Canterbury, whose interest was flies and carabid beetles; C. J. R. Robertson and Dr Gerald van Tets, who together observed albatrosses, mollymawks, and the Campbell Island shag; and Dr Peter Wilson, of the Ecology Division, DSIR, and W. R. Regnault, of Massey University, who studied the condition of the feral sheep.

The frigate HMNZS *Canterbury* anchored off the basalt cliffs at the south-west end of Enderby Island. The Navy accommodates scientists when it can, on its visits to the islands during regular fisheries patrols.

The Auckland Islands, as the largest and most diverse group, has had many expeditions since 1954, when the DSIR and the Dominion Museum mounted two visits, followed by others in 1962 and 1966. The New Zealand Oceanographic Institute also made several visits, in 1963, 1964, and 1973.

The fifteen scientists on the 1962 expedition, led by Dr Falla, included Dr Eric Godley of the Botany Division, DSIR; Professor George Knox and Peter Johns of the University of Canterbury; Dr Linsley Gressit from Bishop Museum, Hawaii; Dr John Yaldwyn, then a marine biologist at the Australian Museum and now Director of the National Museum in Wellington; marine biologist J. M. Moreland; and Brian Bell of the Wildlife Service.

The 1966 Auckland Islands Expedition, again of fifteen scientists, was divided into two parties, the northern party being led by Dr Falla and the southern, to Adams Island, by Dr Godley.

At Port Ross, Dr Brian Fineran of the University of Canterbury studied the distribution of *Olearia lyallii*, a plant which has led to a good deal of present day controversy over its potential to spread and alter the environment, and Rowley Taylor continued his work on the effect of introduced mammals on the island's ecology.

The Adams Island group included three entomologists, Dr G. ("Willie") Kuschel, Peter Johns and Keith Wise, and John Kendrick of the Wildlife Service, who filmed and made, with Peter Morrison, the 16 mm documentary film *Adams Island*. A rare Auckland Island rail was captured and taken back to Mount Bruce, near Masterton, for study. The island impressed the expedition members. Eric Godley wrote in his diary for 26 January:

> Brian [Bell] and I kept to the high ground and came upon a garden of *Pleurophyllum speciosum* in full flower. A breath-taking sight, the plants so numerous that it was impossible to avoid treading upon them. We sat down to look about us and a Sooty Albatross glided out of the mist and alighted within arm's reach to keep us company. Further east the weather on the tops cleared for a time, but the mist descended again and we lost our way. However we found a rock bivouac about 4.30 p.m. and got into our sleeping bags to pass the night. Dinner of chocolate and biscuits.[1]

The 1972–73 Auckland Islands Expedition was another important scientific milestone. The leader was Brian Bell, and the expedition's ships were Alex

A mother right whale and albino calf at Northwest Bay, Campbell Island. Although uncommon, albino animals have been recorded with this species in the past. The characteristic excrescences, or "bonnets", of right whales can be seen on the animals' heads. *Photo: Ramari Stewart, Fisheries Research Division.*

In 1887, the survivors of the *Derry Castle* built a punt, to get from Enderby Island to the castaway depot at Erebus Cove. Later, a government steamer transferred the punt to a new boatshed on Rose Island, against the slim chance of people being marooned there. By 1973 the boatshed had collapsed, and the RV *Acheron* helped in the tricky task of transferring the punt, balanced on a dinghy, back to the boatshed at Erebus Cove, where it is still. *Photo: Department of Lands & Survey.*

Black's *Acheron* and the nine and a half metre Wellington ketch *St Michael*.

The expedition was organised into overlapping groups, and its total complement of twenty-eight exceeded the Philosophical Institute of Canterbury's twenty-two man expedition of 1907. The purpose was to establish a base knowledge of the general ecology of the Auckland Islands as a reference for future research and management, in view of the growing interest of the area for tourism, mineral prospecting, and fisheries. Among those taking part were Dr Mike Rudge and D. J. Campbell of the Ecology Division, DSIR, who carried out research into the range and effect of feral goats; C. J. R. Robertson of the Wildlife Service and Rowley Taylor of the Ecology Division; Dr Chris Challies, who studied the impact of pigs on the vegetation of the main island; Dr Gerald van Tets of the Commonwealth Scientific and Industrial Research Organisation, Australia, and Dr Milton Weller of Iowa State University, who observed respectively Auckland Island shags and flightless teal; and Canterbury University's husband and wife team Dr Don Horning and Carol Horning, who studied insects and invertebrates. As usual, collections were made of flora and fauna for a large number of scientists and institutions back in New Zealand, and the results of the expedition were published in a substantial volume, *The Preliminary Results of the Auckland Islands Expedition, 1972–73*, edited by Dr John Yaldwyn of the National Museum for the Department of Lands and Survey.

The Snares Islands experienced a long spell of thirteen years between the last post-war expedition of 1948 and the first of what was to become an almost biennial series of expeditions from the Zoology Department of the University of Canterbury, in 1961.

In that year a party of four, led by Dr John Warham, built the biological station on the nucleus of the old castaway depot and studied sooty shearwaters and invertebrates. A team of six stayed for a month in 1967, and another party of six, with four staying the whole period, was on the Snares for more than three months from 14 November 1968 to 25 February 1969. Don and Carol Horning spent thirteen months on the island from November 1971 to November 1972, carrying out biological observations and research. Canterbury University, under the guidance of Dr Warham and his associate Peter Johns, has continued its close interest in the Snares up to the present time.

An interested sea lion watches University of Canterbury entomologist Peter Johns searching for wingless kelp flies on the shore of De la Vire Point, on the northern side of Perseverance Harbour.

The first substantial scientific expedition to the Antipodes was there from 28 January to 10 March 1969. The expedition, which had first called at Campbell Island, was organised and led by Dr John Warham, and it studied the island's plants, marine and land invertebrates, birds, mammals, and evidence of past human contact. The expedition included Brian Bell of the Wildlife Service, ecologist Rowley Taylor, entomologists Dr Guillermo ("Willie") Kuschel and Peter Johns, marine biologist Ian Mannering, and botanist Dr Eric Godley.

The Bounty Islands, which had been visited only briefly in passing, had to wait until 1978 for their first major expedition, which included the first party to camp on the group for ninety-eight years.

From 7–20 November, a three-man team of Chris Robertson, Dr Don Horning, and Dr Gerald van Tets, who were members of the 1978 BAAS Expedition aboard HMNZS *Waikato*, camped on barren Proclamation Island,

Huts used by the Fisheries Research Division of the Ministry of Agriculture and Fisheries, at the western end of Sandy Bay, on Enderby Island.

to study the ecology and behavioural patterns of the birds breeding there, and to report on visiting birds such as giant petrels, gulls, and starlings. Underwater collections of marine plants and invertebrates were also made. During the expedition a photographic survey was carried out by Rowley Taylor and John Newton in the *Waikato*'s helicopter and also in an RNZAF Orion, to record, from the air, the numbers and distribution of birds and seals.

BAAS stood for the Bounty, Antipodes, Auckland, and Snares Expedition, and most of the expedition's time was spent on the first two groups. The new Lands and Survey hut was built alongside the old castaway depot on the Antipodes, and a television crew (Neil Harraway, Bob Brown, and Errol Samuelson from the Natural History Unit at Dunedin) filmed the documentary *Island of Strange Noises* for the "Wild South" series. Also on the expedition were Brian Bell, Dr Phil Moors, Mike Imber, and John Kendrick of the Wildlife Service, photographer and medical officer Dr Mike Soper, Rowley Taylor of the DSIR, and Dr Cameron Hay of the Oceanographic Institute. It was on the *Waikato*'s second circuit to pick up the parties ashore that Sir Robert Falla made his last visit to the subantarctic.

Short of being parachuted in, scientists have always used considerable initiative in getting down to the subantarctic. The ability to cook can land a year at Campbell Island! Dr Alan Baker of the National Museum was a crew member on the *Acheron* on the 1972–73 Auckland Islands Expedition, and was able to make shoreline collections at Ranui Cove and at the Snares. But one of the most determined researchers must be Martin Cawthorn, the acknowledged authority on the Hooker's sea lion. He has been studying the

Sandy Bay colony since 1975, concentrating on the breeding season, which covers the period from November or early December through the Christmas–New Year holidays into January — a difficult time for a family man, although some years ago his wife Francis was able to accompany him. He recalls on one occasion being engrossed in making notes on the sea lions crowded on the beach when she put a hand on his knee and said, "That was nice." Surprised, he asked, "What was nice?" and turned to see an enormous sea lion bull, which had been sniffing the back of her neck, looking down at them! They sat quite still and, curiosity satisfied, it ambled off.

Martin Cawthorn usually travels down on one ship and returns on another, whether it is a naval frigate, a fishing boat, the *Acheron* while it was so active in the subantarctic, the fisheries research ship *James Cook*, or a luxury tourist liner like the *Lindblad Explorer* — with lectures aboard paying for the trip. He has been down every summer except the 1982–83 season, when there was no transport. However, that year he was able to take advantage of an April visit aboard HMNZS *Otago*.

A Snares crested penguin.

The Navy's hydrographic research ship HMNZS *Monowai* has also helped scientists on several occasions, linking their requirements with its own tasks. In 1980 it enabled an expedition to be dropped off at the northern end of the Auckland Islands so that John Newton and Paul Dingwall of the Department of Lands and Survey could examine the feasibility of a ranger's house being built at Port Ross and other management options. DSIR botanist Dr Colin Meurk, geologist Dr Chris Adams, and Dr Murray Williams, Duncan Cunningham, and Ray Pierce of the Wildlife Service were with them, the last three studying flightless teal and the mice and coastal birds on Enderby Island.

In 1982 the *Monowai* left two groups of scientists and Lands and Survey staff at Port Ross and Carnley Harbour; the groups were later picked up by HMNZS *Tui*. Archaeological sites were mapped at Port Ross, and the four geologists at Carnley Harbour, Dr Chris Adams and Dr John Gamble, Dr Ian Turnbull and Duncan Ritchie, investigated the Carnley caldera.

HMNZS *Otago*, on fisheries patrol in 1983, dropped off parties of scientists on the Campbell and Auckland Islands on its first circuit, and picked them up again on its second round some nine days later. Dr Peter Wilson, son of Cape Expeditioner R. F. Wilson, continued his study of the sheep on Campbell Island, while the others, led by Martin Cawthorn, went to the Aucklands: Dr Murray Williams and a party from the Wildlife Service to observe the nocturnal behaviour of the Auckland Island teal, *Anas aucklandica aucklandica*, by attaching small radio transmitters to them; Martin Cawthorn to study sea lions and Dr Talbot Murray to collect the small, white-footed marine paua on Enderby Island; Dr Mike Rudge and John Campbell of the Ecology Division, DSIR, to continue their investigations into the effect of goats on vegetation and the environment; and Martin Foggo, of the Central Institute of Technology, to take soil samples from a wide range of sites.

At the end of 1983, the National Film Unit chartered the *Acheron* for its first season of filming in the subantarctic for the documentary *Beyond the Roaring Forties*, a co-production with the Department of Lands and Survey. The *Acheron*, skippered by Alex and Colleen Black, sailed from Dunedin on 29 December for the Snares, the Aucklands, and Campbell Island. The film crew had Peter Johns of Canterbury University and Ron Nilssen of the Wildlife Service as their advisers, and Alex Black's intimate knowledge of the inshore waters and seamanship enabled superb footage to be filmed from the sea, sometimes within metres of the shore, as well as underwater sequences on the wrecks of the *Dundonald* and what was thought to be the *General Grant* but may in fact prove to be the *Anjou*.

The film crew returned to Bluff on HMNZS *Canterbury*, failing to film the boarding of trawlers by the Navy due to heavy sea mist, and sailed again with the *Acheron* on the 14th, for the Snares, Aucklands, and Campbell Island, this

The Wasp helicopter from the Navy's hydrographic research vessel HMNZS *Monowai* about to touch down on the summit of Beeman Hill.

time with Hugh Best of the Wildlife Service as adviser. The film crew finally returned from Campbell Island on the *Lindblad Explorer*, and reached Bluff on 29 February.

The following summer, the National Film Unit visited all New Zealand's subantarctic islands on HMNZS *Monowai*, under the command of Commander Ken Robertson, with myself as expedition leader, on a major hydrographic, surveying, filming, and scientific expedition. Lands and Survey and naval staff achieved the hydrographic and land information necessary for the precise charting of the islands for the first time, with the exception of the Snares, which had been charted by the *Monowai* in 1981, and was thus able to delineate the exact limits of New Zealand's Territorial and Exclusive Economic Zone.

The Department of Lands and Survey's objective was to establish ground control points, and with the aid of full aerial photographic coverage enable modern, accurate topographical maps to be prepared for the Campbell, Auckland, Bounty, and Antipodes Islands. Deputy expedition leader and senior surveyor Ron Keen's instructions were to carry out as much of the survey work as the region's notorious weather would allow. Good conditions and planning, and the close co-operation of naval staff, enabled all requirements to be completed satisfactorily, which was certainly more than anyone had expected. On the Aucklands, Allan Eden's triangulation of 1944 was used as the basis for establishing additional control points. On Campbell Island only a few of the original stations could be found, and mapping was virtually done from scratch, as it was on the Antipodes. The Bounties were correctly surveyed for the first time.

The very reasonable weather also enabled the Film Unit to complete its work for *Beyond the Roaring Forties*, with valuable additional footage. The Wasp helicopter was used to land the crew ashore, sometimes in marginal

Ecologist Rowley Taylor of the Ecology Division, DSIR, disentangles an Antipodes red-crowned parakeet from his net. Note the blood on his finger! Antipodes red-crowned and green parakeets were taken back to mainland New Zealand to supplement the captive breeding stock at Mount Bruce, near Masterton.

conditions, and for aerial photography. Fifteen scientists accompanied the expedition, and only highlights of their full programme can be given here.

Ecologists Rowley Taylor and Dr Richard Sadleir found seven fur seal pups on the Antipodes, first confirmation that breeding is once more taking place there, 140 years after the fur seal population was wiped out by the early sealers, and thirty years after seals started to return as occasional visitors. One male and four female Antipodes Island green parakeets were captured to supplement the captive breeding stock at the National Wildlife Centre at Mount Bruce.

More than one hundred soil samples, numerous plants, and vegetation and environmental data were taken at differing latitudes and altitudes by Dr Colin Meurk and Martin Foggo, and their work will add considerably to the now extensive botanical knowledge of the subantarctic islands. Lichens and algae were collected at the Bounty Islands. "Grab-bag botany on the fast trot" is not easy, especially when "wading through eye-high Draco",[2] and Colin Meurk can be sympathised with for what he did *not* have time to find when he records that "I snatched at a sedgy tuft as I clambered aboard the helicopter in the middle of Auckland Island to later confirm a new record of *Lepidosperma australe*."[3]

Marine scientist Dr Cameron Hay of the Oceanographic Institute, Department of Scientific and Industrial Research, sorts out specimens after a dive at Anchorage Bay on the Antipodes.

The Wildlife Service was represented by Brian Bell, Chris Robertson, and Dr Murray Williams. Attempts were made to capture three female Campbell Island teal on Dent Island, with the help of some of the ship's crew, but in spite of intensive efforts over the steep, tussock-covered terrain, the mission was unsuccessful. The Antipodes were assessed for possible teal liberation sites, but because of the lack of running streams were not considered appropriate. Chris Robertson made extensive aerial photographic surveys of albatross, mollymawk, and penguin colonies to compare with previous records, took detailed notes of birds sighted at sea, and continued his work on the darker wandering albatross of the Antipodes. New Zealanders have always been prominent in studying the great albatrosses. Dr Lance Richdale's pioneer research into royal albatrosses between 1938 and 1952 was followed by that of J. H. Sorensen and Professor Kaj Westerskov.

Dr Kim Westerskov, Kaj's son, was able to dive at all islands except the Snares on the *Monowai* expedition, and to make valuable marine collections for Auckland University and the National Museum. Dr John Yaldwyn of the Museum also made collections of seaweeds, as well as ground litter samples of ferns from the Antipodes, and Dr Cameron Hay carried out comprehensive intertidal collections at the Antipodes and Bounties. These efforts did much to fill a substantial gap in the knowledge of subantarctic shorelines.

Dr Murray Gregory of the University of Auckland was able to assess the oil-spill sensitivity of the islands. He found plastic containers and other litter, such as ship refuse, cordage, and floats, to some degree on all shores visited — an indication that there can now be nowhere in the world free of such unwelcome signs of civilisation.

Dr Chris Adams extended previous work carried out on Campbell Island and the Aucklands, and made important new finds on the Bounties and

The *Acheron*

The research vessel *Acheron* at the wreck site of the *General Grant*, or possibly the *Anjou*, during diving and underwater filming of the wreck for the National Film Unit documentary *Beyond The Roaring Forties*. The RV *Acheron*, of twenty-three metres and eighty-seven tonnes, was built at Port Chalmers in 1971, and was owned and skippered by Alex and Colleen Black from then until its sale in 1985.

Alex Black began his long association with the subantarctic with the MV *Alert*, when he took R. A. Falla and an expedition to the Snares in 1947. The *Alert* was sold several expeditions and twelve years later.

One of *Acheron*'s first major tasks was to support and service the Auckland Islands Expedition of 1972–73, and the Blacks' knowledge of the islands and skill at manoeuvring close inshore made the *Acheron* ideal for scientific, diving, and exploring expeditions, from Campbell Island and the Aucklands and Antipodes to the Great Barrier Reef and the Coral Sea.

Antipodes, which have already been discussed, while geomorphologists Paul Dingwall of the Department of Lands and Survey and Dr Ian Owens of Canterbury University mapped glacial landforms on the Auckland Islands, and the series of massive landslides on Campbell Island. An ongoing survey of the earth's magnetic and gravity fields continued while the *Monowai* was at sea.

Whether large or small, such expeditions have added to what is now a very detailed knowledge of these subantarctic islands, which provide us not only with magnificent natural laboratories for ecological studies, but also with a better understanding of the wider problems of people's impact on the environment, and in turn the information we need to protect that environment from ourselves.

PART FOUR

Towards the Future

Crayfish boat off the stark islands of the Western Chain, at the Snares.

17
Options for the Future

The Canadian photographer, writer, and naturalist Fred Bruemmer, visiting the Auckland Islands in 1980, was strongly impressed with their beauty, wealth of wildlife, and isolation. With experience, amounting to many years, of numerous arctic and subarctic islands off Alaska, Canada, Greenland, and northern Europe, he was able to make some rather surprising comparisons with New Zealand's subantarctic.

The islands of the north tend to be bleaker, and their wildlife shyer and more dispersed, and there are vast regions devoid of people, yet Bruemmer considered these northern islands to be generally more accessible than the islands of the Southern Ocean. Scientific interest in the Canadian Arctic alone is intense. In the summer of 1980, eighty-six field parties from universities and government departments were working on Canada's high arctic mainland and arctic islands; in 1985, the number had risen to 268.[1] At present, despite the presence of oil in neighbouring Alaska, mineral exploration and the exploitation of the Arctic's resources remains in its infancy, but the situation could change rapidly. Relating his experience to the Auckland Islands, Bruemmer concludes,

> the very isolation of the Auckland Islands is perhaps their best protection. But the arctic islands, too, were extremely isolated and little known until about 30 years ago. Change, unfortunately, came in a rush and commercial exploration and exploitation often preceded detailed scientific studies. This resulted in a considerable amount of destruction and a lot of *ad hoc* legislation to deal with acute problems in certain areas. What was painfully missing, was a scientifically based management plan for the entire region.[2]

Most New Zealand scientists familiar with the subantarctic have sounded similar warnings of future pressures — political pressures, competition from commercial fisheries, the impact of tourism, pressure for oil and mineral exploitation in the Great South Basin, and threats to the environment.

Sandy Bartle, Curator of Birds at the National Museum, is one of the few New Zealanders to have worked at France's Kerguelen Islands. He was there

A catch of barracouta on a Korean trawler. The main commercial catches of the Southern Ocean are orange roughy, squid — caught by trawl or line — southern blue whiting, mackerel, wharehou, barracouta, sharks, oreo dory, and blue cod. *Photo: Chris Thomas.*

A bellbird in full song by the shore, on Rose Island, at Port Ross.

in 1981 and 1985. Although there is still only a small wharf and lighters have to be used, foreign trawlers anchor off Port aux Français, and there are 120 people at the substantial scientific and meteorological base during the summer, and seventy in winter. Prospecting has been carried on round the marine shelf, and there are at least moderate indications of oil. There has already been an oil spill caused by the recent wreck of a small tanker. The large main island has introduced cats, rats, and mink, which have swum to the surrounding islands, and sheep and rabbits. Although there are still burrowing petrels on the barren rock above 300 metres and the vegetation zone, Bartle considers much of the main island environmentally "devastated".

Macquarie Island is another environmental disaster and example of massive modification. It has been subjected to introduced rats, cats, mice, dogs (which have since died out), wekas, which with the cats are thought to be mainly responsible for the extinction of the Macquarie Island parakeet, and rabbits, which have stunted vegetation and caused severe erosion.

Nearer home, the Auckland Islands came under extreme pressure in 1981 for the construction of a land-based communications facility as part of oil exploration in the Great South Basin, an oil prospecting concession on the Campbell Plateau. Equipment, including a mast, as well as a generator shed and living accommodation, were in fact ready to leave New Zealand when the oil companies concerned withdrew and the crisis was averted. The Department of Lands and Survey was closely involved, and well aware of the inherent dangers. Today, it is just as aware of conflicts with the environment in other countries, and of New Zealand's mistakes with its own subantarctic islands in the past.

In its present administration of these islands, the Department draws considerably on the help and recommendations of its Outlying Islands Reserves Committee, of which several of the leading subantarctic scientists are, or have been, members. Research and precise knowledge are essential to good management decisions, which must also be based on the specific requirements of the different island groups.

The story of the wild sheep on Campbell Island is a good example of the need for care and long-term study before making what might have seemed a clear-cut management decision. When the number of sheep was found to have increased between 1961 and 1969, concern was expressed about their effect on nesting albatrosses and native vegetation, until it was found that in

A Japanese trawler just north of the Auckland Islands. Foreign vessels fishing in New Zealand's Exclusive Economic Zone are granted licences and quotas, and work under strictly regulated conditions.

the same eight years the number of breeding albatrosses had actually doubled. It was then argued that grazing could be beneficial to the birds. However, damage to the island's flora was undeniable, and so the fenceline dividing the island in half was built in 1970 and the sheep shot out to the north. Had the sheep been completely eliminated, there would have been no chance for a later study of the interaction between sheep, albatrosses, and vegetation, or of maintaining a stock of what could still prove genetically valuable sheep. Observations have in fact revealed that the elimination of the sheep has made very little difference to the nesting or distribution of royal albatrosses on the island, and this made the decision to restrict the sheep to a quarter of the island much easier. The policy is now to maintain the present population of about 400 ewes, continue research upon them, and review the situation in five years time.

A careful watch is also being kept on the status of *Olearia lyallii*, thought to have been introduced to the Auckland Islands at the time of the Enderby Settlement. Some scientists thought it might spread to dominate the coastal vegetation of Port Ross and replace the southern rata. However, further research has suggested that so far it has only colonised previously disturbed sites and is not in competition with the rata. For this reason a decision has been made not to mount an expensive eradication programme, but to ensure that *Olearia* does not spread to other islands in Port Ross, or to Adams and Disappointment Islands. With the recent decision to eliminate the cattle and rabbits from Enderby Island, and the subsequent changes this will bring to the island's ecology, a careful watch will be kept on the possible spread of *Olearia* there.

The Antipodes is another group which could support dwarf or low forest, and as *Olearia* seeds are small and numerous, there is a particular danger that they might be unwittingly transported there on the clothing or boots of people going ashore after visiting the Snares or Auckland Islands.

The controversy as to whether introduced animals should be allowed to remain on Rose and Enderby Islands has been a long-standing one, and was finally resolved in 1985 with the decision to remove or exterminate them as soon as possible. Caution has long been advised in taking this step, as modified environments do not necessarily revert to their original state. But the steady replacement of grass sward by native tussock on nearby Rose Island, and the regeneration of megaherbs on Campbell Island, indicate that there is a high chance of success on Enderby.

A crayfishing boat from Stewart Island, moored at Ho Ho Bay, the Snares. Although the number of boats with permits to moor is strictly limited, many conservationists feel that any is too many. Whatever decisions are taken, an element of risk to the environment, and of rats getting ashore, remains.

The recent run of warmer summers and modifications to browsed vegetation may have led to changes in another supposedly stable situation. For many years, introduced goats of potential genetic interest had been confined to a small range at the northern end of the main Auckland Island and allowed to remain there. But as a result of their 1983 visit Dr Mike Rudge and John Campbell had revised their previous observations and noted signs that the goats were beginning to spread south. In 1985 the HMNZS *Monowai* Expedition reported sightings from the helicopter of goats on the Hooker Hills, which indicated further movement southwards, and soon afterwards a recommendation was made to either remove them for research purposes, as they are the southernmost herd of feral goats in the world, or to exterminate them as soon as possible. Rudge and Campbell returned in February 1986, and eleven goats were brought back to the South Island for study purposes. They were found to be larger than any of the goats in New Zealand, and may prove of considerable value as mohair breeding stock. As a result, those remaining on the Auckland Islands have been granted a reprieve until 1990.

In the strict sense, introduced animals have no place in nature reserves, however interesting they may be genetically, but the options are not always straightforward, and many factors have to be considered before decisions are reached.

A rare yellow-eyed penguin, found with a discarded nylon fishing net entangled round its neck, on Enderby Island. *Photo: Martin Cawthorn.*

It is this type of careful judgement based on scientific investigation and advice that has given New Zealand a high international reputation for the successful management of island reserves. But protection is not enough. What is needed, and is being applied, is what was lacking in the sub-Arctic — a scientifically based and positive management plan.

At the time of writing, a management plan has been in operation for Campbell Island Nature Reserve since 1983, for the Snares since 1984, and for the Auckland Islands since 1986. Draft management plans are available for the Antipodes and the Bounty Islands. The management planning process enables scientific and public comment and objections to be made, before plans are finally approved and implemented.

One planning and management issue which raised a storm of protest from many conservationists was the decision to limit rather than ban the mooring of crayfishing boats at the Snares. The conservationists' concern was shared and understood, but it was considered better to gain the support of fishermen rather than alienate them or reach a confrontation which could increase the number of illegal visits and therefore the risk of rats getting ashore. Those fishermen with mooring permits are well aware of the environmental disaster which would occur if this should ever happen. Existing licences will not be transferable and will therefore be gradually phased out.

Further research is needed before the policy to exterminate cats and pigs can be implemented, as the task will be far more difficult than shooting the goats or getting rid of the cattle and rabbits which are on small islands. Removal would have to be complete, and not just a reduction in numbers, as the remaining few would quickly increase to the present balance and be a continuing problem.

There are perhaps fewer than fifty cats on Campbell Island. They tend to keep away from the scrub and buildings, and are confined to localised areas on the open ridges, where there are dry rock caves. Because of the exposed and open nature of Campbell Island they could be eradicated more easily there than on the main Auckland Island.

Rats are a more difficult problem. Graeme Taylor of the Ecology Division of the Department of Scientific and Industrial Research spent a year on Campbell Island, in 1984–85, studying the distribution and feeding habits of the brown rat, *Rattus norvegicus*. While a rat has been known to tunnel up through a nest and disembowel a royal albatross chick, this is apparently

The southern spider crab, found in shallow waters at Port Ross, has excellent meat, but does not occur in sufficient numbers to support a crab fishery, even if such an industry were considered desirable

unusual,[3] and royals have increased in numbers in places such as Faye Ridge, where the rat population is high. Analysis of stomach contents indicates that rats, having killed off almost all ground-burrowing birds, mostly eat insects, larvae, flowers, seeds, and berries. Rats have been eliminated on some small offshore New Zealand islands with anticoagulant bait, but Campbell is a much larger island. Introducing predators such as male stoats, which would die out, is out of the question because of the bird population, and there may be no answer until there is a breakthrough in international research into an ecologically safe method of control.

Research is also continuing into sea lion mortality. The five percent mortality rate of pups suffocated in rabbit burrows was one of the factors leading to the decision to eliminate rabbits from Enderby Island. Sea lions are also in direct competition with trawlers, and they risk getting caught and drowned in the nets. At the height of the squid fishery, which coincides with the latter part of the sea lions' breeding season, this is particularly serious, as each female lost represents three animals — the pregnant mother and the orphaned pup it is still suckling, which will starve to death. The German research vessel *Wesermunde* caught ten sea lions in fifty-one tows in 1979.[4] However, recent research suggests that sea lions may have actually started to learn that trawlers are dangerous and have become more careful in approaching the nets. Research continues, but in the meantime a buffer zone restricting all fisheries and commercial activities within twelve nautical miles has been declared round the Auckland Islands, and similar protective zones will in time be established round the other groups.

This restriction would affect any development of the potential southern spider crab fishery, which was investigated for the shallow waters of the Auckland Islands in 1971. Although stocks were considered too small to support a viable industry, this crab, *Jacquinotia edwardsii*, has excellent eating qualities only slightly inferior to the commercially fished North Pacific king crab, the taking of which has been greatly scaled down by the United States, Russia, and Japan because of the serious depletion of stock. However, there is still a potential fishery for the southern king crab, *Lithodes murrayi*, which is only slightly smaller than the Alaskan and sub-Arctic variety and found at over 200 fathoms on the Campbell Island Rise, Pukaki Rise, and other shallower parts of the Campbell Plateau, well away from the islands.

The seas round the islands are generally unsuitable for inshore fisheries. The closer fish are infested with parasitic worms, and the only sizeable crayfish at the Snares are found in deep water well offshore. Moreover, conditions are treacherous.

In spite of a growing volume of statistics, we still know very little about the resources of the deep water fisheries of the Southern Ocean. Reserves tend to be regarded as limitless, but the experience of inshore fisheries in New Zealand and other parts of the world has shown that too great a pressure can result in a sudden, drastic, and irreversible collapse, with less preferred species moving in to replace exhausted stocks, if indeed they are replaced at all; sometimes, the result is an ecological desert. On the Californian coast, the collapse of the sardine industry in the late 1950s had an immediate adverse effect on the bird population. The same thing happened with the anchovy catch and cormorant colonies off the coast of Peru.

In the open ocean, long-lived species such as orange roughy cannot maintain numbers when subjected to a high catch rate because their replacement rate is slow, whereas squid, with a short life cycle, can replace heavy losses rapidly. Krill is another resource for which there is a growing demand, and with the decline in the number of whales the supply has increased and seems limitless. But nothing in the sea is infinite, and krill holds a vital place in a food chain which ultimately affects all sea birds and marine mammals. The problem is knowing when stocks are in danger, and while fish gutting and filleting at sea has led to an increase in some Northern Hemisphere sea

A Japanese crab fishing boat at the Auckland Islands. A large number of pots was put down here, but the fishery was found to be unprofitable. Vessels are also allowed to take shelter from adverse seas, and some risk to the environment could always accompany such close contacts with the land. *Photo: New Zealand Wildlife Service.*

birds such as fulmars and skuas, the British Nature Conservancy Council's Seabirds at Sea Team, which has done an enormous amount of research in the North Sea, points out that the commercial exploitation of their prey is a major threat to many sea birds, and that the first warnings of a wider disaster may well sound on the ledges of sea bird colonies.

Another commercial pressure already mentioned could be the demand for shore-based facilities for offshore petrochemical or mineral exploration. Manganese nodules and phosphate deposits occur on the sea bed in several areas on the Campbell Plateau, although only in light concentrations. In 1972, seismic surveys for oil were carried out as far south as Campbell Island. The latest of several unsuccessful exploratory holes was drilled 130 nautical miles east-south-east of the Snares in 1983. It is not unlikely that oil will eventually be found and that pipeline terminals and shore-based storage facilities could again be requested, possibly on a much greater scale, involving buildings, roads, shipping, and disposal of refuse and waste, in harbours ideal for bringing pipelines ashore, such as Perseverance, Carnley, and Port Ross. These harbours and their wildlife would be particularly vulnerable to a major ecological disaster through oil pollution.

It is fortunate that in the case of a rig blowout at sea, the subantarctic islands have predominantly high energy shores, which means that vigorous wave action would break up dangerous slicks into tar balls within forty-eight hours. The indication is that most slicks would also degrade within 150 nautical miles, and that they would tend to be carried away from the islands.[5] The Bounties and Antipodes, although lying downwind from possible disaster areas, are so distant that little impact on them is likely.

A Naval officer examines the *Stella* depot on Enderby Island, built in 1880 to house emergency food and supplies for castaways.

A greater public appreciation of the special value of the subantarctic islands is one of the strongest defences against future demands and pressures upon them. Some islands, like the Snares, are so vulnerable that tourists are not allowed ashore, but a very good idea of the islands and their wildlife can be gained from inflatables travelling close to the shore.

Tourism is not new. Fare-paying passengers were often carried on the early government steamers. In recent years, organised "adventure tourism" has become fashionable, with specially equipped ships such as the *World Discoverer* and *Lindblad Explorer* visiting subantarctic islands and the Antarctic Continent, and although there is a lull at the moment, this trend is likely to continue.

Tourists and Hooker's sea lion pups on Enderby Island, during a brief visit, by inflatable dinghies, from a ship moored off Sandy Bay. The pups are naturally curious, but they also have extremely sharp teeth!

Landing on New Zealand's subantarctic islands is by permit only, but because of their isolation a high degree of co-operation and goodwill is still needed; on organised trips there is always a Department of Lands and Survey ranger or representative aboard, to give tourists a fuller appreciation of what they are seeing, as well as a sympathetic attitude towards reserve management. The number of people allowed ashore each year has to be carefully controlled, as the ground is easily damaged because of the wet climate and peat soil, and is slow to recover. Paths could become quagmires, and the right approach and respect has to be taken towards wildlife.

A group from the Royal Forest and Bird Society chartered the *Acheron* to visit the Auckland Islands for six days in December 1983, and an enthusiastic article with excellent photographs appeared in *Forest and Bird* magazine the following May. Fred Bruemmer's visit to Enderby Island in 1980 was also encouraged because of the articles he would later write in such publications as the American magazine *Natural History*. The Television New Zealand film crew which was on the Antipodes in 1978 was there at the same time, to acquire footage for the BBC and for the "Wild South" documentaries *Sealion Summer* and *As It Wasn't in the Beginning* (Enderby Island). The National Film Unit's *Beyond The Roaring Forties* has been sold to a large number of countries.

A wider appreciation of these islands, and an associated degree of access for the general public, as well as for scientists, is extremely important. The extent of protection given to the islands has steadily increased, from Adams Island being made the first flora and fauna reserve in 1910 to all subantarctic islands reaching this status in 1961, and then proceeding to a higher degree of protection as nature reserves with the passing of the Reserves Act in 1978. Among other things, this Act requires detailed management plans to be prepared for the various island groups.

In 1983, the Snares was the first group to be made a National Reserve, and the remaining islands reached this highest degree of protection under New Zealand law in 1986. An Act of Parliament is now needed to change the precise guidelines laid down to safeguard them, with penalties for unauthorised entry, for example, doubled. It is extremely likely that UNESCO may eventually consider the New Zealand subantarctic islands as World Heritage sites, and this would give them international recognition. Even so, the environment is for ever vulnerable, and constant care and vigilance is needed to protect them in the future.

Tourists admire a nesting royal albatross on Campbell Island. The isolation of the islands means that the number of people able to visit them will always be limited, but tourism has a place in increasing public awareness of the rare value of New Zealand's subantarctic islands.

18
A Heritage of Islands

We live in an extraordinary world. The tropical rain forests are being destroyed at the rate of twenty hectares every minute: every year, an area three times the size of Switzerland is lost. Twenty-five thousand of the world's flowering plants are on the verge of extinction.[1] In just under forty years, Britain has lost half its lowland fens, thirty to fifty percent of its ancient woods, and ninety-five percent of its lowland herb meadows.[2] In the Mediterranean countries of Malta, Cyprus, Lebanon, Portugal, Spain, France, and Italy tens into hundreds of millions of migratory birds are killed each year by shooting, netting, and trapping, not for food or the protection of crops, but for sport.[3]

New Zealand has a much greater appreciation of wildlife, and conservation has for years been a powerful emotional and political issue, but it has not always been so in the subantarctic. R. E. Malone of HMS *Fantome*, at Port Ross in 1852, noted briskly, "We had some good pot-shooting here. Toois [sic] were the most numerous . . . two guns have brought down four dozen in a few hours. While there our fellows (the officers) killed 302 toois, 144 wild duck, 12 sea lions, 6 parrots, 2 snipe."[4] Henry Armstrong, J.P., wrote that on the Snares, "the penguins (ludicrous birds) in hundreds drawn up in rank and file, stood to oppose us in our march, and it required not a little vigorous kicking to force our way through them."[5] And while James P. Joyce appreciated the "arrowy swiftness" of sea lions, he saw no reason to continue to protect them, as "they simply occupy and defile considerable areas on the coast that could be utilised for pastoral purposes".[6]

It was not long, fortunately, before values began to change. In 1907 B. C. Aston wrote,

> One realises at every turn that one is in close touch with nature. The tameness of the animals on the shore and waters, the numerous sea and land birds, the creeping life of the woods, the unique plants of the forest and meadow, the enormous cliffs with their successive scores of lava flows . . . and above all the history of the islands rich in stories of . . . shipwreck and disaster, of heroism and endurance rewarded by rescue — these are enough to attract and hold spell bound the naturalist, the artist, the historian or the man [and one should add, the woman!].[7]

Yellow-eyed penguins at Derry Castle reef on Enderby Island. Shy, and much more wary than most species, they are probably the world's rarest penguin.

197

A royal albatross, surrounded by tussock grass and the seed heads of *Bulbinella*, on its solitary nest on Campbell Island, the major breeding ground for this majestic sea bird.

In 1967, Dr Eric Godley cited Adams Island as an example of the New Zealand subantarctic's rare heritage:

> Here one can see the striking endemic plants of the Subantarctic islands in their proper situations, densities and proportions; and observations here help us to understand the kind of changes that have taken place on the main island. Unmolested by cats, the tiny flightless Auckland Island rail still survives on Adams Island, and the Auckland Island snipe is here in abundance. Bellbirds flew into our tents to catch flies and perch on heads and microscopes. This island is a great treasure and all efforts must be made to keep it undisturbed.[8]

His reference to the changes which have taken place on the adjoining main Auckland Island are a reminder of how easily virgin environments can be destroyed, and their original state just as readily forgotten. Of mainland New Zealand, H. Guthrie-Smith wrote in the 1930s that "grass — not flax, toetoe

Left: The yellow flowers of the rare giant herb *Stilbocarpa robusta*, confined to the Snares and a few small islands off Stewart Island. Beyond it are the broad-leaved grass *Carex trifida*, and *Hebe elliptica*.

Below: Hooker's sea lions, rarest of the world's sea lions, among the stunted trees on Figure-of-Eight Island, their main breeding colony in the south of the Aucklands.

A sleek female Hooker's sea lion comes ashore on the rocky northern coast of Enderby Island.

and rush — began to seem the natural covering of the land",[9] and Colin Meurk noted in 1983 that

> generations of New Zealand scientists have become used to the modified vegetation on the subantarctic islands, just as they have on the New Zealand mainland. Deer have been in our forests so long that to most hunters, trampers and even many ecologists the emasculated eaten out understorey is the "natural bush" the way it always was. Relating this to the subantarctic, the wilderness needs to be preserved in all its oozing balance. It is vital we should always have that infinite remoteness to escape to as the pressures of civilisation increase.[10]

On the subantarctic islands, the few remaining traces of civilisation are, in fact, slowly crumbling away. A few momentos of the past, such as the *Dundonald* survivors' coracle and the sealskin clothing and shoes of ship-wrecked mariners, have been brought back to museums and are of great interest. But space, even for storage, is limited, as are the funds to restore crumbling historic huts and depots; and so, over the years, several structures have fallen into disrepair, until they are now too far gone to save. The Cape Expedition buildings have withstood the climate well, but floors and walls are rotting, and weather and sea lions have found their way in. Soon these buildings will be in their final decline. Efforts to save relics *in situ* are seldom successful: the A-frame shelter over the truncated remains of the *Victoria* tree does nothing for it; the modern headstone for the *Derry Castle* grave lacks the pathos of the original site, which was marked with spars and the weathered figurehead from the ship; and that same figurehead, spick and span with fresh paint in the Canterbury Museum, conveys very little of the disaster, and the wild shore from which it was brought.

As the past fades, the subantarctic islands have in some ways become more remote than ever. They are no longer needed as stepping stones to Antarctica. None of them has an airstrip, and while bases on the Antarctic Continent and most parts of the Arctic can be reached in an emergency within a few hours, the islands' only access remains the sea.

Leonard Cockayne predicted in 1907 that as the primitive world became smaller and smaller, the subantarctic islands would be prized beyond present belief.[11] Yet they remain little known, seldom visited, "the homes of such seabirds as love the storm".[12] Protected by the Southern Ocean, diverse, wonderful, and lonely, they possess some of the last few unspoilt environments on Earth.

REFERENCES

Chapter 1   The Elemental Islands
(pages 5 to 11)

1. Musgrave, Thomas. *Castaway on the Auckland Islands*. Wellington, A. H. & A. W. Reed, 1943, p. 72.
2. Warham, John, and Wilson, Graham J. *The Size of the Sooty Shearwater Population at the Snares Islands, New Zealand*. University of Canterbury Snares Islands Expeditions Paper No. 45. Reprinted from *Notornis*, Vol. 29, Part I, March 1982, p. 23.
3. Aston, B. C. Previously unpublished report to Secretary of Agriculture, 7 December 1907, published by E. J. Godley in *The 1907 Expedition to the Auckland and Campbell Islands*. Botany Division, DSIR, Christchurch. Reprinted in *Tuatara*, Vol. 23, No. 3, May 1979, pp. 146–149.
4. Armstrong, Henry. Official Report on Cruise of the Brig *Amherst. New Zealand Government Gazette, Province of Southland*. 11 April 1868, Vol. 6, No. 9, p. 53.

Chapter 2   Specks in the Ocean
(pages 13 to 25)

1. Chilton, C. ed. *The Subantarctic Islands of New Zealand*. Wellington, Philosophical Institute of Canterbury: New Zealand Government Printer, Vol. 2, 1909, p. 455.
2. Wilson, E. A. *Edward Wilson: diary of the Discovery expedition to the Antarctic region 1901–1904*. Ed. Ann Savours. London, Blandford Press, 1966, p. 347.
3. Clifton, L. Official Report of the Cape Expedition. Unpublished typescript. Aerodromes Branch, Public Works Department, Wellington, 24 October 1946, p. 3.
4. Bates, F. A Hundred and Three Days on a Desert Island. *Chambers Journal*, London, 30 January 1892, p. 79.
5. Robertson, C. J. R., New Zealand Wildlife Service, personal comment.
6. *Guiness Book of Records*. London, Guiness Superlatives Ltd., 1973.
7. Robertson, C. J. R., personal comment.
8. ibid.
9. Warham, John. The Incidence, Functions and Ecological Significance of Petrel Stomach Oils. Department of Zoology, University of Canterbury, Christchurch. Reprinted from *Proceedings of the New Zealand Ecological Society*, Vol. 24, 1977, p. 84.
10. Travers, H. H., and Travers, W. T. L. On the Birds of the Chatham Islands. *Transactions and Proceedings of the New Zealand Institute*, 5, 1873, pp. 212–222.
11. Warham, John, and Wilson, Graham, J. *The Size of the Sooty Shearwater Population at the Snares Islands, New Zealand*. University of Canterbury Snares Islands Expeditions Paper No. 45. Reprinted from *Notornis*, Vol. 29, Part I, March 1982, pp. 29–30.
12. Robertson, C. J. R. ed. *Reader's Digest Complete Book of New Zealand Birds*. Sydney, Reader's Digest, 1985, p. 120.
13. Robertson, C. J. R. ed. op cit. p. 122.

14. Falla, R. A. Antarctic Birds. *In*: Simpson, Frank. ed. *The Antarctic Today*. Wellington, A. H. & A. W. Reed, 1952, p. 223.
15. Moors, Philip, New Zealand Wildlife Service, personal comment.
16. Darby, J. Hoiho — World's Rarest Penguin. *Forest and Bird*, May 1985, p. 18.
17. Reischek, A. Notes on the Islands to the South of New Zealand. Read before the Auckland Institute, 30 July 1888. *In: Transactions of the New Zealand Institute*, Vol. 21, p. 388.

Chapter 3   Creatures of the Sea
(pages 27 to 37)

1. Cawthorn, Martin, Fisheries Research Division, Wellington, personal comment.
2. Kerr, Ian S. *Campbell Island: a history*. Wellington, A. H. & A. W. Reed, 1976, pp. 83–84.
3. Cawthorn, Martin, personal comment.
4. Bailey, Alfred, M., and Sorensen, J. H. Subantarctic Campbell Island. Denver Museum of Natural History. Proceedings No. 10, 1 February 1962, pp. 49–50.
5. Mackworth, William. Unpublished diary, 8 September 1950.
6. Sorensen, J. H. *Wild Life in the Subantarctic*. Christchurch, Whitcombe & Tombs, 1951, p. 70.
7. Cawthorn, M. W., Crawley, M. C., Mattlin, R. H., and Wilson, G. J. *Research on Pinnipeds in New Zealand*. Pinniped Research Review Subcommittee, Fisheries Research Division, Wellington, 1985, p. 15.
8. Taylor, R. H. New Zealand Fur Seals at the Bounty Islands. *New Zealand Journal of Marine and Freshwater Research*, Vol. 16, 1982, p. 3.
9. Bailey, A. M., and Sorensen, J. H., op. cit. p. 60, and Management Plan for the Campbell Islands Nature Reserve. Wellington, Department of Lands & Survey, 1983, p. 25.
10. *New Zealand Environment*, No. 40, Environmental Publications Trust, Summer 1983, p. 3.
11. Cawthorn, Martin, personal comment.
12. Wilson, E. A. *Edward Wilson: diary of the Discovery expedition to the Antarctic region 1901–1904*. Ed. Ann Savours. London, Blandford Press, 1966, p. 351.
13. Cawthorn, M. W., *et al.*, op. cit. p. 9.
14. D'Urville, Dumont. *The Voyage of the Astrolabe — 1840; an English rendering of the Journals . . .* Ed. Olive Wright. Wellington, A. H. & A. W. Reed, 1955, pp. 10–11.
15. Sorensen, J. H., op. cit. p. 72.
16. Wilson, E. A., op. cit. p. 349.
17. Grams, Capt. Alfred. *Voyage of the Erlangen*. Diary of Captain of SS *Erlangen*. Bremen, North German Lloyds, 16 July 1967.
18. ibid.

Chapter 4 The Nature of the Subantarctic
(pages 39 to 51)

1. John, Dilwyn. Lecture reprinted in The Second Antarctic Commission of the RRS *Discovery II. The Geographical Journal*, LXXXIII, pp. 381–398. Quoted in Sir George Deacon, The Antarctic Ocean. *Interdisciplinary Science Reviews*, Spectrum House, Vol. 2, No. 2, June 1977, pp. 116–117.
2. Gamberoni, L., Geronimi, J., Jeannin, P. F., and Murail, J. F. Study of Frontal Zones in the Crozet-Kerguelen Region. *Oceanologica Acta*, Vol. 5, No. 3, 1982, p. 289.
3. Meurk, Colin, Botany Division, DSIR, Christchurch, personal comment.
4. Hooker, Joseph. Contributing to Ross, Capt. Sir James Clark. *A Voyage of Discovery and Research in the Southern and Antarctic Regions During the Years 1893–43*. London, John Murray, 1847, Vol. I, p. 144.
5. Cockayne, Leonard. The Southern Islands. Christchurch *Press*, December 1907, p. 7.
6. ibid.
7. ibid.
8. Hooker, J. Contributing to Ross, op. cit. p. 160.
9. Cockayne, Leonard. *New Zealand Plants and Their Story*. 4th ed. Wellington, New Zealand, Government Printer, 1967, p. 176.
10. Hooker, Sir Joseph D. *The Botany of the Antarctic Voyage of H. M. Discovery Ships Erebus and Terror in the Years 1839–43*. Part I, Vol. I, *Flora Antarctica*. London, Reeve, 1844–1860.
11. Meurk, Colin, personal comment.
12. Meurk, Colin. Address on Botany of Subantarctic Islands to personnel on HMNZS *Monowai*, 1985.
13. Meurk, Colin, personal comment.
14. Chapman, F. R. Illustrations from Sub-Antarctic New Zealand. *Otago Witness*, 19 December 1895.
15. Guthrie-Smith, William Herbert. *Sorrows and Joys of a New Zealand Naturalist*. Wellington, A. H. & A. W. Reed, 1936, pp. 229–230.
16. Aston, B. C. Previously unpublished report to Secretary of Agriculture, 7 December 1907, published by E. J. Godley in *The 1907 Expedition to the Auckland and Campbell Islands*. Botany Division, DSIR, Christchurch. Reprinted in *Tuatara*, Vol. 23, No. 3, May 1979, pp. 144–145.
17. McCormick, R. *Voyages of the Discovery in the Arctic and Antarctic Seas, and Round the World*. London, Sampson Low, 1884, p. 132.
18. ibid.
19. Cockayne, Leonard, op. cit. p. 176.
20. McCormick, R., op. cit. p. 132.
21. Hooker, Sir Joseph D., op. cit. *The Botany of the Antarctic Voyage . . .* pp. *vi-vii*.
22. Enderby, Charles. *Description of the Outlying Islands South and East of New Zealand*. London, Hydrographic Office, Admiralty, 1868.
23. Hay, C. H., Adams, N. M., and Parsons, M. J. *Marine Algae of the Subantarctic Islands of New Zealand*. National Museum of New Zealand, Miscellaneous Series No. 11, August 1985, pp. 1–70.

Chapter 5 Origins
(pages 53 to 63)

1. Malone, R. E. *Three Years' Cruise in the Australasian Colonies*. London, Bentley, 1854, p. 68.

2. Raynal, F. E. *Wrecked on a Reef or Twenty Months in the Auckland Isles*. London, Nelson, 1885, p. 202.
3. McNab, Robert. *Murihiku*. Invercargill, William Smith, 1907, p. 188.
4. Adams, C. J., Institute of Nuclear Sciences, DSIR, personal comment.
5. Adams, C. J. Migration of Late Cenozoic Volcanism in the South Island of New Zealand and the Campbell Plateau. *Nature*, Vol. 294, No. 5837, 12 November 1981, pp. 153–155.
6. Cheeseman, T. F. *In*: Chilton, C. ed. *The Subantarctic Islands of New Zealand*. Wellington, Philosophical Institute of Canterbury: New Zealand Government Printer, Vol. II, 1909, pp. 453–471.
7. Wegener, Alfred. *The Origin of Continents and Oceans*. London, Methuen, 1967.
8. Gregory, Murray. *Plastics and Other Seaborne Litter on Subantarctic Island Shores*. Department of Geology, University of Auckland, 1985, p. 5.
9. Darlington, Philip J., Jr. *Biogeography of the Southern End of the World*. Boston, Harvard University Press, 1965, p. 107.
10. Fleming, C. A. Two-Storied Cliffs at the Auckland Islands. Transactions of the Royal Society of New Zealand. *Geology*, Vol. 3, No. 11, 8 December 1965, pp. 171–174.
11. Fleming, C. A. An Outline of the Geology of the Auckland Islands. *In*: Yaldwyn, J. C. ed. *Preliminary Results of the Auckland Islands Expedition 1972–73*. Wellington, Department of Lands and Survey, 1975, pp. 411–415.
12. Fleming, C. A., and Mildenhall, D. C. Quaternary Sediments and Plant Microfossils from Enderby Island, Auckland Islands. *Journal of the Royal Society of New Zealand*, Vol. 6, 1976, pp. 433–458.
13. Management Plan for the Campbell Islands Nature Reserve. Wellington, Department of Lands and Survey, 1983, p. 19.
14. Adams C. J. *Geological Studies on the 1985 Cruise of HMNZS Monowai (i) to Campbell, Auckland and Snares Islands; (ii) to Antipodes and Bounty Islands*. INS-R-300 and INS-R-341, 1985, Institute of Nuclear Sciences, DSIR, Lower Hutt, New Zealand.

Chapter 6 Islands of Contrasts
(pages 65 to 75)

1. Reischek, A. Notes on Islands to the South of New Zealand. Read before the Auckland Institute, 10 July 1888. *In: Transactions of the New Zealand Institute*, Vol. 21, p. 388.
2. Taylor, R. H. Parakeets. *New Zealand's Nature Heritage*, Part 84, 1975.
3. Aston, B. C. Previously unpublished report to Secretary of Agriculture, 7 December 1907, published by E. J. Godley in *The 1907 Expedition to the Auckland and Campbell Islands*. Botany Division, DSIR, Christchurch. Reprinted in *Tuatara*, Vol. 23, No. 3, May 1979, p. 148.
4. Fleming, Sir Charles A., personal comment observed by Sir Robert Falla.
5. Auckland Islands Nature Reserve, Draft Management Plan. Wellington, Department of Lands and Survey, 1985, p. 59.

6. Darlington, Philip J., Jr. *Biogeography of the Southern End of the World.* Boston, Harvard University Press, 1965, pp. 35–37.

7. Wilson, E. A. *Edward Wilson: diary of the Discovery expedition to the Antarctic region 1901–1904.* Ed. Ann Savours. London, Blandford Press, 1966, p. 348.

8. Musgrave, Thomas. *Castaway on the Auckland Islands.* Wellington, A.H. & A. W. Reed, 1943, p. 69.

9. Turbott, Graham, Cape Expeditioner, personal comment.

10. Eden, Allan, W. *Islands of Despair.* London, Andrew Melrose, 1955, p. 49.

Chapter 7 Discovery and Exploitation
(pages 79 to 87)

1. Bligh, William. *A Voyage to the South Sea.* London, George Nicol, 1792, p. 55.

2. Vancouver, George. *A Voyage of Discovery to the North Pacific Ocean and Round the World in the Years 1790–95.* London, G. G. & J. Robinson, 1798.

3. Collins, David. *Account of the English Colony in New South Wales.* London, T. Cadell Jr. and W. Davies, 1798–1802.

4. Bristow, Abraham. Log of the *Ocean,* Enderby & Co. Quoted in Ross, Capt. Sir James Clark. *A Voyage of Discovery and Research in the Southern and Antarctic Regions During the Years 1839–43.* London, John Murray, 1847, Vol. 1, pp. 137–138.

5. McNab, Robert. *Murihiku.* Invercargill, William Smith, 1907, pp. 152–154.

6. *Historical Records of New South Wales.* Vol. 1, p. 273..

7. Furnas, J. C. *Anatomy of Paradise.* London, Gollancz,

8. McNab, Robert, op. cit. p. 224.

9. McNab, Robert, op. cit. pp. 258–259.

10. *Sydney Gazette,* 29 July 1826. Quoted in McNab, Robert, op. cit. pp. 347–348.

11. Morrell, Capt. Benjamin. *A Narrative of Four Voyages, 1822–1831.* New York, Harper, 1832, pp. 363–364.

12. Falla, R. A. Exploitation of Seals, Whales and Penguins in New Zealand. *New Zealand Ecological Society Proceedings,* No. 9, 1962, p. 37.

13. Cumpston, J. S. Sub-Antarctic By-Ways: the history of Macquarie Island. Typescript MS of 1955. The book, published in 1968, does not contain the references to penguin skins referred to on pp. 203–208 of the MS. Cumpston, J. S. *Macquarie Island.* Antarctic Division, Department of External Affairs, Australia, 1968.

Chapter 8 The Antarctic Explorers
(pages 89 to 97)

1. Bellingshausen, Thaddeus. Account of Macquarie Island, translated from German. *In:* McNab, Robert. *Murihiku.* Invercargill, William Smith, 1907, pp. 276–284.

2. Morrell, Capt. Benjamin. *A Narrative of Four Voyages, 1822–1831.* New York, Harper, 1832, p. 360.

3. Morrell, Capt. Benjamin, op. cit. p. 361.
4. Morrell, Capt. Benjamin, op. cit. p. 363.
5. Morrell, Capt. Benjamin, op. cit. p. 361.
6. ibid.
7. Morrell, Capt. Benjamin, op. cit. p. 363.

8. Kerr, I. S. *Campbell Island: a history.* Wellington, A. H. & A. W. Reed, 1976, p. 30.

9. Wilkes, C. *Narrative of the United States Exploring Expedition During the Years 1838, 1839, 1840, 1841, 1842.* London, Ingram, Cooke & Co., Vol. 1, 1852, pp. 282–283.

10. Wilkes, C., op. cit. p. 284.
11. Wilkes, C., op. cit. p. 283.
12. Wilkes, C., op. cit. p. 284.

13. D'Urville, Dumont. *The Voyage of the Astrolabe — 1840; an English rendering of the Journals . . .* Ed. Olive Wright. Wellington, A. H. & A. W. Reed, 1955, p. 6.

14. D'Urville, Dumont, op. cit. p. 8.

15. Ross, Capt. Sir James Clark. *A Voyage of Discovery and Research in the Southern and Antarctic Regions During the Years 1839–43.* London, John Murray, 1847, p. 136.

16. McCormick, R. *Voyages of the Discovery in the Arctic and the Antarctic Seas, and Round the World.* London, Sampson Low, 1884, p. 135.

17. ibid.
18. Ross, Capt. Sir James Clark, op. cit. p. 151.
19. Hooker, J. *In:* Ross, Capt. Sir James Clark, op. cit. p. 159.
20. Ross, Capt. Sir James Clark, op. cit. pp. 139–140.
21. Ross, Capt. Sir James Clark, op. cit. p. 140.
22. Hooker, J. *In:* Ross, Capt. Sir James Clark, op. cit. p. 144.
23. Hooker, J. *In:* Ross, Capt. Sir James Clark, op. cit. p. 147.

Chapter 9 The Enderby Settlement
(pages 99 to 107)

1. Enderby, Charles. *The Auckland Islands: a short account of their climate, soils, and productions; and the advantages of establishing there a settlement at Port Ross for carrying on the southern whale fisheries.* London, Pelham Richardson, 1849. Quoting Sir James Clark Ross, p. 51.

2. Enderby, Charles, op. cit. p. 26.
3. Enderby, Charles, op. cit. p. 41.
4. Enderby, Charles, op. cit. pp. 37–38.
5. Enderby, Charles, op. cit. pp. 18–19.

6. Mackworth, William. Unpublished private diary. Entry of 14 October 1850.

7. Mackworth, William, op. cit. Entry of 27 October 1850.
8. Mackworth, William, op. cit. Entry of 28 May 1851.

9. Bishop Selwyn to Dean of Ely, 1851. Quoted in McLaren, Fergus. *The Eventful Story of the Auckland Islands.* Wellington, A. H. & A. W. Reed, 1948, p. 59.

10. Mackworth, William, op. cit. Entry of 13 May 1851.
11. ibid.
12. Mackworth, William, op. cit. Entry of 14 June 1851.
13. Mackworth, William, op. cit. Entry of 25 February 1851.
14. Mackworth, William, op. cit. Entry of 7 February 1851.
15. Mackworth, William, op. cit. Entry of 25 February 1852.

16. Malone. R. E. *Three Years' Cruise in the Australasian Colonies.* London, Bentley, 1854, p. 63.

17. Malone, R. E., op. cit. p. 64.
18. Malone, R. E., op. cit. p. 69.
19. ibid.
20. Mackworth, William, op. cit. Entry of 4 August 1852.
21. Malone, R. E., op. cit. p. 77.
22. Mackworth, William, op. cit. Entry of 12 February 1850.
23. Mackworth, William, op. cit. Entry of 24 August 1850.
24. Mackworth, William, op. cit. Entry of 7 July 1851.

25. Mackworth, William, op. cit. Entry of 29 May 1852.
26. Ross, Capt. Sir James Clark. *A Voyage of Discovery and Research in the Southern and Antarctic Regions During the Years 1839–43*. London, John Murray, 1847, p. 134.

Chapter 10 The Shipwreck Era
(pages 109 to 121)

1. Raynal, F. E. *Wrecked on a Reef or Twenty Months in the Auckland Isles*. London, Nelson, 1885, p. 64.
2. Musgrave, Thomas. *Castaway on the Auckland Islands*. Wellington, A.H. & A.W. Reed, 1943, p. 35.
3. Letter from Commissioner of Trade and Customs, Melbourne, of 3 October 1865, to Capt. Thomas Musgrave. *In*: Norman, W. H., and Musgrave, T. *Journals of the Voyage and Proceedings of H.M.C.S. Victoria in Search of Shipwrecked People at the Auckland and Other Islands*. Melbourne, Victoria Government Printer, 1866, p. 5.
4. Eunson, K. *The Wreck of the General Grant*. Wellington, A.H. & A.W. Reed, 1974, p. 61.
5. Eunson, K., op. cit. p. 79.
6. Armstrong, Henry. Cruise of the Brig *Amherst*. *New Zealand Government Gazette, Province of Southland*, Vol. 6, No. 9, 11 April 1868, p. 52.
7. Armstrong, Henry, op. cit. p. 56.
8. ibid.
9. ibid.
10. Escott-Inman, H. *The Castaways of Disappointment Island*. London, Partridge, 1911, p. 56.
11. McLaughlin, D., 2nd Mate of the *Dundonald*. *New Zealand Times*, 7 December 1907.

Chapter 11 Farming and Whaling
(pages 123 to 129)

1. Armstrong, Henry. Cruise of the Brig *Amherst*. *New Zealand Government Gazette, Province of Southland*, Vol. 6, No. 9, 11 April 1868, p. 54.
2. Chilton, C. ed. The Subantarctic Islands of New Zealand. Wellington, Philosophical Institute of Canterbury: New Zealand Government Printer, Vol. II, 1909, p. 599.
3. Monkton, F. A. Manuscript No. 429, Folder No. 6, Alexander Turnbull Library, Wellington.
4. *Illustrated London News*, 24 December 1887, p. 749.
5. Carrick, Robert. New Zealand's Lonely Lands. A Report for Department of Lands and Survey, New Zealand Government Printer, 1892. Enclosed Report of John Hay, District Surveyor, Province of Southland.
6. Joyce, James P. Report on Auckland, Campbell and Other Islands to the Hon. the Minister of Marine, Invercargill, 28 May 1894.
7. ibid.
8. Records of District Lands and Survey Office, Invercargill, 31 January 1895.
9. Letter from Moffett and Sons to the Minister of Marine, Invercargill, 27 June 1896. File M2/6/1, National Archives, Wellington.
10. Kerr, I. S. *Campbell Island: a history*. Wellington, A.H. & A.W. Reed, 1976, p. 74.
11. Kerr, I. S., op. cit. p. 89.
12. *Otago Daily Times*, 4 August 1931.

Chapter 12 People and Change
(pages 131 to 139)

1. Foggo, M. N., and Meurk, Colin D. Notes on a Visit to Jacquemart Island in the Campbell Island Group. *New Zealand Journal of Ecology*, Vol. 4, 1981, pp. 29–32..
2. Joyce, James P. Report on Auckland, Campbell and Other Islands to the Hon. the Minister of Marine, Invercargill, 28 May 1894, p. 2.
3. *Southland Times*, 3 July 1933, p. 175.
4. Armstrong, Henry, Cruise of the Brig *Amherst*. *New Zealand Government Gazette, Province of Southland*. Vol. 6, No. 9, 11 April 1868, pp. 51–52.
5. Armstrong, Henry, op. cit. p. 55.
6. Boyle, D. *In*: Norman, F. M. ed. *Memoirs of the Life of the Right Hon. David, Seventh Earl of Glasgow, 1833–1915*. Edinburgh, T. & A. Constable, 1918, p. 269.
7. Ross, Capt. Sir James Clark. *A Voyage of Discovery and Research in the Southern and Antarctic Regions During the Years 1839–43*. London, John Murray, 1847, p. 153.
8. Norman, W. H., and Musgrave, T. *Journals of the Voyage and Proceedings of H.M.C.S. Victoria in Search of Shipwrecked People at the Auckland and Other Islands*. Melbourne, Victoria Government Printer, 1866, p. 32.
9. Armstrong, Henry, op. cit. p. 52.
10. Muerk, C. D., Foggo, M. N., and Lee, W. G. Conservation on New Zealand's Subantarctic Islands: a botanical perspective. Paper to 15th Pacific Science Congress, Dunedin, February 1983.
11. Armstrong, Henry, op. cit. p. 54.
12. Ross, Capt. Sir James Clark, op. cit. p. 150.
13. ibid.
14. Enderby, C. Report in *The New Zealand Pilot*. 4th ed. London, Hydrographic Office, Admiralty, 1875, p. 315.
15. Fleming, Sir Charles, Cape Expeditioner, personal comment.
16. Ross, Capt. Sir James Clark, op. cit. p. 149.
17. Musgrave, Thomas. *Castaway on the Auckland Islands*. Wellington, A.H. & A.W. Reed, 1943, p. 92.
18. Pollock, Laurie. Unpublished personal diary.
19. Enderby, C., op. cit.
20. Raynal, F. E. *Wrecked on a Reef or Twenty Months in the Auckland Isles*. London, Nelson, 1885, p. 182.
21. Falla, R. A. Exploitation of Seals, Whales and Penguins in New Zealand. *New Zealand Ecological Society Proceedings*, No. 9, 1962, p. 37.
22. Cumpston, J. S. *Macquarie Island*. Antarctic Division, Department of External Affairs, Australia, 1968.

Chapter 13 The Early Scientists
(pages 143 to 153)

1. Warham, John, and Johns, P. M. *The University of Canterbury Antipodes Island Expedition 1969*. University of Canterbury Antipodes Island Expedition Paper No. 7. *Journal of the Royal Society of New Zealand*, Vol. 5, No. 2, 1975, p. 105.
2. Sailing instructions to Charles Wilkes, authorised by Act of Congress 14 May 1836. *In*: Wilkes, C. *Narrative of the United States Exploring Expedition During the Years 1838, 1839, 1840, 1841, 1842*. London, Ingram, Cooke & Co., Vol. I, 1852.

3. Godley, E. J. *Botany of the Southern Zone*. Botany Division, DSIR, Christchurch. In *Tuatara*, Vol. 13, No. 3, November 1965, p. 168.
4. Chilton, C. ed. *The Subantarctic Islands of New Zealand*. Wellington, Philosophical Institute of Canterbury: New Zealand Government Printer, 1909, Vol. I, p. 23.
5. Godley, E. J., op. cit. p. 173.
6. McCormick, R. *Voyages of Discovery in the Arctic and Antarctic Seas, and Round the World*. London, Sampson Low, 1884, Vol. I, p. 135.
7. *British Navy Record Society's Naval Miscellanies*. Vol. 3, 1928.
8. Judd, N. Protection of Historical Information in the Subantarctic. Diploma thesis, Parks and Recreation, Lincoln College, January 1983, pp. 13, 38.
9. Godley, E. J., op. cit. p. 152.
10. German Transit of Venus Expedition. *In: Voyage of Exploration of the Gazelle*. Part I, 1874. Translated by New Zealand Department of Internal Affairs, Wellington, 1975.
11. ibid.
12. ibid.
13. Reischek, A. Notes on Islands to the South of New Zealand. Read before the Auckland Institute, 30 July 1888. *In: Transactions of the New Zealand Institute*, Vol. 21, p. 381.
14. Reischek, A., op. cit. p. 384.
15. Reischek, A., op. cit. p. 385.
16. Warham, John, and Johns, P. M., op. cit. p. 108.
17. Wilson, E. A. *Edward Wilson: diary of the Discovery expedition to the Antarctic region 1901–1904*. Ed. Ann Savours. London, Blandford Press, 1966, pp. 347–348.
18. Godley, E. J., op. cit. p. 135.
19. Godley, E. J., op. cit. p. 136.
20. Oliver, W. R. B. Solitary Isles: the Dominion's outposts. Wellington *Evening Post*, 16 April 1927.
21. Guthrie-Smith, William Herbert. *Sorrows and Joys of a New Zealand Naturalist*. Wellington, A.H. & A.W. Reed, 1936, Introduction and p. 128.

Chapter 14   The "Cape" Expedition
(pages 155 to 163)

1. Grams, Capt. Alfred. *Voyage of the Erlangen*. Diary of Captain of SS *Erlangen*. Bremen, North German Lloyds, 16 July 1967.
2. Clifton, L. Official Report of the Cape Expedition. Unpublished typescript. Aerodromes Branch, Public Works Department, Wellington, 24 October 1946, p. 1.
3. Clifton, L., op. cit. p. 2.
4. Balham, Ron, Cape Expeditioner, personal comment.
5. ibid.
6. Stead, E. F. The Supposed Flightless Duck from Campbell Island. *Transactions of the Royal Society of New Zealand*, Vol. 68, 1937, pp. 100–101.
7. Pollock, Laurie. Unpublished personal diary.
8. Wilson, R. F. Unpublished personal diary.
9. D'Urville, Dumont. *The Voyage of the Astrolabe — 1840; an English rendering of the Journals . . .* Ed. Olive Wright. Wellington, A.H. & A.W. Reed, 1955, p. 5.
10. Eden, Allan W. *Islands of Despair*. London, Andrew Melrose, 1955, p. 115.
11. Eden, Allan W., op. cit. p. 86.

12. Turbott, E. G., Cape Expeditioner, personal comment.
13. Balham, Ron, personal comment.
14. Clifton, L., op. cit. p. 7.
15. Fleming, Sir Charles. Obituary of Sir Robert Falla. *Emu 80*, 1980, pp. 41–42.

Chapter 15   Campbell Island Weather Station
(pages 165 to 171)

1. Harper, Grant, Campbell Island staff 1983–84, personal comment.
2. Management Plan for the Campbell Islands Nature Reserve. Wellington, New Zealand Department of Lands and Survey, 1983, p. 20.
3. Kelburn Meteorological Office staff, personal comment.
4. Management Plan, Campbell, op. cit. p. 20.
5. Ministry of Transport. A Year of Your Life on Raoul or Campbell Island. (Pamphlet), Wellington, 1976.
6. Ross, Capt. Sir James Clark. *A Voyage of Discovery and Research in the Southern and Antarctic Regions During the Years 1839–43*. London, John Murray, 1847, pp. 154–155.
7. Mackworth, William. Unpublished private diary. Entry of 10 January 1850.
8. Brownie, Mr., quoted in letter from C. W. Chamberlain, Acting Director of Customs in Dunedin, to Secretary of Marine, 25 August 1886.
9. Auckland Islands Nature Reserve, Draft Management Plan. Wellington, New Zealand Department of Lands and Survey, 1985, p. 45.
10. Draft Management Plan, Aucklands, op. cit. p. 46.
11. Snares Islands Nature Reserve, Management Plan. Wellington, Department of Lands and Survey, 1983, p. 10.
12. Raynal, F. E. *Wrecked on a Reef or Twenty Months in the Auckland Isles*. London, Nelson, 1885, p. 202.
13. Wilkes, C. *Narrative of the United States Exploring Expedition During the Years 1839, 1840, 1841, 1842*. Vol. I. London, Ingram, Cooke & Co., 1852, p. 282.
14. Stewart, Ramari, Campbell Island staff 1982–83, personal comment.
15. ibid.
16. Crompton, Mark, Officer in Charge, Campbell Island staff 1983–84, personal comment.

Chapter 16   Scientists Today
(pages 173 to 183)

1. Godley, E. J. *In*: Yaldwyn, J. C. ed. *Preliminary Results of the Auckland Islands Expedition 1972–73*. Wellington, Department of Lands and Survey, 1975.
2. Meurk, Colin. Report in Botany Department, DSIR, Newsletter No. 102, 7 May 1985.
3. ibid.

Chapter 17   Options for the Future
(pages 187 to 195)

1. Bruemmer, Fred. In letter, personal comment, 1 November 1985.
2. Breummer, Fred. Impressions from the Auckland Islands. *Landscape 10*, Wellington, Department of Lands and Survey, November 1981, pp. 3–4.

REFERENCES

3. Crompton, Mark, personal comment.
4. Donoghue, Mike. In letter, personal comment, 4 February 1985, concerning World Wildlife Fund on sea lion research.
5. Gregory, M. R. *The Sub-Antarctic Islands and Oil-Spill Persistence (or Physical Sensitivity) Index Mapping.* Geology Department, University of Auckland, 1985.

Chapter 18   A Heritage of Islands
(pages 197 to 200)

1. World Wildlife Fund advertisement for World Conservation. *Time*, 8 July 1985.
2. Mills, Stephen. The Thin Green Line. *BBC Wildlife*, May 1984, p. 235.
3. Oddie, Bill. Big Fun with Bullets. *BBC Wildlife*, June 1984, pp. 293–295.
4. Malone, R. E. *Three Years' Cruise in the Australasian Colonies.* London, Bentley, 1854, p. 66.
5. Armstrong, Henry. Cruise of the Brig *Amherst. New Zealand Government Gazette, Province of Southland*, Vol. 6, No. 9, 11 April 1868, p. 51.
6. Joyce, James P. Report on Auckland, Campbell and Other Islands to the Hon. the Minister of Marine, Invercargill, 28 May 1894, p. 2.
7. Aston, B. C. Previously unpublished report to Secretary of Agriculture, 7 December 1907, published by E. J. Godley in *The 1907 Expedition to the Auckland and Campbell Islands.* Botany Division, DSIR, Christchurch. Reprinted in *Tuatara*, Vol. 23, No. 3, May 1979, pp. 156–157.
8. Godley, E. J. Notes on the Main Introduced Animals of the Auckland and Campbell Islands. Report to Department of Lands and Survey, Wellington. Botany Division, DSIR, Christchurch, March 1967, p. 1.
9. Guthrie-Smith, William Herbert. *Tutira.* Edinburgh, Blackwood, 1921.
10. Meurk, Colin, Botany Division, DSIR, Christchurch. In letter, personal comment, September 1983.
11. Cockayne, Leonard. The Southern Islands. Christchurch *Press*, December 1907, p. 7.
12. Bates, F. As related by. A Hundred and Three Days on a Desert Island. *Chambers Journal*, 30 January 1892, p. 79.

BIBLIOGRAPHY

Books

Bailey, Alfred M., and Sorensen, J. H. *Subantarctic Campbell Island*. Denver Museum of Natural History. Proceedings No. 10., 1 February 1962.

Bligh, William. *A Voyage to the South Sea*. London, George Nicol, 1792.

Chilton, C. ed. *The Subantarctic Islands of New Zealand*. Wellington, Philosophical Institute of Canterbury: New Zealand Government Printer, Vols I and II, 1909.

Clark, M. R., and Dingwall, P. R. *Conservation of Islands in the Southern Ocean: a review of the protected areas of Insulantarctica*. Wellington, Department of Lands and Survey, 1985.

Cockayne, Leonard. *New Zealand Plants and Their Story*. 4th ed. Wellington, New Zealand Government Printer, 1967.

Collins, David. *Account of the English Colony in New South Wales*. London, T. Cadell Jr & W. Davies, 1798–1802.

Cumpston, J. S. *Sub-Antarctic By-Ways: the history of Macquarie Island*. MS of 1955 and published version of 1968. Antarctic Division, Department of External Affairs, Australia.

Darlington, Philip J., Jr. *Biogeography of the Southern End of the World*. Boston, Harvard University Press, 1965.

D'Urville, Dumont. *The Voyage of the Astrolabe — 1840; an English Rendering of the Journals . . .* Ed. Olive Wright, Wellington, A. H. & A. W. Reed, 1955.

Eden, Allan W. *Islands of Despair*. London, Andrew Melrose, 1955.[+]

Escott-Inman, H. *The Castaways of Disappointment Island*. London, Partridge, 1911.[+]

Eunson, Keith. *The Wreck of the General Grant*. Wellington, A. H. & A. W. Reed, 1974.[+]

Fraser, Ronald G. J. *Once Round The Sun: the story of the International Geophysical Year*. New York, Macmillan, 1957.

Furnas, J. C. *Anatomy of Paradise*. London, Gollancz, 1950.

Guiness Book of Records. Guiness Superlatives Ltd., 1973.

Guthrie-Smith, William Herbert. *Sorrows and Joys of a New Zealand Naturalist*. Wellington, A. H. & A. W. Reed, 1936.

Guthrie-Smith, William Herbert. *Tutira*. Edinburgh, Blackwood, 1921.

Hooker, Sir Joseph D. *The Botany of the Antarctic Voyage of H. M. Discovery Ships Erebus and Terror In the Years 1839–43*. Part I, Vol. I. *Flora Antarctica*. London, Reeve, 1844–1860.

Kerr, Ian S. *Campbell Island: a history*. Wellington, A. H. & A. W. Reed, 1976.[+]

McCormick, R. *Voyages of the Discovery in the Arctic and the Antarctic Seas, and Round the World*. London, Sampson Low, Vol. I, 1884.

McLaren, Fergus. *The Eventful Story of the Auckland Islands*. Wellington, A. H. & A. W. Reed, 1948[+]

McNab, Robert. *Murihiku*. Invercargill, William Smith, 1907.

Malone, R. E. *Three Years' Cruise in the Australasian Colonies*. London, Bentley, 1854.

Morrell, Benjamin. *A Narrative of Four Voyages, 1822–1831*. New York, Harper, 1832.

Musgrave, Thomas. *Castaway on the Auckland Islands*. Wellington, A. H. & A. W. Reed, 1943.[+]

Norman, F. M. ed. *Memoirs of the Life of the Right Hon. David, Seventh Earl of Glasgow, 1833–1915*. Edinburgh, T. & A. Constable, 1918.

Raynal, F. E. *Wrecked on a Reef or Twenty Months in the Auckland Isles*. London, Nelson, 1885.[+]

Robertson, C. J. R. *Reader's Digest Complete Book of New Zealand Birds*. Sydney, Reader's Digest, 1985.[+]

Ross, Capt. Sir James Clark. *A Voyage of Discovery and Research in the Southern and Antarctic Regions During the Years 1839–43*. London, John Murray, 1847.

Simpson, Frank. ed. *The Antarctic Today*. Wellington, A. H. & A. W. Reed, 1952.

Sorensen, J. H. *Wild Life in the Subantarctic*. Christchurch, Whitcombe & Tombs, 1951[+]

Vancouver, George. *A Voyage of Discovery to the North Pacific Ocean and Round the World in the Years 1790–95*. London, G. G. & J. Robinson, 1798.

Wegener, Alfred. *The Origin of Continents and Oceans*. (Translated by Biram, John from *Die Ehtstehung der Kontinente und Ozeane*. 4th German ed. rev.) London, Methuen, 1967.

Wilkes, C. *Narrative of the United States Exploring Expedition During the Years 1838, 1839, 1840, 1841, 1842*. London, Ingram, Cooke & Co., Vol. I, 1852.

Wilson, E. A. *Edward Wilson: diary of the Discovery expedition to the Antarctic region 1901–1904*. Ed. Ann Savours. London, Blandford Press, 1966.

Scientific Papers, Abstracts, and Reports

Adams, C. J. *Geological Studies on the 1985 Cruise of HMNZS Monowai (i) to Campbell, Auckland and Snares Islands; (ii) to Antipodes and Bounty Islands*. INS-R-300 and INS-R-341, 1985, Institute of Nuclear Sciences, Lower Hutt, New Zealand.

Adams, C. J. Migration of Late Cenozoic Volcanism in the South Island of New Zealand and the Campbell Plateau. *Nature*, Vol. 294, No. 5837, 12 November 1981.

Aston, B. C. Previously unpublished report to Secretary of Agriculture, 7 December 1907, published by E. J. Godley in *The 1907 Expedition to the Auckland and Campbell Islands*. Botany Division, DSIR, Christchurch. Reprinted in *Tuatara*, Vol. 23, No. 3., May 1979.

Beardsell, Mike. The Future of Deepwater Fishery. *Catch '85*, December 1985

Bell, B. D., and Taylor, R. H. The Wild Sheep of Campbell Island. *Forest and Bird*, November 1970.

Blake, Barry. Threats to Birds of the Sea. *New Scientist*, 20 October 1983.

Bruemmer, Fred. Sealion Shennanigans. *Natural History*, American Museum Natural History, No. 7, 1981.

[+] Recommended for general reading.

BIBLIOGRAPHY

Bruemmer, Fred. Impressions from the Auckland Islands. *Landscape 10*, Wellington, Department of Lands and Survey, November 1981.

Campbell, D. J., and Rudge, M. R. A Case for Controlling the Distribution of the Tree Daisy, *Olearia lyallii. Proceedings of the New Zealand Ecological Society*, 23, 1976.

Cawthorn, M. W., Crawley, M. C., Mattlin, R. H., and Wilson, G. J. *Research on Pinnipeds in New Zealand.* Pinniped Research Review Sub-committee, Fisheries Research Division, Wellington, 1985.

Challies, C. N. Feral Pigs on Auckland Island. *New Zealand Journal of Zoology*, Vol. 2, No. 4, 1975.

Cockayne, L. A. Botanical Excursion During Midwinter to the Southern Islands of New Zealand. *Transactions of the New Zealand Institute*, Vol. XXXVI, 1904.

Dingwall, Paul. The Changing Image of the Auckland Islands. *Landscape 9*, Wellington, Department of Lands and Survey, May, 1981.

Enderby, Charles. *Description of the Outlying Islands South and East of New Zealand.* Hydrographic Office, Admiralty, London, 1868.

Falla, R. A. Exploitation of Seals, Whales and Penguins in New Zealand. *New Zealand Ecological Society Proceedings*, No. 9, 1962.

Fleming, C. A., Mildenhall, C. D., and Moar, N. T. Quaternary Sediments and Plant Microfossils from Enderby Island, Auckland Islands. *Journal of the Royal Society of New Zealand*, Vol. 6, No. 4., December 1976.

Fleming, C. A. Two-Storied Cliffs at the Auckland Islands. Transactions of the Royal Society of New Zealand. *Geology*, Vol. 3, No. 2, 8 December 1965.

Fleming, C. A. *Sea Lions as Geological Agents.* (Erratic pebbles of basalt carried as gastroliths in sea lions' stomachs from the Auckland Islands 130 miles to the Snares Islands.) J. Sediment, Petrol, 1951.

Foggo, M. N., and Meurk, Colin D. Notes on a Visit to Jacquemart Island in the Campbell Island Group. *New Zealand Journal of Ecology*, Vol. 4, 1981.

Gamberoni, L., Geronimi, J., Jeannin, P. F., and Murail, J. F. Study of Frontal Zones in the Crozet-Kerguelen Region. [Ocean convergences] *Oceanologica Acta*, Vol. 5, No. 3, 1982.

German Transit of Venus Expedition. *In: Voyage of Exploration of the Gazelle.* Part I, 1874. Translated by New Zealand Department of Internal Affairs, Wellington, 1975.

Godley, E. J. *Preliminary Results of the Auckland Islands Expedition 1972–73.* Ed. J. C. Yaldwyn. Department of Lands and Survey, 1975.

Godley, E. J. Notes on the Main Introduced Animals of the Auckland Islands. Report to Department of Lands and Survey, Wellington. Botany Division, DSIR, Christchurch, March 1967.

Godley, E. J. Botany of the Southern Zone. *Tuatara*, Vol. 13, No. 3, November 1965.

Gregory, M. R. *Plastics and Other Seaborne Litter on Subantarctic Island Shores.* Department of Geology, University of Auckland, 1985.

Gregory, M. R. *The Subantarctic Islands and Oil-Spill Persistence Cor Physical Sensitivity) Index Mapping.* Department of Geology, University of Auckland, 1985.

Hay, C. H., Adams, N. M., and Parsons, M. J. *Marine Algae of the Subantarctic Islands of New Zealand.* National Museum of New Zealand, Miscellaneous Series No. II, August 1985.

John, Dilwyn. Lecture reprinted in The Second Antarctic Commission of the R.R.S. *Discovery II. The Geographical Journal*, LXXXIII. Quoted in Sir George Deacon, The Antarctic Ocean. *Interdisciplinary Science Reviews*, Vol. 2, No. 2., June 1977.

Management Plan (Rough Draft) for the Antipodes Islands Nature Reserve. Wellington, Department of Lands and Survey.

Management Plan (Draft) for Auckland Islands Nature Reserve. Wellington, Department of Lands and Survey, 1985.

Management Plan (Rough Draft) for the Bounty Islands Nature Reserve. Wellington, Department of Lands and Survey.

Management Plan for the Campbell Islands Nature Reserve. Wellington, Department of Lands and Survey, 1983.

Management Plan (Draft) for the Snares Islands Nature Reserve. Wellington, Department of Lands and Survey, 1983.

Meurk, Colin D. *Report on the 1985 Southern Islands (NZ) Expedition.* Botany Division, DSIR, Christchurch, 5 July 1985.

Meurk, Colin D. Report in Botany Department, DSIR, Newsletter No. 102, 7 May 1985.

Meurk, Colin D. Alien Plants in Campbell Island's Changing Vegetation. *Mauri Ora*, 5, 1977.

Meurk, C. D., Foggo, M. N., and Lee, W. G. Conservation on New Zealand's Subantarctic Islands: a botanical perspective. Paper to 15th Pacific Science Congress, Dunedin, February 1983.

New Zealand Environment, No. 40, Environmental Publications Trust, Summer 1983.

Penniket, A. W. and Dingwall, P. R. *The Contribution of Research to the Management of Island Reserves: an overview.* Wellington, Department of Lands and Survey, 1983.

Reischek, A. Notes on the Islands to the South of New Zealand. Read before the Auckland Institute, 30 July 1888. *In: Transactions of the New Zealand Institute*, Vol. 21.

Ritchie, L. D. *Commercial Fishing for Spider Crab (Jacquinotia edwardsii) at the Auckland Islands.* Fisheries Technical Report No. 101. Wellington, Ministry of Agriculture and Fisheries, 1973.

Scientific Results of Cape Expedition Series 1941–45. A series of reports based on collections of data and specimens during wartime coastwatching activities. Wellington, DSIR.

Stead, E. F. The Supposed Flightless Duck from Campbell Island. *Transactions of the Royal Society of New Zealand*, Vol. 68, 1937.

Taylor, R. H. New Zealand Fur Seals at the Bounty Islands. *New Zealand Journal of Marine and Freshwater Research*, Vol. 16, 1982.

Taylor, R. H. Influence of Man on Vegetation and Wildlife of Enderby and Rose Islands. *New Zealand Journal of Botany*, Vol. 9, No. 2, June 1971.

Taylor, R. H. Introduced Mammals and Islands: priorities for conservation and research. *Proceedings of the New Zealand Ecological Society*, 15, 1968.

Taylor, R. H., Bell, B. D., and Wilson, P. R. Royal Albatrosses, Feral Sheep and Cattle on Campbell Island. *New Zealand Journal of Science*, Vol. 13, No. I, March 1970.

Travers, H. H., and Travers, W. T. L. Birds of the Chatham Islands. *Transactions and Proceedings of the New Zealand Institute*, Vol. 5, 1873.

Warham, John. *The Incidence, Functions and Ecological Significance of Petrel Stomach Oils.* Department of Zoology, University of Canterbury, Christchurch. Reprinted from *Proceedings of the New Zealand Ecological Society*, Vol. 24, 1977.

Warham, John, and Johns, P. M. *The University of Canterbury Antipodes Island Expedition 1969.* University of Canterbury Antipodes Island Expedition Paper No. 7. *Journal of the Royal Society of New Zealand*, Vol. 5, No. 2, 1975.

Warham, John, and Wilson, Graham J. *The Size of the Sooty Shearwater Population at the Snares Islands, New Zealand.* University of Canterbury Expeditions Paper No. 45. Reprinted from *Notornis*, Vol. 29, Part I, March 1982.

Yaldwyn, J. C. ed. *Preliminary Results of the Auckland Islands Expedition 1972–73.* Wellington, Department of Lands and Survey, 1975.

Records, Reports, Diaries, Letters, etc.

Armstrong, Henry. Official Report on Cruise of the Brig *Amherst*. *New Zealand Government Gazette, Province of Southland*. Vol. 6, No. 9, 11 April 1868.

British Navy Record Society's Naval Miscellanies. Vol. 3, 1928. Brownie, Mr., quoted in letter from C. W. Chamberlain, Acting Director of Customs in Dunedin, to Secretary of Marine, 25 August 1886.

Carrick, Robert. *New Zealand's Lonely Lands.* Report for Department of Lands and Survey. New Zealand Government Printer, 1892.

Clifton, L. Official Report of the Cape Expedition. Unpublished typescript. Aerodromes Branch, Public Works Department, Wellington, 24 October 1946.

District Lands and Survey Office, Invercargill, 31 January 1895, offering pastoral leases on Bounty Islands.

Donoghue, Mike, letter to author concerning World Wildlife Fund and sea lion research.

Enderby, Charles. *The Auckland Islands: a short account of their climate, soils, and productions; and the advantages of establishing there a settlement at Port Ross for carrying on the southern whale fisheries.* London, Pelham Richardson, 1849.

Grams, Capt. Alfred. *Voyage of the Erlangen.* Diary of Captain of S. S. *Erlangen*. Bremen, North German Lloyds, 16 July 1967.

Historical Records of New South Wales. Vol. 1. (Early sealing trade.)

Joyce, James P. Report on Auckland, Campbell and other Islands to the Hon. the Minister of Marine, Invercargill, 28 May 1894.

Judd, N. Protection of Historical Information in the Subantarctic. Diploma thesis, Parks and Recreation, Lincoln College, January 1983.

Mackworth, William. Unpublished private diary of the Enderby Settlement.

Ministry of Transport. A Year of Your Life on Raoul or Campbell Island. (Pamphlet), Wellington, 1976.

Moffett and Sons, letter to Minister of Marine, Invercargill, 27 June 1896, re farming. File M2/6/I, National Archives, Wellington.

Monkton, F. A. Manuscript No. 429, Folder No. 6, Alexander Turnbull Library, Wellington, re farming.

Norman, W. H., and Musgrave, T. *Journals of the Voyage and Proceedings of H.M.C.S. Victoria in Search of Shipwrecked People at the Auckland and Other Islands.* Melbourne, Victoria Government Printer, 1866.

Pollock, Laurie. Unpublished personal diary of the Cape Expedition.

Wilson, R. F. Unpublished personal diary of the Cape Expedition.

Newspapers, Magazines, and Periodicals

BBC Wildlife, June 1984. Oddie, Bill, "Big Fun With Bullets".

BBC Wildlife, May 1984. Mills, Stephen, "The Thin Green Line".

Chambers Journal, London, 30 January 1982. Bates, F. "A Hundred and Three Days on a Desert Island".

Christchurch *Press*, December 1907. Cockayne, Leonard, "The Southern Islands".

Emu 80. 1980. Fleming, Sir Charles, "Obituary of Sir Robert Falla".

Forest and Bird, May 1985. Darby, J., "Hoiho — World's Rarest Penguin".

Forest and Bird, May 1984. Eagle, Audrey, "The Auckland Islands Visited".

Illustrated London News, 24 December 1887. (Nelsons at Port Ross.)

New Zealand's Nature Heritage, Part 84, 1975. Taylor, R. H., "Parakeets".

New Zealand's Nature Heritage, Part I, 1974. Stevens, Graham, "A Land Is Made".

New Zealand Times, 7 December 1907. Diary of McLaughlin, D., Second Mate of the *Dundonald*.

Otago Daily Times, 4 August 1931. (End of Farming on Campbell Island.)

Otago Witness, 19 December 1895. Chapman, F. R. "Illustrations From Subantarctic New Zealand".

Southland Times, 3 July 1933. (Remnants of sealers' potato plot on the Snares.)

Sydney Gazette, 29 July 1826. (Collapse of sealing trade.)

Time, 8 July 1985. World Wildlife Fund advertisement for world conservation.

Wellington *Evening Post*, 16 April 1927. Oliver, W. R. B., "Solitary Isles: the Dominion's outposts".

Films

Adams Island. NZ Wildlife Service, 1966, 24 minutes.

An Island Alone (Campbell Island). Television New Zealand, 1979, 24 minutes.

Antarctic Outpost: Campbell Island. National Film Unit, Weekly Review No. 284, 1947. B&W. 9½ minutes.

As It Wasn't In the Beginning (Enderby Island). Television New Zealand "Wild South", Natural History Unit, 1982, 24 minutes.

Beyond the Roaring Forties (All New Zealand's Subantarctic Islands). National Film Unit, 1986, 58 minutes.

54–40 South. National Film Unit, Weekly Review No. 438, 1950, B&W, 10½ minutes.

50° South (Campbell and Macquarie Islands). New Zealand Public Works Department, 1945. B&W, 38 minutes.

Gift of the Sea (The Snares). Television New Zealand "Wild South", Natural History Unit, 1984, 24 minutes.

Island of Strange Noises (Antipodes). Television New Zealand "Wild South", Natural History Unit, 1981, 24 minutes.

Sealion Summer (Enderby Island sea lions). Television New Zealand "Wild South", Natural History Unit, 1982, 24 minutes.

INDEX

INDEX

tussock grass (*see* grass)
Tutanekai 128, 139, 148, 152
TVNZ Natural History Unit 178, 194

University of Canterbury 174, 175, **176–7**, 183
University of Otago 174
unmodified islands **131, 138, 198**

Vancouver, Capt George 79; discovers Snares **80**
van Tets, Gerald 174, 176, 177
Venus Bay, C Id 68 (*see* French Transit of Venus Expedition)
Victoria, HMCS 113, 116, 123, 124, 133
Victoria Passage 2, 70; M 67
Victoria tree **113**, 200
volcanic dykes *56*
volcanic origins **54–6, 58–63**

Waikato, HMNZS 163, 177, 178
Waite E. R. 148, 150
wandering albatross *17*, **16–8**, 66, 182
Warham, John 176, **177**; on uses of petrel oil 22–3
Warren, Arthur 128
Waterhouse, Capt, discovers Antipodes **80**

Webling, Capt 156
Wegener, Alfred 56
weka (woodhen) 134, 138, 188
welcome swallow 72
Western Chain Islands, Snares *15*, 22, 73, *184*
western cliffs, Ak Is 9–10, *71*, 71, *108, 115, 152, 153*
weta 57
whales 27, *28*, **28–9**; *see also* right whale
whaling: at Ak Is 100, 103, 105; at C Id 28, 68, *125*, **127–9**, *128, 129*; international 28, 89, **92–5, 96, 99**, 100, 128; ships: *Eliza Scott* 92, *Enterprise* 85, *Fancy* **105,** *Hardwicke* 105, *Nancy* 94, *Ocean* 82, *Sabrina* 92, *Sarah* 82; Southern Whale Fishing Co 100
Whitchurch, Peter 160
wild cabbage (*see Stilbocarpa polaris*)
Wildlife Service 169, 174–9 *passim*
Wild South TV series 178, 194
Wilkes, Charles **92–4**, **143**, 168
Williams, Murray 179, 182
Wilson, Edward: describes aurora **16**; describes blowflies **72**; cockles and mussels **36**; Hooker's sea lions **33**; Port Ross **149**
Wilson, Peter 174, 179

Wilson R. F., diary **160**
women in subantarctic **106**: Black, Colleen 106; Mrs Cook 106; Farr, Elizabeth 85; Guthrie-Smith, Barbara 106; Miss Hallett 102; Jewell, Mary Ann 106; "Lady of the Heather" 106; Mrs Morrell 89; Mrs Nelson 106, 124; Younger, Isabel *106*
woodhen (weka) 134, 138, 188
wool 127, 128; *see also* sheep
World Discoverer 193
World Heritage sites 194
World War II v, **155–8**, 165; *Erlangen* **155–6**; German raiders 156; Japan 156, 158; liberty ships 158; *see also* "Cape Expedition"
worms, parasitic in fish 35, 94

Yaldwyn, John 175, 176, 182
yellow-eyed penguin v, **25**, *191, 197*
Young and Ford 124
Younger, Isabel *106*

Zalophus californianus (*see* California sea lion)
Zelée 94, 94
zooplankton 35

V. R. WARD, GOVERNMENT PRINTER, WELLINGTON — 1986